DODGING POTHOLES

PROLOGUE

I have always been fascinated by faraway places. As a boy, I kept maps hanging up on the walls so that I could dream of exotic lands and distant adventures. When I was three, I climbed the garden gate and boldly told the milkman that I was going to be a cartographer, such was my interest in maps. He told me, in his inimitable way, that he was going to bite my bum. So far neither prediction has borne fruition.

In primary school I remember racing through maths so that I could do extra geography and I was able to recite all of the capitals of Europe.

Yes, I was a nerd.

However, my interest in travel never diminished. So once I had qualified as a teacher I began to take more notice of the newspaper section for overseas jobs. I recalled working as a barman and being told by an ageing hippie that Latin America was the last land of magic and romance. It certainly had an alluring mystique, and I began applying for jobs there: Lima, Peru; Santiago, Chile; Mexico City.

With a geographer's keen precision, I was soon writing off to a school in Gilgil, a sleepy, rural location in the Kenyan Rift Valley, to accept the post of junior class teacher.

My first year in Africa was unbelievable! At the earliest opportunity I joined some colleagues for a long weekend at Naro Moru in the foothills of Mt. Kenya. On the way there I saw my first big game animals: white rhinos and giraffe.

At the half term holiday I joined a group camping in the national parks of Shaba and Samburu, where I saw my first lions, leopard, cheetah and elephants. We bathed in a dam surrounded by armed Somali camel-herders and were more concerned about the camels peeing into the water than the herdsman's AK-47s. When I returned home for Christmas and Millennium-eve, my friends and family were fascinated by the tales I told.

In the new year I climbed Mt. Kenya for the first time, travelled with university friends to the Masai Mara and went camping in the Aberdares mountains.

When I came home to attend a couple of weddings that summer, I found myself telling these stories over and over to friends and relatives. It was flattering that they were interested, but telling the same stories, twenty-odd times, started to get a bit dull and I started to feel guilty at abbreviating them the more often I told them.

Then I hit upon an idea! As email had (relatively) recently come into existence, I decided to write a detailed journal of my travels and send it to interested parties back home. It felt like a bit of a cop out to someone who prefers face-to-face story-telling but after my trip to Uganda, I sent back the first of my journals. I suppose nowadays we'd call this a blog.

This is a collection of journals from a year spent travelling in East Africa between October 2000 and August 2001. I love travelling and I love telling stories: what follows is a combination of these two passions.

DODGING POTHOLES

MPWHEELHOUSE

<u>All names have been changed from their originals.</u>

UGANDA

I had been planning to go to Uganda for quite a while and had intended to go during the summer holidays, but my funds had run out. However, by October I had the money and a travelling partner, Bowen, a gap year student working at the school. We shared a similar interest in travelling and studying the results of the local brewing industries.

The highlights of our trip to Uganda were trekking to see chimpanzees and mountain gorillas (though Bowen was unfortunately unable to afford the latter as it came above the gap student budget) and white water rafting from outside a town called Jinja, in eastern Uganda.

We had intended to meet up with Rob and Sean, two fellow teachers from the school. However, Rob was on duty looking after the kids until they had all been picked up and this was normally a time consuming job; not every parent considers punctuality in this regard to be a priority.

I was borrowing Rob's car until we met up at the border to finalise plans and deal out permits for the gorilla park, but as often happens in Africa, not everything went according to plan.

On a sunny Saturday afternoon, we waved goodbye to the students and took off, hell for leather, for Uganda in Rob's car. As Rob was on duty until Lord only knew what time, he and Sean were going to follow on and catch us up at the border in Sean's speedier, sexier wagon. However, the best laid plans...

We arrived at the border early in the afternoon and were whirled through a maelstrom of documentation, red-tape and unnecessary headache by a group of 'well-meaners' who were obviously after a quick buck for their well-meaning. We snoozed for an hour or so while we waited for the boys to catch up, but there was no sign of them, and so, fearing that the border would close, we took off for Uganda.

Arriving on the other side, we were promptly charged the Ugandan Shilling equivalent of £20 apiece for what seemed to be bribes and were sent in dizzying circles for yet more paperwork before finally breaking through to Uganda.

And what a contrast...

The first thing we noticed was how green everything was. As if the two sides of the frontier had been painted from different palates, the Ugandan side was a rich emerald to the Kenyan tired dun. Throughout the trip, not one bit of the country deviated from this description and we spent the whole week surrounded by this fresh, invigorating shade.

Everywhere along our route we saw banana palms, thatched mud huts, rolling hills, grassy fields, reed-filled marshes and friendly faces. The people of Uganda had a charming naivety that was a cool breath of fresh air coming from Kenya, where nothing seems to be offered for nothing. We stopped at a sleepy village called Bugiri to sample our first Ugandan brew: Bell, a cheeky little number with a hoppy taste. We were informed by the locals that only women drank it, as it had a mere 4% alcohol. Quite right too, but possibly this made it a good choice given that we still had a good distance to drive.

A random chap pointed out the horizontal affliction that one of our tires was suffering, probably caused by a pothole that had thrown us across the road shortly before. Fairly sharpish, another fellow was there to help jack up the car as I changed the wheel. When I offered to buy him a soda for his help, he agreed, smiled cheerily and wished us a pleasant journey. In Kenya we were used to being asked for a month's local wages, sometimes on the tenuous premise that a 'helpful' stranger had told you of the problem, without actually fixing it. We were told that there were signs posted by the government reminding Ugandans to be friendly to tourists. Revenue from tourism was a big foreign income contributor, but the intent was evident throughout our trip and was very welcome.

Unfortunately, the country seemed to have taken so many body blows to its tourism industry that I suppose it had to try to make up the ground somehow. We were less than a decade removed from the Idi Amin years, where, quite apart from the despotic reign of terror of the leader, the armed forces of the Ugandans, then the Tanzanians, blasted most of the wildlife to oblivion, dispensing of a high tourist earner. Then there had been problems with the Ebola virus, a disease of two strains that were both thought to have originated in Uganda. More recently the kidnapping and subsequent murder of tourists from the Bwindi Impenetrable Forest Park, one of our intended destinations, had caused a stir.

We carried on and rocked up at our hotel in Jinja where we camped, quite literally, on the lawn. We had a couple of beers and were pestered by a promiscuous local girl before we disappeared for food. The first place we looked for (selected from the guidebook) didn't exist any longer, so we headed on to our second choice. We ordered chicken and chips (chicken, it turns out, is what you eat everywhere in Uganda) and waited patiently. Well, I say patiently, but after a 10½ hour drive, we interrogated the waiter quite a bit and he, playing his part, smiled each time and told us, "It will not be long." During the hour and a half wait for dinner, we discovered a note in the menu which read: *"Please your requested to pardon for 15 minutes before served on the table,"* which seemed to suggest that our food had been delayed by 6 times the norm. When it finally arrived, we fell on our dinner like vultures and appropriately appeased our appetites.

Next morning we had the luxury of a proper shower before setting off through Kampala to change money (where I discovered I had come £20 short of being a Uganda shilling millionaire) and up the trail to Mubende. Upon our return to Kenya the following week, we read in their national papers that in a village on the road to Mubende, a person had died from Ebola at about the time we passed through. This awful disease causes the internal organs to melt and bleed out of every orifice, killing the sufferer within 24 hours. Thankfully, the speed at which the disease kills its host stunts its ability to spread and kerbs its virility, though I suppose this is of little consolation to the afflicted.

Up until Mubende we had had a perfect tarmac road to cruise along but shortly after the town, and as we plunged into the rainforest, the tarmac ended and we were guided to zigzag across the unfinished new highway. An optimistic sign read: "Diversion for 80km." We would hurtle into the dense green growth, scattering villagers and churning up billowing brown dust clouds in our wake, as we took to the temporary dirt road that filled in while they finished the tarmac on the highway to our side. Though it was excruciating to inch along the old zigzag road when the highway being built had a good surface that could offer greater speed, it did add to the sense of adventure as we were consumed on either side of the dirt road by the deep, pulsating jungle. At one point, sick of the morale-sapping pace we were achieving, we did err onto the highway for a short while, but two truckers waved their fingers at us admonishingly and we were humbled into better behaviour.

Suddenly, there was tarmac again! We stopped in a village to recover from the shock with a sugary soda, but our presence (or more likely the weirdness of our white skin) caused some nearby nipper to start wailing and so we scuttled off on our way again. The tarmac heralded our arrival in the tea plantations. The perfectly manicured bushes rolling over the hills gave one the impression of sculptured Japanese gardens, where not a blade of grass or a millimetre of elevation in the landscaped vista is out of place. Its emerald welcome invited you to roll down it like a child on a grassy, summer slope.

Fort Portal proved to be your average shabby African town with grubby shops and (thankfully for us!) a petrol station or four to keep the local population employed and our tank filled. From there we headed for the potholes that led to Kibale National Park, another magical rainforest with the world's highest density of primates, which was on our agenda for its chimpanzees. In fact, the place is festooned with every kind of monkey, baboon and other animals, including forest elephants and wild piggy things, which sadly remained an anathema for the duration of our stay. Spoiled by the long range visibility of the savannah game parks we were used to, we hadn't realised just how easy it was for beasties, even as big as elephants, to stay hidden in the jungly depths. Despite this, the bloke who met us at the Kibale information centre, 11 bone-jarring hours after leaving Jinja, was full of enthusiasm for our impending chimpanzee search.

"Oh yes, you will see them in an hour. You will be back by midday. They are just here," he exclaimed, gesturing a close proximity. Like fools, we failed to treat this with the usual scepticism you show for any African telling you something isn't far away. The Swahili word for near, "karibu", is extensively used to describe distances varying from right in front of you to several days' travel away.

The famous studies of Jane Goodall began to shed light on just how 'human' chimpanzees are. They go bald and grey in old age, and have been observed manipulating their environment in various ways including the use of sticks to dig insects out of holes and the selective use of plants for medical purposes, including curing disease and expelling intestinal parasites. Chimpanzees are found in a broad swathe from Senegal to the forests bordering the Rift Valley, meaning that we would be looking for the easternmost populations. To the south, the river Congo separates chimpanzees from their close relatives, bonobos.

Next morning we woke up to find that there was no shower unit... or shower head or evidence of pipes in the shower. Our curiosity increased when we were asked if we would like a shower. Replying in the affirmative, we were greeted with a washing up bowl of hot water, from which we derived the term 'Ugandan shower', for a wash from a tub of hot water. At every subsequent stay in Uganda, we were offered a bowl of hot water when we asked for a shower.

We gathered with the rangers to begin our chimpanzee trek. Believing we'd be back in time for a late breakfast, we didn't take any food and only 500ml of water each when we set out. But what did it matter? After all, "They are just here!" and we'd be back in a jiffy.

The scheme on these trips is that advance scouts have been out in the morning to locate the chimps and then they radio your guide to get you to the location in all due haste. We tramped through the forest for two hours waiting for the radios to work. Then our guide picked up the signal from the guide of a different tourist group and we spent an hour trying to find them instead. When we got to them, it became pretty clear that these guides didn't have any more idea where the chimps were than our guides did. I only hoped that they knew where *we* were!

And then, we heard them!

Though most of the time we appeared to be logically following the screams of the primates, there were times where we would stand for what seemed like ages listening and then charge off in the opposite direction to the calls we eventually heard. This, on top of the fact that we were hungry and thirsty - having brought such scant reserves for what we had imagined would be a two hour jaunt at most - was, shall we say, somewhat grating. I swear there were times when we were within arms reach of the chimps: they seemed to scream in our ears, but with a cacophonous rustle of the bushes they'd be gone!

After another three hours of leaping through dense jungle, snagging ourselves on thorns, wading through swamp, getting tied in knots by vines and sweating profusely our guide stopped us. He drew himself up to his full height, plus mud-stained wellie boots, and proclaimed, "This group is not habituated (scientist-talk for 'they are scared witless by humans') and they keep running away when we get close." I could have slapped him. Without wishing to overstate my own underdeveloped tracking skills, I could have told him that three hours ago!

And so, with heavy hearts and after 6 hours and 15 minutes of scrambling through some of the most unforgiving terrain in the world, we clambered onto the dirt road and set off for camp, defeated. It wasn't just defeated either. We're supposed to be an evolutionary step or two ahead of these guys, but they had repeatedly enticed and eluded us even when they seemed to be so near. I guess their home-field advantage had really paid off.

Just then, we heard a screaming from the opposite side of the road to the one we had just come from and it seemed to come from close by. Wasting only the briefest moments on useless conversation, Bowen and I plunged back into the maze, hotly pursued by the guide. We met up with the other trekking group shortly thereafter; they having come to the same decision that the chase wasn't over if another primate group had presented itself, and a tap on the shoulder alerted me to the presence of our prey.

Now, one doesn't wish to sound ungrateful, because these chimps had let us get close enough to see them, but they were not in the mood to be photographed. Therefore, what ensued was the most arduous chase of my life. It was great! The chimpanzees would sit tantalisingly close, enjoying a chomp on some delicacy, but, as if sensing the raising of the camera to the eye, they would scarper further into the beyond before settling down for another feed. But it was as if Gandalf had uttered his charm and the spell was cast. This was what we were here for.

It felt just like being a child again. You play tag in the school yard; you play hide and seek in the woods; and you play soldiers in the fields. This was all rolled into one. You'd found them, now you were chasing them to get the shot. The exhilaration cannot be given justice by the written word. Wow!

Eventually, just when we were getting really knackered, as luck would have it, they whipped up some trees while we caught up with them. Unfortunately they got too high for us to photograph using our limited zoom capacity, but at least they weren't running further away. They were still for a while and we got to observe them through the binoculars calling to each other. When we had finally had enough, we departed with a wistful farewell, knowing that this would probably never happen again in our lives, and retreated to camp with faces like we'd seen our first Christmas. The celebratory beer was an anticlimax, welcome as it was.

We ordered our evening meal: the traditional chicken and rice, and jested that the chicken clucking about in the yard in front of us could be our dinner. Just then a burly African came out, grabbed the chicken by the neck and took him behind the shed/kitchen, from where we heard a muffled crunching noise. Perhaps unsurprisingly, given the little we had eaten that day and the exercise we had partaken in, this didn't put us off our food in the slightest. This last minute butchering is quite commonplace in Africa as it keeps your meat fresh in the absence of refrigeration. Following much revelling in our eventual success, we turned in with a glow of contentment and listened to the sounds of the jungle all about us: the insects, the wind in the trees and our new friends, the chimpanzees.

As the sunrise glittered through the trees, and following a Ugandan shower, we packed up camp to head off for Bwindi. Our route took us into the courtroom of the Ruwenzoris, the dominating range that forms the border with the Democratic Republic of Congo (formerly Zaire). These mountains are big and include Point Stanley, the third highest peak in Africa at 5,109 m (16,763 ft). They form an impressive backdrop to the farming communities with their patchwork of *shamba* plots rolling towards the jagged blue hardness of the range.

We went from the foothills of the Ruwenzoris to Queen Elizabeth National Park, which is by Lake Edward. Unusually, there didn't seem to be any barrier to our entering the park. The landscape changed and the grasslands reminded me of Kenya's Masai Mara. The low, rolling hills levelled into plains, the farmland turned into waist high grass and we hurtled towards our destination. Whilst passing through the park we saw some gazelles which we mistook for impala, but turned out to be Uganda Kob. Of course to an avid wildlife watcher like me, this was very exciting news, as this was another new beasty to add to the 'seen' list! The kob, a fine looking chap with beautifully curving horns, appears on the Ugandan coat of arms alongside the grey crowned crane. The male kob entices the female to join his mating group by making soft noises and whistling through his nose. The old smoothie.

With the exception of the stretch between Tororo and Jinja, Uganda's main highways were far better than those of Kenya, which resembled a cratered warzone. What is more, the Ugandan roads appeared to be well maintained. Every so often you saw a lorry full of gravelly dirt crawling along with a bloke on top liberally lobbing the stuff off in the direction of the potholes and a gang following behind to whack it all in tight. Their Kenyan counterparts seemed to be doing something a bit more independent. They just sat around with spades in their hands and asked passersby for donations. However, because this wasn't an official program, the road never got fixed, because that would take away their income source. The Ugandan system seemed to work much better. No scrounging, just hard graft: an inspired concept!

Soon after going through Katunguru we made a right turn onto a dirt track that was to take us to Ishasha and our next turn-off. The track continued through the grasslands before plunging into a forest where another spectacle was unveiled for us. The road changed colour to a reddish-orange of butterfly wings that consumed the car as we drove through, causing thousands of these insects to take off. Macrolepidopteran clouds danced about the car and, though I felt guilty that I had probably killed a few thousand of them by the end of the 20km stretch they occupied, it was clear that this would make no impression on their overall population, as it would only be possible to count them in their millions. They were predominantly reddish-orange, but were heavily interspersed with black and greens, bright blues and iridescent yellows. It was like driving through a rainbow.

Shortly after the butties, a chap with a Kaleshnikov waved us down. Not wishing to deny an armed man my hospitality, I dutifully pulled the car to a halt and rolled down my window. This bloke turned out to be a bit of a stone-face, who didn't speak much English, so most of the conversation carried on in Swahili, a language not native to Uganda but adopted by Idi Amin's military as a lingua franca during his reign and still used by much of the military.

"Unataka kwenda wapi?" (Where do you want to go?), I asked.

"Ishasha."

"Ah, sawa sawa. Sisi tunaenda hii. Wewe na yeye unakaa juu na mama yako keti kwa gari na mimi. Ndio?" (Ah, okay. We are going there. You and him <Bowen> sit on the roof and your wife can sit in the car with me. Yes?)

So the bloke turned out to be harmless enough, but unfortunately Bowen didn't speak a word of Swahili and all he could see was the chap's stone face and loaded assault rifle. It turned out that for the rest of the journey, not another word was spoken between the two of them. They shared the small space on the roof of the car, as we had no more room inside. Just to make matters a little more friendly, the muzzle of the Ugandan soldier's AK47 kept prodding Bowen's ribs as we bounced along the road, causing Bowen to believe that we were being held up for this ride. You can imagine the hilarity this caused me when Bowen relayed his version of the story to me about an hour later, when we had dropped off the soldier and his wife.

We got to a little village where a barrier blocked the road and another could be seen 100 yards away. A policeman came out of his office to see us. When we had explained where we wanted to go, he told us that we had come too far, that we had to go back and look for a village called Kihihi. From there we could take the road to Bwindi. Ishasha was on the border with Congo and we had stood a mere hundred metres or so from one of the most volatile places on earth. At that time eastern Congo was full of Tutsis, Hutus and Ugandans, all tooling up and training for the day they could return to their respective countries to overthrow the government and restore 'democracy' through their genocide.

Since it was gorillas and not guerillas we were interested in, we turned back and went to Kihihi.

Having passed this village, we entered a rural Uganda of small farms, ruby soil and emerald vegetation. We weren't far from our destination (we could see the mountains that gave the gorillas their name) when the heavens opened and unleashed one of those truly tropical storms in which we couldn't see for more than ten metres through the intensity of the rain beating down. We also discovered that one of the windscreen wipers had dropped off at some point...

Visibility became problematic for the rest of our journey, but as there wasn't a lot of traffic in that sprawling metropolis of rural Uganda, we only had to stay on the road. Directing the car along the brown blur discernible from the green blur didn't prove too tricky, though spotting the potholes wasn't easy. We pulled up at the gates to Bwindi Impenetrable Forest some time later, rattled to the core.

There then ensued a bit of a scramble. We had intended to meet up with Rob and Sean at the border and it was they who had the details for the gorilla trekking. We had not managed to do this, so we didn't have a clue whether we had been booked in, what day we were booked for or whether any money had changed hands. To cut a long story short, nothing had been arranged in advance, but there was one place left for the next day and if no-one in the capital Kampala had bought it by 8:30 tomorrow, I could go.

Unfortunately Bowen, as a gap student, didn't have the money to go. We had hoped that the 50% off reduction for East Africa residents, which we were entitled to in the other game parks, would count for gorilla trekking. If this had been the case, I had offered to use my saved half to pay for Bowen to go, but sadly, we got the reduction on the park entry (making it about £1.50) but had to pay full whack for gorillas (£160). So, with that disappointment and every limb and digit crossed for my prospects in the morning, we turned into our tent for the night.

The view that greeted us when we stuck our head out of the tent next morning was of a hillside smothered in steaming jungle and swirling fog. It certainly gave one a taste of what was to follow.

The park official didn't seem enthusiastic for me to go on the trip, but having waited an exasperating 10 minutes past the deadline and when no-one had materialised, he grudgingly conceded that it didn't appear as if there was any obstacle to selling me the last ticket. In my experience, clips round the ear have been rendered for less. However, I wasn't going to let a small matter such as this mar my day and so it was that, with slightly better provisions than last time (1.5l of water and some emergency chocolate), I was heading into the forest at 9am.

It immediately became apparent why this place was called impenetrable. Both sides of the track presented a solid wall of green, which even the most eternal optimist would have thought twice about before attempting to get through. The plant that intrigued me the most was a sort of fern tree, which is supposed to be one of only a handful of species to have survived the last Ice Age. Apparently, the whole of Bwindi forest had survived that period and was pretty much the same now as it had been a million years previously, before the start of the Pleistocene period. It made you think that at any moment a stegosaurus might leer at you from the foliage, or an archaeopteryx could swoop overhead. But it didn't come to pass, that was just an overactive imagination getting the better of me.

We deviated from the main track and followed a much narrower one that wound its way through the montane tropical forest, scaling rises and then dropping down to cross rivers. Then the path became vertical and we scrambled up the slippery, mud path, stopping frequently as members of the group ran out of puff. Having reached the top of this ridge we plunged back into the impenetrable bit. This task was made a little easier by the fact that the trackers had hacked a path through the day before. Gorillas don't move very fast, perhaps only covering a mile in a day, so the trackers start their search where they left the gorillas the day before, fairly confident that they will be close at hand and will have left them a trail to their current whereabouts.

Despite the makeshift traverse, we still snagged ourselves on bushes: reaching out for handholds and finding them full of thorns. It was quite tough going. We stopped a moment for some to breathe and for me to nurse my shredded legs (must remember not to wear shorts next time I'm in an impenetrable forest - sweating like a pig suddenly gains appeal when your legs are in bloody tatters!). The rainforest was also extremely humid. Moisture from the daily rainfall gets trapped below the upper canopy and turns the air into an almost tangible sweat box. All this means you lose a lot of water which needs to be replaced to avoid dehydration.

The guide turned around and asked us how long we thought it would be before we found them, to which I was tempted to reply that we were hoping he would know that! Different members of the group ventured estimates ranging from three hours to hopefully very soon. I had noticed that the advance trackers had returned and wondered if this was a bit of a clue, but I didn't like to steal this bloke's thunder. Our lead tracker seemed to find it quite a good wheeze to ask half a dozen sweating, panting tourists how much further they think they have to go and then watch their faces as the pessimism sets in.

However, it turned out that the return of the advance trackers was the clue and twenty yards further along we saw a female gorilla stuffing her face up a tree. She was shorter than I had imagined, fat, hairy and farted an awful lot. In fact, she was reminiscent of a few girls I have had narrow escapes from in my time. But more to the point, she was at home and didn't seem to mind that we had called round to see her, which was a welcome change after the chimpanzee experience.

We were warned not to get in the path of the gorillas, as this would scare them and make their behaviour more erratic, possibly violent. So we settled down behind them to watch the female in the tree as our cameras were sent whirring. We were alerted to the presence of the youngsters, four of them, and the silverback, who rather unsportingly wasn't showing himself. The young were great though. At times you'd be appreciating their almost human characteristics as they enjoyed a bit of rough and tumble or picked their noses, but then you would be reminded that these were wild beasties, as they hung upside-down from a branch using just a hand or foot.

The pattern emerged that the silverback would get comfortable and start eating everything within reach, before moving on to the next buffet with the females and kids in tow. Interestingly, it wasn't the females who took care of the young ones, but the more mature juveniles. As dad moved off, the tiny ones would clamber onto their older siblings' backs, grab a handful of hair and enjoy the ride.

I wondered if this looking after the younger siblings served as a training ground for sexual maturity when the young gorillas would have offspring of their own to look after. This affection is an example of the close and endearing familial ties existing in the gorilla groups. In her book, 'Gorillas in the Mist', Dian Fossey made several harrowing reports of the shows of grief displayed by gorillas who had lost a member of their group, either through poaching or the often violent interactions with other males. When a male takes over a new group, he will often kill all the offspring of the previous alpha both to ensure the survival of his own genes through the elimination of rival ones and because the females in the group normally become fertile once they are deprived of their young. This behaviour is not unique to gorillas in the animal kingdom.

Gorillas generally seem to spend most of their time eating and resting, in what seems to amount to an idyllic lifestyle. The only fly in this ointment is that they see thistles and wild celery as delicacies, which comprise the greater part of their diet and somewhat jades their otherwise nirvana-like existence.

I went back to watch the female again and before long she climbed out of her tree and walked right past me. If I had reached out, I could have stroked her as she walked past. It was a magical moment. They moved off down the hill and we followed as the trackers cut through the undergrowth with their *pangas.* There the gorillas met up with more members of their Habinyanja group (or H group for those of us who couldn't remember the name, let alone spit the mouthful out).

Gorilla groups tend to have two male silverbacks. The primary male has the task of forming and then leading the group and has the pick of the females. The secondary male, often an eldest son, acts as his minder and can mate with some of the peripheral females. He will usually be expected to take over control of the group upon the death of the primary male. The group can comprise as many females as the male can maintain in his group, protecting them from the sequestering sorties of marauding males with dastardly designs. These females are ranked in importance, usually according to when they joined the group, and give birth roughly every three to five years.

The silverback was frustratingly keeping too far ahead to photograph, but after about 45 minutes the guides and I circled into a good position to get the photos I wanted. This put us in front of the group. As I got the viewfinder to my eye, I saw a blur of black rushing at me.

Now it is said that when a male gorilla charges, you must on no account run away, as this signifies weakness on your part and prompts him to attack with sometimes fatal consequences. However, when 25 stones of muscle and teeth gets it in his head to ward you off with a little threatening frollicking in your direction, I am afraid to say that my first reaction was not to stand and look danger squarely in its furry face. No, my shoulders turned as I made ready to leap into the jungle and get as much distance as possible between myself and the hairy brute. But in the split second that I turned I noticed that neither of the guides had flinched, so, feeling a little sheepish, I forced my feet to stay put and slowly turned back. I was relieved to find that the gorilla had not actually carried through the charge, probably due to the stoic trackers, and he seemed to enjoy an ape-ish chuckle to himself at the whiff of fear he had caused to simper through the trees.

Gorillas are gentle, amiable creatures but they have the power to defend themselves if they feel threatened. They are commonly misunderstood, probably due to a combination of their secrecy and the film industry casting them as blonde-kidnapping super-fiends. I had not deliberately provoked the silverback, and I even wondered afterwards if the rangers had been having some fun with me, but fortunately the animals were unhurt and so was I.

The silverback climbed a nearby tree, the group all scampered up trees after him and that was where we left them as our time was up. Again it was with great regret that we left, as we knew that it had been a once in a lifetime experience. Also, these (approximately) 20 gorillas comprised about 5% of the world's population of these seriously endangered animals. Gorillas share 98% of their genetic make-up with humans, making them our closest animal relative. For this reason, they are particularly susceptible to contracting human diseases and illnesses. The park authorities take the precaution of not allowing people under the age of 16 to view the gorillas as they are more likely to be carrying these germs, a point of view no teacher would argue. Even this seemingly innocuous threat can have a major impact on mountain gorilla populations, and it is taken seriously by park authorities.

The walk back down was much easier than the ascent and it was pleasant to enjoy the feeling of satisfaction from our trekking success. However, it dawned on me towards the end that Bowen was about to set off on another walk shortly and that if he did I would be locked out of the car and tent as he had the keys to both. With this in mind I quickened my pace, leaving the main group behind, and caught up with the well-armed lead group. They knew I spoke Swahili as I had nattered with them on the way up, and one guy told me to go back to the main group, gesturing helpfully with his Kaleshnikov the direction he desired me to take.

"Hapana," I replied. *"Mimi nataka terudi kwa cambi haraka sana, sababu rafiki yangu iko fungua kwa hema na gari!"* (No, I want to return to the car quickly because my friend has the keys to the tent and the car). Since we were nearly back anyway, he responded with a smiling, cheerful *sawa sawa* (okay), and I carried on my forced march.

When I got back Bowen did not seem ready to go anywhere, as he was half way down a beer and had his shoes off. He expressed surprise at my early return and explained that he had just got back from a withering combination of all the walks suggested in the park guide pamphlet. He said that there was no way he was going anywhere. It turned out that his guide had been in radio contact with my guide and the poor sod had been tortured through a running commentary of my successful trip, which he had been unable to to go on. I did feel sorry for him, so we remedied the situation in the only way possible and drank some more beer together.

Following a short booze snooze, we got talking to a guide who was sat meditatively by the campfire. He told us that it was the second anniversary of the Rwandan guerillas attacking the Bwindi camp that day and went on to explain the whole action (it turned out that his dates must have been confused - the events took place on 2nd March 1999 and we were there about 18 months later, though it's very likely he was being vague with his timings).

"They came down from there," he said, pointing behind us, up the hill. "They went into those *bandas* and took some people from a tent just there. They went off into the forest. We followed them but they were armed and we had to stop."

31 tourists of mostly US and British nationality were taken, and a game warden and three of his rangers were killed trying to prevent the guerillas' escape. The rebels wanted to make the point that they did not like the British and American support of the Tutsi minority, 800,000 of whom were butchered by the Hutu majority in Rwanda. The prisoners were tortured and raped, and 8 were murdered. In fairness to the Ugandan government, since then they had stationed one of only four tanks owned by the state down the road, and we had been escorted into the forest by half a dozen well-armed guards (that we knew of - there could easily have been more in the forest unseen by us). So while it was evident that the government was taking security measures, the story was a somber reminder of how the magical African experience can become a nightmare in the blink of an eye.

It must have been our night for stories, as we got talking to a Swedish/Russian guy in the bar who had first attracted our attention due to his brilliant T-shirt which read: "It's Mr. Mzungu to you!" Everywhere you go in Kenya, children call out "Mzungu" to you, in case you were not properly appraised of your skin colour. Mzungu is a term used for white people but is said to originate from a missionary who annoyed a local with his church bell-ringing. The local moved to another village but encountered another bell-ringing missionary. The word *mzungu* is therefore supposed to derive from the term bell-ringer.

Over dinner and beers afterwards Mr. *Mzungu* began telling us about his experiences around the world, which were quite literally beyond belief. He also introduced us to Kasese, a locally brewed spirit which tasted and smelled like tequila, but gave the impression of being more damaging. Despite the fact we were told it had been watered down, I was still amazed to find that I had retained full ocular faculties by the next morning.

Mr. *Mzungu* span a story so full of bravado and self-aggrandising that we sat in dumbfounded silence, allowing him to go on creating his nebulous fiction, staggered by the claims he was making with such a straight face. It reached a point (where he was in Iraq with Saddam Hussein in his sniper's crosshairs) that Mr. *Mzungu*'s storytelling got a bit beyond that point where you're happy to listen to the story for its entertainment value, in spite of its obvious deviation from the truth. Bowen and I bade him a goodnight and made our way back to the tent. On our way, Bowen was about to begin the conversation about the absolute bull we had listened to at the same time as I was about to warn him that I had seen a ruddy great drainage ditch somewhere in the vicinity. Unfortunately, he went first, both with his topic and, consequently, into the ditch. Naturally, in the ensuing hilarity Mr *Mzungu* and his fantastic stories were forgotten.

I had discovered that three members of my group on the gorilla trek were teachers at Greensteds school, about half an hour up the road from where we worked in Kenya. I had thought they looked vaguely familiar when I had first seen them. Greensteds used to have a *makuti* hut staff bar which I had frequented once, though from these occasions it isn't always possible to remember names with crystal clarity. They were planning to take the public transport bus back to Kampala the next day, but since we were going that way, we offered to give them a lift and they accepted. We juggled luggage and they had their rucksacks on their laps, but everyone was better off than the roof rack, which Bowen related had been uncomfortable even for the comparatively short time he'd been up there.

I fancied the idea of going to Kisiizi Falls, which was in a very rural location but would offer a beautiful vista and cut a corner for us to get onto the main road for Kampala. The others agreed and, since we didn't have a very detailed map, I sat down to copy the relevant part of the map in park headquarters onto a piece of scrap paper.

Accordingly, we set off next morning to find Kisiizi and it so happened that somewhere early in the journey an insect stung me just where a bloke least wants to be stung. Indeed, at the next stop for improvised toilet facilities (pee on the verge) I was quick to get my valuables out and inspect the damage. You can only imagine my horror at finding a 10mm sting hanging out of my right testicle!

As everyone else urinated with contented faces, mine was etched in agony as I tried to wrestle the menace free. At first I only succeeded in breaking half of it off, making it more difficult to get at the rest, but I spent some time trying to squeeze out the remainder between my thumb nails, wriggling and writhing partly with the effort and partly with the pain. I can only imagine that the two locals who walked past, pausing to observe the tussle by the roadside, thought I was either mad or perverse.

Oddly, the Greensteds teachers didn't seem to appreciate my relief at having finally removed the offending alien body. Bowen was much more sympathetic, or at least he laughed heartily for a good few hours afterwards at my misfortune, which is what you can expect from a mate under the circumstances.

Our trip through the countryside proved thoroughly worthwhile as we passed through beautiful tea farmland, picked our way along tiny mountain tracks and were constantly amazed at the size of the local bovine horns, which sometimes doubled the height of the cow. My hand drawn map proved effective for the most part (there were a few disputes about this along the way, but those people can write their own account!), though assistance was asked for and given by several friendly locals who kept us going the right way. I maintain that the conversations with locals confirmed the accuracy of my map, but this wasn't the universally held view.

Kisiizi Falls proved to be rewardingly impressive. There is a story that unmarried pregnant girls were thrown from the top into the swirling pools below. Whether this was for their spiritual cleansing, to abort the fetus or to kill the girl wasn't clear, but the brick red colour of the water that cascaded from the 50 foot cliff suggested that the blood of these poor lasses still coursed over the rocks. Luckily, due to a huge mission we saw being built in the town, wayward local girls need only fear for their eternal damnation rather than the loss of their lives, for which I'm sure they are grateful.

Quite some time later we reached the tarmac road, to which there was much rejoicing, but we still had quite a trek left to get to Kampala, to which there was understandably much woe. We thrashed the car up these superior roads and were setting up camp in a Kampala backpackers place by nightfall.

Having assessed our waning kitty, we asked the tour operators if we could bring the white water rafting forward a day. The phone call was made and the fixture changed, though as we watched videos of previous rafting trips on the screen in the backpackers bar that night we did wonder if we had lost all grip on our sanity.

Strangely, Bowen was up bright and early the next morning and, as much as it pained me to quell this enthusiasm, it was only 6am and we really ought to get the extra hour's sleep. However, his bowels were as excited as his nervous system and weren't letting him sleep. We were packed up and ready to go at 7.

At about half past, two long haired Aussies turned up, talking gibberish and generally getting everyone in the mood. We paid and arranged to meet again at Bujagali Falls, where the River Nile leaves Lake Victoria and our rafting was to commence. We had decided to go by car as it got us nearer to the border for the next day's return to Kenya.

The staff were a mix of Ugandans and Antipodean hippies, flowing locks seeming to be a sort of uniform amongst the *mzungu* employees. The chap with the camera proved to be particularly taxing, as he had a habit of coming right up into your face and talking crap at you. He also had a predilection for shots of people taking big bites out of things. During the course of the day, I was filmed swallowing a whole banana and taking an enormous bite out of a Scooby-snack-esque sandwich, both of which I willingly performed, as he seemed to buzz off and leave you in peace once you'd satisfied this particular whim. I should point out that, even though they had these odd quirks, all the staff were brilliant and really added an extra energy to the day - though it really didn't need too much livening up!

We finally got into the rafts, wearing our helmets and life jackets, and were talked through all the procedures by our guide, Juma. These included rowing left, right and straight ahead, grabbing hold of the sides and GET DOWN! Juma was a brilliant guide with a love of life only equalled by the love of his job, the latter ironically endangering the former. He wore a fixed, maniacs grin in the face of everything and laughed at all occurrences: getting thrown in the water, getting clobbered by a stray oar, it didn't matter. He was great and the success of the trip was in a large part down to his personality.

White water rapids are graded from 1 to 6. A grade 6 rapid is likely to kill you and should only be attempted by a professional rafter, so Muppets like us were allowed to try rapids up to grade 5. It was explained that there would be three kayakers waiting at the bottom of each rapid to come and get us in case of any trouble. We might need to hold out breath for 5 seconds, "But you can hold your breath for 5 seconds, right?" asked Juma, wearing the smile of the clinically insane. We all nodded back mirroring his facial expression.

After our instruction, we set off into a grade 3 to whet our appetites before heading straight into a grade 5, presumably to get wet. After all there is no substitute for getting stuck right in!

Some of the group said they didn't remember much about this rapid as it happened so quickly, but I remember it vividly, which I suppose is because time seemed to stand still in the terror! We hit the rapid fairly quickly and were turned sideways as we went in. The boat tipped sideways and I held onto the rope around the side until the raft landed on top of me and I assumed there wasn't much point in holding on any longer.

Juma had said we would be under the water for 5 seconds, but it seemed like weeks. I saw black, then green, then blue, then white before I came to the surface. Before I could take a breath I was taken by a wave, carried to the crest of the swell and then dropped back to the bottom. Again I came up and this time got a half breath before the procedure was repeated.

I was just wondering whether the rescue team would get to me before I drowned, when a heavy thump over the back of the head heralded the arrival of a kayaker. I grabbed hold. The kayakers were damned good, to give them their due. Not only were they in grade 5 rapids but they were naoeuvering through them to get to the stragglers and then dragging them out. When I got hold of the kayak I was the third person clinging to it and he paddled us effortlessly to safety. It may seem like a strange reaction to what I have just described, but it was brilliant! I coughed up half the river, laughed raucously and clambered back into the raft looking forward to the next rapid.

The next one to tip us was a grade 3. This time I was on the side that got tipped up and I was thrown into the rush. I was at least able to hold onto my paddle, a feat of which I was very proud, but in throwing it back onto the boat I nearly beaned another member of the group who was climbing back on! We were chastised for this potentially dangerous action.

We stopped for lunch at an island in the middle of the river. We moored the rafts and walked up a wooden staircase to a little clearing in the underbrush. There we found a four-foot monitor lizard, which was a most impressive sight and scared some female members of our group silly. The lunch was great, with an enormous selection of sandwich fillings that we stacked high and attacked ferociously. During the lunch break a Guatemalan chap and his wife decided they'd had enough and returned home. He reckoned it was because his wife couldn't swim, but she hadn't seemed too upset. He had taken a dunking in the first capsize and had clearly not enjoyed swallowing a lot of water. I think he was using her as a scapegoat to cover his own anxiety, particularly as she couldn't speak English to defend herself!

Shortly after lunch the sun disappeared, fog rolled in from the lake and a hail storm started. Not only this but the rain was so heavy you could hardly see and the wind kept blowing us back upstream. Funnily enough, the best place to keep warm throughout this was in the river, which maintained its warmth - a far cry from the British river water that I was used to!

The wind meant that we had to paddle really hard between rapids, just to maintain our forward progress. Between rapid sets, Juma told us that the record for the most times tipped into the water was four times, and that there were two more sets of rapids to come that could have us overboard. Considering ourselves to have the requisite lack of boating ability, we thought there was a good chance we could equal that record and it was with much enthusiasm that we splashed our way to the next big one.

Unfortunately, we were close but no Havana. The boat tipped, we all prepared for a dip, but then it righted itself and we slipped away. We were disappointed not to be able to challenge for the record, but looked forward to the next rapid, which was another grade 5.

The run up to the last rapid was too dangerous for non-pros to attempt - it was a grade 6, an award it achieved when someone drowned there when they were grading it - so we got out of the river and, having lugged the boat along the bank, re-entered just above the grade 5. The rapid looked fearsome. There was a big dip and then a swell rose up in front of it like an enormous dune.

We got in and heard Juma shout, "Paddle hard forward!" I looked and thought to myself, 'But that will lead us straight into that bloody great dip,' and with a wave of understanding, it occurred to me that this was the plan! The nose of the boat went into the swell; the nose popped up so the boat was standing on its rear part, and then flipped over backwards. Being at the front, I was thrown from a height of about four metres above the water and back into the swell. This time I had plenty of time, whilst airborne, to realise what was happening and take a big breath before tumbling in.

We swam to the side as we had been instructed to and wondered where the boat had gone. Juma appeared with the raft soon after and was in great cheer. He proclaimed that he had never before been able to flip the boat backwards like that and we were justifiably proud for him. We climbed back into the raft to continue to our pick up point, but as one lady threw her oar aboard the handle caught me squarely in the groin. As I lay in a crumpled heap on the deck, I reflected that although I had had a brilliant time in Uganda, maybe my genitals had not.

We took the bus back to Bujagali with the guides and kayakers. They had laid on a full crate of beer on the bus and since the staff weren't drinking, they plied us with beer after beer. We "grudgingly" complied and were absolutely legless by the time we returned to the campsite. There we tried to converse with the campsite staff but were reduced to giggling like school girls for the most part. They didn't see the humour in this. We then compounded the problem by trying the ESB (an acronym for Extra Strong Brew at 7.5%). This didn't help us achieve sobriety but was a splendid way to see out Uganda.

Next morning we discovered that our ability to set up the tent had been adversely affected by the beer as we were woken by the tent flooding in the early hours. We packed up in the rain and made off.

To us, Uganda had been the 'Pearl of Africa' - a quote most associated with Winston Churchill following his visit in 1907 but which was probably first used by Henry Morton Stanley, the Welsh/American journalist more famous for the line, "Mr. Livingstone, I presume?", in the late 19th century. The sapphire skies, emerald vegetation and ruby soils makes for a jewellery box of colours and yet the friendliness of Ugandan people is its winning ticket.

However, it can be difficult to disassociate Uganda from its string of awful post-colonial leaders: Obote, Amin and Museveni. Their achievements include violence, dysfunctional government, ousting the entire Asian population and a catastrophic invasion of Tanzania that was not only repelled, but ended in the Tanzanian occupation of Uganda. With the Lord's Resistance Army, recruiting child soldiers in the North of the country under its leader, Joseph Kony while we were there, it wasn't entirely surprising to witness a child of surely no more than 11 wielding a rifle by the roadside as we left. Though Museveni had achieved a level of stability at the time we were there, it had come at the expense of any recognisable democracy.

At the border we were required to pay £2 to leave the country on the solid grounds that it was a Saturday! When we arrived back at school we had covered 2300km. The week had been perfect from start to finish (perhaps excepting THOSE two injuries) and I will always harbour fond memories of Uganda.

ETHIOPIA

When I booked my flights home for Christmas 2000, Ethiopia Airways had very good prices which I jumped on. Unfortunately, there had been a mistake in the booking which was going to keep me in Addis Ababa for a few days waiting for my onward flight. Before changing the tickets, however, I read a little bit about Ethiopia, as I had toyed with the idea of visiting before. As well as the endemic animal species roaming the Bale mountains and high altitude mountains of Ras Dashen, Ethiopia had churches carved out of the rock at a place called Lalibela; the Ark of the Covenant was said to rest under a stele at Axum; palaces and castles had been built in the African equivalent of Camelot in Gondar; and monasteries clung to islands in Lake Tana. I was intrigued! This wasn't the Africa I knew to date and I wanted to find out more.

The easy part was changing the ticket to allow me a week in Ethiopia - the difficult part was the red tape to get in! As most UK travellers will be aware, it is normally quite straightforward to buy or be given your visa upon arrival in many countries, but Ethiopia was not an adherent to this system. I dutifully sent off to the embassy to find out the details and waited to hear from them.

Two weeks later I had heard nothing, which was a bit of a problem, as I was flying the next day. In a hasty rehash of the original plan, a friend took me to the embassy to try to get the visa through in one day, instead of the four it usually takes. The lady at the desk gasped in shock at what I was proposing. I gasped back, so she wouldn't feel self-conscious.

As I waited outside the locked embassy door the next day, with about *an hour to get to the airport, it did occur to me that maybe I had pushed it a bit far this time, but when the door opened everything seemed okay. With the wind from the open car window drying the ink on the visa, we rushed to the airport having pulled off a get-out-of-jail stunt!*

My first job upon entering Ethiopia was to stash one of my bags at the airport for the week, as I reckoned it would be more comfortable to only be shouldering one pack around. The only problem with this was that I didn't speak the native Amharic and the lady in charge of baggage didn't speak any English or Swahili. However, I couldn't have found a nicer lady to help me and, with a few smiles and helpless looks, it was like having your mum there to look after you!

Another area in which my planning had fallen down was in not realising that you could book internal flights from Britain. I had intended to just turn up and jump on a plane. However, I was informed that, as it was Orthodox Christmas in Ethiopia, all the flights to anywhere with churches were fully booked and that about wiped out my planned destinations for air travel! I hung about at the airport in the hopes that someone wouldn't turn up and that I could take their seat, but they all did. Naturally this was a bit disappointing. Refusing to be beaten, I took a taxi to the bus station to get a ticket to Lalibela for the festive celebrations.

It was great to see the fleets of Lada taxis, all painted a uniform blue and white, parked down one side of the car park, while the classier taxis (I forget what model of car they were) were all parked down the other side, decorated in a garish New York-cab yellow. Ladas turned out to be a very popular make of car in Ethiopia, rivalled by the sturdy VW Beetle, of which I am a fan.

The cabby was a bit of a card who couldn't speak a lot of English, though in fairness it vastly overshadowed my abilities in Amharic. I have to confess that Amharic seemed more difficult to get the tongue round than Swahili. A lot of Swahili words tend to be quite simple and short, whereas the words in the Ethiopian language were predominantly the opposite. However, I am proud to say that I had mastered a few of the basics by the end of my stay: hello; how are you?; fine; thank you; where is; I want; goodbye. Nothing too swish, just enough to keep food on a plate before me and a smile on the face of the people I met.

I finally got over to the taxi driver where I wanted to go and we set off while he gave me a lecture on communism, from which I derived that he was not a fan. He asked me what my name was. I am often amused by the difficulty it gives people, considering that the name I give is monosyllabic,

"Max?"

"No, Matt."

"Ah, Mash?"

"No, Matt."

"Ah, Mats?"

"No, Matt."

"Math?"

"Yes, I suppose that'll do nicely."

While I considered the possibility that I had a speech impediment, he told me his name was Zeri, promptly grollied up, with a sound like a jet aeroplane waiting for takeoff, and spat out of the window. I wondered if this was some Ethiopian "pleased to meet you" custom I had transgressed on, or if he just didn't like his own name. Who knows?

Zeri dropped me off next to the bus station right next to a leaking drain, which stank to high heaven. It is said that every country has its own unique stinky drain smell. If this is true, then put me in the camp that doesn't favour the Ethiopian version much! This was to be a common occurrence in the towns of Ethiopia, but undeterred I jumped out and bought my ticket. The girl at the desk thought it was fantastic that the bus would be carrying four white people and could barely suppress her excitement!

I tipped the youngster who had shown me to the correct door for my purchase, but I was rather surprised when he laughed at it, and I'm sure I heard him throw it away when I turned my back. I later worked out that I had given him a note worth just less than a penny. Oops! Upon arrival in a new country it is quite easy to get a bit confused by the value of the currency.

I left to find the hotel I had selected from my guidebook, or 'Bible' as they are often known, for the almost religious fervour with which they are carried everywhere by nomadic tribes of backpackers. It was described as 'clean, well-run and good value'. Opening the door of the taxi again revealed the almighty stench of an overworked drain, but the hotel room looked okay for just under 4 quid.

Having secured the lodgings for the night, I toddled off into town for a word with the good people of Ethiopia Airways and a final revamp of my travel plans. The only available flight that was of any use to me was my return from Gondar to Addis Ababa to get me back in time for my flight to Nairobi. This meant that I was going to have to cut Bahar Dar out of my itinerary leaving me with just Lalibela and Gondar, with a two day bus journey between each. I resolved that this wouldn't be so bad, as I'd get to see some of the country from the wagon. However, the buying of a ticket was a bit of a pain. I didn't have enough cash to pay and had to nip over the road to change some Birr (pronounced as if there was no 'i', a bit like expressing a degree of cold) into US dollars.

The paperwork to buy 11 bucks was unbelievably vast! They wanted to stamp my passport, air tickets, backside, everything! All just for some exchange! I then had to go back to the EA office and wait to see a chap and his computer, who sent me to someone else to pick up the ticket, who sent me to someone else to pay for it. Travel in Africa requires a certain sense of humour and a great deal of patience, though I was ably entertained by a Rasta fellow who was singing quite happily at his office desk.

The term Rastafarian comes from the former Emperor of Ethiopia who, before taking the imperial name Haile Selassie, was called Ras Tafari. The former slaves in the Caribbean believed that one day they would return to their homelands of Africa, and settled upon Ethiopia as their Promised Land because it was relatively untainted by European powers. Indeed, Ethiopia had been one of the few African success stories in repelling European powers when they decisively won the Battle of Adwa of 1895-96, bringing to a close the First Italo-Ethiopian War.

Italy did gain control of Ethiopia following the Second Italo-Ethiopian War in 1938, having secured victory through the use of chemical weapons, on the expressed authority of Italian dictator Benito Mussolini. However, this occupation was short-lived, as events in the wider East African Campaign of the Second World War removed Italy from Ethiopia and reinstated Haile Selassie as Emperor in 1941.

I was having a quiet drink in the hotel (Castle <not to be confused with the South African brand>: a quite reasonable flavour with no lurking aftertaste), when the manager came over and we started talking. Darien was a very friendly fellow, who, as it turned out was common with Ethiopians I met, was extremely keen to know what a foreigner thought of the

Ethiopian people and their hospitality. This is a source of huge national pride for Ethiopians and made my visit all the more enjoyable. He wanted to know where I was from and why I had come to his country.

He asked me if I would like to come back to his house to see the coffee ceremony and I readily agreed. I had been a coffee enthusiast for some time. A girlfriend at university had expressed great disdain at my drinking instant and had bought me my first French press. I was an instant convert! My imagination of faraway places was stimulated as I bought Arabica from exotic places around the globe and I even had a vivid dream in which I was a coffee plantation owner. I had heard of the Ethiopian coffee ceremony and couldn't believe my luck at being invited to attend one on my first day in the country.

First we went to a cafe and ate a traditional Ethiopian meal which was really filling, so much so that the two of us couldn't finish it. The meal consisted of injera bread (like a fluffy, bitter pancake tasting like it had lemon in it) used as a plate, upon which a selection of minced meats, flavoured with different spices and sauces, was served. You tear off strips of the injera and use it to pick up the meat. The injera is made from flour and fills you up very quickly, though I confess that I wasn't overly keen on the bitter, slightly acidic flavour.

From there Darien took me to some chat dens to try to purchase some of the local leaf. Bundles of leafy chat twigs are wrapped in a palm frond and then the chat user picks off all the leaves and chews them up. This is normally accompanied by drinking soft drinks or milk and smoking tobacco from a shisha. The dens themselves looked great! There were shelves, covered in palm leaves and chat stalks, all full of blokes nattering away under a fog of shisha smoke.

Chat, also known by several other spellings of the same word (khat, qat, quatt, ghat), is a translation from Arabic into romanised letters. It is native to the Horn of Africa and the Arabian Peninsular and contains the alkaloid cathinone, said by the World Health Organisation to be a drug of potential abuse but on the other hand not problematic. Chat is supposed to be one of Ethiopia's main exports, most of which goes to Djibouti. Darien assured me that if the delivery comes late then the mood among the fellas of Djibouti is much akin to that of their brothers in Wales following rugby defeat to their neighbours: utterly foul!

Anyway, armed with our stash we made off for Darien's lair, which wasn't such a bad pad. He had a concrete built, blockish abode, built in a residential neighbourhood of Addis Ababa. I tried the chat, which is supposed to induce a relaxed but awake feeling, though I didn't like it much as the taste made your mouth very dry. However, chat was not the reason I had accepted his offer to come back. I was there for coffee.

The coffee ceremony is said to be an ancient tradition in this country, which claims to be the first to have used the berries from the plant (a claim disputed by Yemen, a short hop over the Red Sea from Ethiopia). A goatherd was said to have noticed his flock being naughtier and more lively than normal after they had eaten the red berries from the bush and for a long time the berries were eaten rather than drunk. The procedure I observed obviously hadn't reached the politically correct age, as the woman seemed to do all the work while the men reap the reward. Darien's partner, Eshe, carried out the whole process, which went as follows:

A small clay pot was filled with charcoal and over this little inferno, the beige, dried coffee beans were dry roasted in a pan. The most endearing part of the process was when Eshe held the pan of roasted beans before us, and we wafted the aroma towards our eager nostrils, "mmm"-ing our appreciation. This gesture of appreciation was somewhat sullied when Darien sent his partner outside to pummel the beans in a pestle and mortar out of earshot, so that the sound did not interrupt our discussions inside.

Eshe returned to add the coffee grounds to some boiling water in a charming little vase/jug thing - an Ethiopian coffee pot, no less - which had been heating up on the same charcoal brazier that had previously been used to roast the beans. Once the coffee grounds were in the coffee pot, the vessel was placed back on the heat to steep. The finished product was then poured into small cups, copious amounts of sugar was added and it was served up. Sometimes cinnamon is added too, which gives a pleasant flavour. This seems quite commonplace nowadays, but at the time was the first time I had ever encountered it. Apparently, some tribal groups, notably in the western and southern areas, add butter to the coffee, which didn't sound so good.

I returned to the hotel to catch up on my journal entries, to ensure I could recount the coffee ceremony just given in full detail, but I got somewhat side-tracked when I asked the waiter to soak the beer bottle in water so that I could get the label off. At the time, I collected beer bottle labels of new beers I encountered on my travels. No amount of play-acting and buffoonery could overcome the language barrier between us and convey my meaning, so I went to get the jerry can from under the bed to demonstrate.

When I asked him to fill the jerry can with water, he gave me a look like I was insane and even when I had successfully shown him the technique, I'm still not sure I had proved to him that I had a secure hold on my marbles. However, the waiters immediately took to this new pastime, bringing all kinds of bottles out from various receptacles to prize off the labels in order to please the foreign guest and they seemed justifiably proud of their prowess in this new-found technique. This led to a more wide-ranging debate on all sorts of traveller's topics before I left to get some sleep preceding the big trip to Lalibela on the morrow.

I woke up an hour after I had asked to be woken and at the exact time that the bus was scheduled to leave. In my haste to pack my bag I may have left my camera in the room or dropped it from an insufficiently secure pocket or had it nicked while I was flustered and not paying due attention, but somehow by the time I had taken my seat on the bus, I was down one camera. As I rushed for the hotel door, the chap who I had asked to raise me in time hailed me with a smile, "Don't worry! There is plenty of time!" I am afraid that, on the back of only three hours sleep (perhaps due to the chat?) and the potential ruining of my holiday (due to the fact that there simply wasn't another bus going north for me to catch if I missed mine), my reply was not as polite as it could have been.

Anyway, we both rushed off to the station and, lo and behold, the hotel chap was right. Always trust Africa to run its public transport off the timetable! In fact, I sat on the bus for an hour and a half before it had filled sufficiently to set off.

This journey north, I reasoned, was my first look at the real Ethiopia: Addis Ababa had given me a feel for it and I was looking forward to this next step despite the smelly open drains and profusion of crippled beggars, which were a bit upsetting of stomach and heart respectively. We travelled through lots of different terrains during the course of the day. The land dropped in altitude to an arable farming plain before gradually climbing to pastoral heights. They both looked pretty dry but quite healthy. I was surprised by the volume of wheat growing throughout the country, though the flour for the injera has to come from somewhere.

As a child of the '80s, it is difficult to separate Ethiopia's image from the pictures of the drought (which were actually several droughts) early in that decade. It therefore came as a bit of a shock to see the fields so full of wheat. In fact, one of the accusations of the Derg government of the time was that it used record harvests to pay for the civil war effort, dedicating 46% of its national budget to the war, mostly paid for through the sale of wheat on the international market. There were many contributing factors to these famines that left half a million dead and 3 million displaced, and these do include rain failure. However, the Ethiopian government had delivered a program of policies that multiplied the effects of the famine, often deliberately. For these crimes, president Mengistu Haile Mariam was sentenced to death in Ethiopia following the defeat of the Derg government, but continues to live in exile in Zimbabwe.

All the time we were climbing and eventually the sun disappeared as we drove into a dense mass of cloud. Visibility was poor but it didn't slow the bus driver down. He carried on bouncing the bus around pot-holed corners with one hand on the horn and one hand gesticulating wildly at oncoming traffic. This rather begged the question, how is the bus being steered?

The terrain took on a decidedly Alpine essence as the temperature dropped, the coniferous trees waved their needly limbs and the road wound its way back and forth along the sheer precipice that was one of its curbs, for what seemed to be the whole journey. The driver obviously fancied himself as a stunt driver for 'The Italian Job', or some such, perpetually posing the question, "Can a fully loaded bus turn a 90 degree corner on two wheels?" Fortunately for us as passengers, this had a positive answer.

The size of these volcanic mountains of the African Rift was breathtaking. They rise like titans from the dry valley and, due to the shape of them, you could see right to the depths and felt as if you were teetering precariously on the edge of an abyss. Descent from these heights was the same breakneck, twisting frenzy as the ascent and soon we were at the valley bottom, walled in on either side by looming mountains. Unfortunately, just then we got a flat tire and were all herded out onto the verge.

Now there is nothing quite like a white person to arouse the interest of a rural African and soon three Israelis and I had quite an audience of locals and fellow travellers. The social stigma of staring doesn't exist here. At first it's a bit unnerving to have a group of about a dozen people just standing and staring at you, but this soon wears off, even if their interest in you does not.

We were soon on our way and passed a wide riverbed that had just a trickle running through it. The stones that littered the bed were the size, not of houses, but warehouses, hinting that a larger volume of water passed through these channels at some point. I thought it looked rather sad, like a skeleton devoid of flesh and life. Two alarming things I saw that day were parts of the bridge we were crossing that had collapsed and a lorry that had plunged off the sheer face we were rushing across the top of. I enjoyed seeing the camels as we got further north, and the table tennis set up by the roadside in many of the villages with cheery locals vigorously whiffing and whaffing.

Dessie was a small town with nothing immediately apparent to recommend it. In fairness, I could have missed something special as it was dark when I arrived and so instead of going off exploring, I settled for a meal in the hotel. The menu was completely in Amharic and the manager didn't speak English. I referred to the guidebook which gave me, not only the translation for chicken, *doro*, but also an idea of what the Amharic symbols for this looked like. Having identified this, I pointed to the word for *doro* and awaited my meal at a little table on my own, with my book for company.

The meal arrived and was half a deep fried chicken in a crispy batter served with warmed up vegetables of some sort. I was so engrossed in my book that it was only as I chomped down the last of my dinner that I turned the chicken over and discovered that the flesh was completely black. I had never seen this before and imagined that this might have unfortunate repercussions in the near future. I sincerely hoped it wouldn't occur while I was on the bus and unable to stop.

Next day we set off for another long drive at about 6am. As I walked from my hotel to the bus station, I noticed lots of people sleeping on the streets. This, and the number of beggars, led me to the conclusion that the economic improvements made by the government had not been far-reaching enough to include the whole population. However, this initial impression of the country may not have been an altogether accurate one. I was travelling at Orthodox Christmas, when many Ethiopian people make pilgrimages to exactly the places I was going to, and many of them only had money to pay for transport. Therefore overnight stays in hotels must be forfeit for the opportunity to reach these religiously important destinations. This would mean that there would be many more people living rough in the places I was staying in, at that precise time of year. It was also true that beggars migrated to these places of worship, intent on collecting the richer pickings associated with pious pilgrims.

I found the beggars particularly upsetting. An old woman begged from me that day and I could understand nothing but the pathetic, pleading manner in which it was carried out. It seems a shame that old people should be reduced to this state, when in other societies either a welfare safety net provides for their needs or social norms require that they are looked after in their families' homes. Having said that, poverty hits the truly vulnerable hardest and Ethiopia is stuck in a long-standing poverty that was readily apparent at the time I was there.

The journey took us through rugged mountain terrain again. The driver was just as mental as the one from the day before and, following an incident where he avoided an oncoming lorry at top speed with the bus inches from where the road slipped away down the hill, I adopted a 'don't look down' policy which helped to keep my trousers clean. We passed four wrecked tanks during the day, relics of the civil war years, as were the destroyed bridges. The older bridges were quite impressive in style, with arched stone traverses, but uninspiring concrete ones took their place where they had had to be rebuilt.

I couldn't get over the mountains! They really were an imposing presence and it is difficult to describe the sort of physical intimidation they inspire in you. It was like being a small child thrust into a huddle of sumo wrestlers. Their tangible power is plain to see, but there is an almost regal, spiritual strength entwined, like kings looking down from a great vantage to pass judgement. As we wove back and forth up the mountain road, I had the impression of climbing God's own ladder into the clouds for a divine audience. Perhaps this was all a part of the pilgrimage taking place around me, which now seemed to include me. The hills were heavily farmed by the local people in spite of the steepness of the incline. The Ethiopian farmers had terraced almost the entire landscape to increase the surface area for planting, to decrease soil run-off when it rains and to stop that precious water disappearing so fast at all. And upon these thousand steps, they planted the wheat to sustain the enormous population of the country.

We stopped off for a bit of breakfast and, as I stood looking up at the hills, a young boy came up to me. We stood for a second, each eyeing the other, me smiling and nodding foolishly, expecting our language barrier to prevent any actual conversation. Then with all the differences between him and I, he pointed to my feet and said, "Green laces." Pleased with his English language practice for the day, he scampered off to who knows what pursuit, leaving me feeling perplexed by this enjoyable vaguery.

As I looked at the scenery around me I felt like I was back in Cross Keys for a moment. There is a rugby pitch there, next to the college I used to play against and then work at, which is overshadowed by a great hill that appears to loom over the top of the park. But for the rugby pitch being a bus station, I could have been standing in that corner of South Wales. This got me thinking about travelling, and why a person does it. Is it to spread your wings, to expand your knowledge of peoples and histories, to learn about yourself, to learn new ways of doing things, to test yourself? I suppose it is all of these things to a greater or lesser degree, but for me at that moment I was struck by being able to see things you can compare as similar to your previous experiences and things you can find that are absolutely different.

When we had finally conquered the ascent, we found ourselves on a mountain plateau. I recall thinking that this was the stuff of the harrowing TV reports I had seen as a kid, though the crops did look quite robust now. However, it was cold and dry: not good conditions for growing crops. It was easier to believe in the harshness of the landscape here, and the great challenge locals must undertake to survive. I later discovered that the main famine had hit further north than I ventured. I had decided against the Axum monument for the fact that there was still seperatist military activity going on there. During the civil war, the government had used famine as a weapon against the Tigray people who lived in the north and there were still disgruntled soldiers willing to carry on the struggle in the region..

From this vantage, you could see for miles. The surrounding hills stood like islands that were missing their sea, or giant's stepping stones. As we came off the plateau the driver thankfully calmed down, but I craned my neck looking back at a different kind of beauty these magnificent mountains had thrown up. This side of the ridge was all cliff face, complete with sedimentary layers to drive a geologist delirious! To me they looked like enormous castles: the rocky outcrops the towers, the lower rock veins the curtain walls, and they would have been impenetrable.

We stopped in a village for some reason, just next to one of the roadside priests. They approach the bus clad in colourful robes with an upside-down umbrella proffered towards the passengers, ready to catch any loot the lay travellers cared to lob their way. Those who made such a contribution were rewarded by being tapped on the bonce with a little wooden cross before being allowed to kiss said cross, top and bottom. There were lots of these birds by the roadside, each leaping carefree into the path of the lunatic bus driver, waving their colourfully embroidered brollies as we sped by. I particularly liked this one though, as he was one of the few who had a big tapestry spread on the roadside next to him. The tapestry depicted the angel St. Mikael, waving his sword about in a manly fashion, as he gave a blue Lucifer his marching orders from God's heavenly abode. I liked Ethiopian art for its simple style and bright colours: a spectacular splash of the spectrum! This makes the unusually wide-eyed characters that much bolder and more easily understood, even for an art dunce like myself.

There was a point when a chappy went around the bus collecting 1 Birr from everyone, to which my first thought was that they were taking bets on whether we would make it to Lalibela alive. However, it turned out that my irony was misplaced, as we pulled up next to this little unmanned kiosk with a cross on its roof and the chap slapped all the money in the collection box. Upon reflection, I pondered whether the passengers were hedging their bets should they fail to make it to Lalibela alive, upon which disaster they could point to their generous contributions to help them pass the pearly gates. Either way, these Ethiopians were a religious lot. Christianity has a long tradition in Ethiopia, having been introduced as the state religion of the ancient Aksum kingdom by King Ezana in AD330. There are stories dating further back than this but their precision is blurred by translations of ancient language usage. For instance, Ethiopian was a common term for any black African 200 years ago, so that references to Ethiopia being Christianised could actually refer to any African group, but more probably ancient Nubians.

As we neared our destination, it appeared that the driver had found himself a new game to replace chicken with petrol tankers, which had apparently become tired and obsolete. The local beasties were clearly not as accustomed to a big bus horn as those nearer the greater cities, and this wonderful instrument sent the animals fleeing in terror, often dragging their unfortunate herdsmen with them. One of the striking things about my experience in Africa was the sometimes odd things they laughed at. I got talking to the bus conductor (or such as they are in Africa) and the locals listened intently. He asked me how old I was, to which I replied that I was 24 years old, prompting not a little mirth from the eager audience. He proceeded to ask me how old I thought he was and I told him I didn't know. "47," he proudly announced and this was greeted with peels of hysterical laughter. Well, I joined in, as it seemed impolite to remain with a perplexed but untickled look upon my face.

Upon arriving in Lalibela I was immediately grabbed by a guide, who had a slick haircut and ponytail, which was unique for this country in my experience. It turned out that as well as guiding tourists (for real money, he explained), he ran a barbers shop too and his buffon was partly advertising. Shemellah was a nice enough guy and once I'd got my tent up, he showed me around the churches.

I had been really looking forward to seeing these, having read about them once I'd decided to go to Lalibela and Ethiopia. They were built out of solid rock using a method where they sunk trenches into the hills in a roughly crucifix form and carved out the stone that remained in the middle. They were extremely impressive buildings, the more so when you consider that if a mistake was made in the carving then it would have messed up the whole job, as opposed to European style churches where the offending block could be taken out and replaced.

The churches were built by a king Lalibela in the late 12th/ early 13th century. He was supposedly given divine help by angels who would come down to work at night as the king's mortal workforce slept. The king, who gave his name to the town upon his death, was part of the short-lived Zagwa dynasty, who briefly overthrew the Solomonic line, which traced back to the fruit of King Solomon and Queen Sheba's loins: Menelik I. The Solomonic dynasty was only supplanted by this one interruption and was otherwise able to trace its ascendancy from Biblical times to its end in 1974 at the hand of the Derg communists.

My guide took me down past the Christmas Eve mass (advising me, as he would many times, to watch my pockets - it seemed that not all contributions were made voluntarily!) and to see the pilgrims gathering for prayer. Tens of thousands had descended on this small town and in the trenches around the churches the floor was thick with people reserving their places ready for the action. I could barely take a step without treading on someone! As preparations were being made for the services, we could not see inside the churches, but could view the outside quite well enough. The decoration was mostly monochromatic, bearing the colour of the rock from which the free-standing churches were hewn. It was odd to see so many swastikas in the windows. In modern parlance, the swastika is a symbol that represents Nazism and is a far cry from the original symbol of divine good luck. It seems a shame that an innocent symbol had been taken by the madmen and bastardised.

Shemellah claimed that it was the Ethiopians under Lalibela who first started using this symbol, though there may be a touch of national pride interfering with this claim's authenticity. The earliest known swastika shape was part of a pattern on a bird carved from mammoth ivory around 10,000BC. The symbol has variously been described as representing a flying stork, the rotation of the north pole or a spinning comet, but the name we now use has been around since 500BC, when the Sanskrit words su ("good, well") and asti ("there is, it is") were combined to describe "health, luck, success, prosperity." The celebrated German archaeologist, Heinrich Schliemann, discovered the swastika on artifacts at a dig in Turkey dating from around 1000BC and recognised their similarity with symbols on German pottery from the 6th century AD. The Nazis later took this and used it to justify their belief in an ancient Aryan master race that ruled Europe and Asia, using Schliemann's finds as evidence of the migration.

I decided to take an early night so that I could be rested for a big day of exploration the next day, but the natives partied very much like we do on Christmas Eve, which made it difficult to get the much-needed zizz. There were also the effects of the black Dessie chicken to keep me from my much-needed. I settled into my sleeping bag with the trusty book and was alarmed by that feeling of passing not only wind. I tied my *kikoi* around me, thrust my feet into my flipflops and rushed to the toilet. African toilets are not everywhere a delight. This one was of the longdrop style (a hole in the floor) and was made that bit more classy by having a board over it to help prevent you from falling into it. As I squatted over the hole making the necessary evacuation, I could feel something oozing over the sides of my flipflops which, in this overcrowded town, could have only been one thing. As I washed my feet clean following the end of chapter one of my toilet troubles, I reflected sadly that I would be back again later, thanks to last night's *doro*.

In the morning I was woken by Shemellah, who had found out that there was a bus leaving that lunchtime for my next destination. I had hoped to spend the whole day in Lalibela, but it seemed prudent to take the bus when it was leaving rather than to hang on and find there was no transport later on. The guidebook suggested that you shouldn't plan too tight an itinerary in case it went toes up due to unreliable transport. I had already been guilty of this crime and it made sense to get ahead of myself if I could. So to give myself more time in Gondar and to ensure that I made my return flight on time, I decided to forego the Eastern group of churches, confining myself to just the main group.

The main group of churches was spectacular and saturated in symbolism that went into both the construction and decoration of the buildings. The first church we visited was that of St. George, the patron saint of Ethiopia, and was easily recognisable in the art by the facts that he is always riding a white horse and is always spearing some poor dragon. There is a story that shortly after king Lalibela had finished his churches, St. George turned up and was a bit miffed that there wasn't one for him! An apologetic king promised to make amends and quickly set his subjects (and presumably his angelic horde) to the task.

The church of St. George, Bet Giyorgis, was my favourite of the ones I saw, perhaps in part because it was whole. The Italians bombed the other three during their invasion and brief occupation in 1936 (another feather in the cap of the far Right!), and UNESCO had to rebuild them in 1954. It seems disgraceful that an army would wantonly destroy sites of historical importance like these but in times of war I suppose one must make pragmatic choices: if your enemy is hiding in the ancient buildings, you have to attack them.

The church is an enormous cross-shaped obelisk with a many layered cross shape on the roof, a bit like a huge potato print. There are twelve cross shaped windows on the first floor, one for each of the apostles, and on the ground floor the windows are filled, or "blind", as the church is supposed to represent Noah's Ark (dirty great lump of rock wouldn't float with holes in the bottom, would it?). Inside the church, where I had to take off my shoes, as I did in all these churches, are three big pictures of the dragon-slaying saint himself, one of which is supposed to date back to when the church was first built, and I will say that it was sufficiently faded as to make it believable.

In a small cavern in the rock that surrounds the church are the skeletal remains of a dead Israelite who, having journeyed to Lalibela from her home, asked to be buried there. Well, they did, only some wag had laid her with her skull detached from her shoulders and laid between her feet, which looks a bit odd...

From Bet Giyorgis, Shemellah took me to the Tomb of Adam, which was not a lot more than a bit of a hollow in a big rock, but opposite is a place called the Hariatt, another chapel with cross-shaped windows only discovered 2 months before I was there! Going on from there were the twin churches of Bet Golgotha and Bet Mikael (Bet being the Amharic word for saint). Inside were some impressive life-size carvings of the apostles, the so-called tomb of Christ and some examples of early Ethiopian Christian art. The tomb of the church-building king is accompanied by his stick, which he would have leaned on, as present-day Ethiopians still do, while prayers and service were being carried out. The stick was T-shaped for supporting the leaning monarch and, judging by the size of it, Lalibela must have been about seven feet tall!

Lalibela's original processional cross was among the artefacts there. A lalibela cross has a sort of bubble around it upon which are placed protrusions for the 12 apostles (six on each side) and below a couple of pairs of wings to speed the messages to their destination. It is said to be made from gold and silver, among other metals. In addition to all this artefact-seeing was the assurance of a place awaiting me in heaven which is apparently due to all who visit Bet Golgotha. That's handy then!

Since Bet Maryam (St. Mary) was heaving and we were short on time, we hurried straight on to the next church, Bet Ghel. An interesting feature of this church were the three joined pillars around one of the corners, said to represent the Trinity. At the foot of these pillars is a pool of holy water in which infertile women occasionally bathe to receive divine intervention in procreative terms. The mind boggled at what caused the water to have an electric green colour.

We then went to the biggest of the lot: Bet Medhane Alem. It is thought to be a copy of the St. Mary of Zion church in Axum, said to be the final resting place of the Ark of the Covenant, though Italian bombs had damaged it and it wasn't looking at its best. Neither did the tin roof over it, held up by a massive scaffold until a more aesthetic replacement could be delivered by the EU.

The church had 36 pillars inside and the same number outside, said to represent the 72 deacons who followed Jesus during his life. I had never heard of these before, but according to Luke (of 'Book of' fame), who is the only person to mention them, these apostles were sent in pairs by Jesus to complete missions of some sort. They apparently have a greater importance in the Eastern Christian faith than the Western, which might explain my ignorance of them.

Inside the church were tombs for Abraham, Isaac and Jacob, who had all invested time in the area before popping their respective clogs. Also there is the Cross of Lalibela, another processional cross, famously nicked by a Belgian (who did in fact pay quite a sum for it), and boy did they bear a grudge against that nation for this crime? Luckily, it was all returned nicely later and they lived happily with a chip on their shoulders ever after. The cross was displayed on almost every available spot throughout these churches, but Shemellah pointed out each and every one, faithfully reminding me that it was a symbol of the crucifixion every time. I found this quite endearing.

My guide's final sentiment was to inform me that the Israeli girl liked me. I thought of the corpse in the chamber and assumed it was a sick joke, but he explained that one of the girls from the bus had been asking for me the night before. On that note, my time was up in Lalibela and, packing up my tent and filling up on drinks, I went to find my bus.

As I boarded the bus I was shouted at by almost everyone and, though I didn't understand a word of what was being said, it seemed that I kept sitting in seats that were already taken. In my defence, I was only sitting and moving to where I was told to, but this seemed an uncharacteristically hostile reception from a nation who prides itself on the warmth of its welcome and I sat down quietly trying to mind my own business. As the stifling African sun combined with the body heat of an increasingly crowded bus, I opened a window to let in some fresh, cool air, but this was quickly snapped shut. Ethiopians seem to have some odd superstition concerning open windows on buses. Consequently, I now know how a chicken feels when it is being roasted. It did rankle a bit that the bus driver had his window open as he snarled at me to shut mine.

We set off down into a semi-arid basin and hell it got hot! I had been wrong the day before to assume that the agricultural land on top of the hills was the place from the TV footage of famine, this was it. There was no obvious sign of any way to make a living in this parched land, though I supposed a few goat herders scratched a survival from it.

We then began the climb back into the mountains, but were hindered by a blowout on both the back left tyres (they were doubled up on the back axle of the vehicle), which sounded like a gun going off. I don't mind admitting that, having seen my fair share of weaponry over the last few days, this made me jump like a deranged flea! We waited around while the driver and his cronies fixed the wheels. I was entranced by a farmer who was winnowing his grain from the chaff. With low to no mechanisation in Ethiopian agriculture, almost all tasks are carried out by hand and here he was using the wind to separate the lighter material from the heavier. It looked like something from a long-gone age and I had certainly never seen it before. I couldn't take my eyes off it.

We were soon back on the road and at the end of our day's journey pulled into a tiny village where I stayed in a room for 1 Birr, or about 90p. I felt fortunate to not be paying British prices at that moment, even if I did sleep in my sleeping bag for fear of potential bed bugs!

I had met a friendly, young student, Kofi (which means "born on Friday" in Amharic, though I only found this out afterwards and never asked him if he had been), on the bus and he offered to wake me at 3:45am the next morning. However, I suppose that even from my own experience as a student, I should have known better than to trust a student's ability to raise anything more than a snore at that time in the morning. I awoke at 3:50, sprang from my bed and rushed to Kofi's room to try to wake him up before charging off to meet the bus before it departed. However, it was another bluff as we didn't set off until about quarter past five, which I suppose I should have expected.

As it was still dark, I tried to get some sleep, but that was easier said than done when you're bouncing along a thoroughly potholed road and packed in tight with people and their luggage. My shoulder was bruised where it had been repeatedly banged from leaning against the window and my head fared little better for trying it as a pillow. I did get some nod, though I forced my eyelids open for a while to watch the sun rise and throw an eerie, golden glow across the mountains.

When I woke again we had stopped in a small town in the middle of a level plain. I got out and had a bottle of soda and wolfed down a packet of biscuits: my first food in twenty four hours. It was unusual for me not to be hungry, but I think it must have been either the physical or psychological effects of the Dessie chicken that had me wondering if I was just going to be feeding myself more ammunition.

As we set off again, we drove through a fertile plain where water was pooled all over the place. Amongst this valuable territory

I also saw four more wrecked tanks and even a few destroyed buildings, which I was later told were military accommodation. It reminded me what a dangerous place this had been until recently. The civil war had begun as a Communist struggle against the monarchy of Haile Selassie, supported with troops and training from the Soviet Union and Cuba, but had then changed direction to a separatist struggle as Eritrea attempted to regain its independence when the Tigray and Wollo people of the north found that the Dirg government were equally oppressive in their policies towards them.

The bus climbed back into the hills shortly after and I saw the first bit of what I thought to be indigenous woodland I'd seen since I'd been in the country. Now I have to confess that I'm at a bit of a moral dilemma over this point because, being a bit of a romantic on the natural history side, I would prefer to see the indigenous flora developed and conserved. This hadn't happened, partly due to a burgeoning population using the wood faster than it could naturally regenerate and partly because of the additional pressure the resource was put under by civil war refugees moving to the capital. The government introduced Australian eucalyptus for its ability to withstand Ethiopian conditions and grow quickly at a time when there was little wood left in the country but particularly around Addis Ababa. In an economy like Ethiopia's, wood is used for cooking, heating and building and it was important to replenish stocks even though it came at the expense of introducing a potentially invasive foreign species.

It was at about this time that a young family got on board: a mother and two little girls. The two nippers just sat next to me and stared. They looked bored out of their minds, so I started to pull faces at them to see if I could prompt a giggle. Sadly, they remained absolutely stone-faced, probably taking me for a loony of some sort.

Ethiopians claim to be racially apart from all other Africans

- they even stand accused of believing themselves superior to others. Certainly in appearance there are differences between Ethiopians and from the Africans I saw further south. Instead of the bulbous or flattened noses of sub-Saharans, Ethiopians have noses that are straighter and thinner, more like European or Arabic ones. Their skin colour is a sort of milky coffee colour rather than the dark chocolate colour of Kenyans, or the paler dough colour of north Africans. The native artwork also reflects the large eyes of Ethiopians too, which adds to their attractiveness. There were a couple of air hostesses on the Ethiopia Airways flights who were decidedly easy on the eye. It is odd then that Ethiopia gets its name from Homer's description of the place being the land of the sun burned faces, when they are not as dark as their more southerly neighbours. Maybe Homer never got to travel that far south. Though again, the change in language usage may have more to do with this discrepancy.

Having carried on through the hills for an hour or two, we came at last to our destination and as this was to be my last bus ride, there would be no more bouncing off windows, no more being cramped by luggage, no more being suffocated by the heat that we couldn't open windows to relieve and no more Ethiopian music. The tunes, if this is how they are going to be termed, involve banging on a drum and hand claps alternately. The good folks on the buses loved to join in and turned the journey into a happy-clapper outing. There are vocals that sound like someone being strangled and every so often, as a change of pace, a woman screams in a way that suggests somebody has just dropped an anvil onto her foot. It would be fair to say that I was not to be counted amongst the fans of Ethiopian music and would go so far as to describe it as something more akin to rhythmic torture. Perhaps I had not fully appreciated the finer subtleties of the genre, perhaps it was a Christmas collection which didn't come out for the rest of the year, but what is certain is that I didn't like it overly much.

It was only later in my journeys that I became aware that there was a huge speaker mounted onto the front of the bus which boomed the music outside the vehicle. For days I had been struggling with the idea that pedestrians we passed were handclapping and, in some instances, dancing in time to the music in our bus. I had drawn the conclusion that I must be suffering sleep deprivation or that my head had been banged off the window too hard, but this realisation provided a more satisfactory explanation, that I wasn't, in fact, going insane. Or at the very least, this wasn't the evidence of it.

Another anomaly of the Ethiopian bus carnival are the chaps who load the luggage onto the roof (yes, in spite of that you are still crushed by the luggage that makes it inside with you). The gentlemen in question climb up and down the ladder with the baggage balanced on their necks. They don't use their hands to carry or balance the weight, because these are fully engaged in climbing the ladder, but some of the loads I saw exceeded a cubic metre in size and looked like they weighed a considerable amount. I found this combined balancing act and feat of strength incredible every time I saw it and was convinced I couldn't achieve it if I had tried.

I made my way into the town of Gondar from the bus station, passing the Royal Enclosure that was to be tomorrow's destination, and headed for my chosen backpacker hotel. This was a hotel built by the Italians during their occupation in the '30s, was uninspiring from the outside and was unredeemed by its inside. From there I struck out up the hill to the more luxurious Hotel Goha for a beer and a gander at the view of town.

The walk was a bit longer than I had thought it was going to be, but when I arrived it was well worth it. The hotel itself looked very nice and it was built in a position on the hill that commanded a marvelous view of the town. I sat at a wooden table in the garden, smelling the combination of dry dust and fresh cut grass as the black kites circled and swooped overhead. I felt no need to envy them their perspective at all, with the whole town laid out at my feet, and the cold beer washed away any vestiges of thirst from my ascent.

I returned to my hotel and took a hot shower that was my first wash in three days. It felt great! At dinner in my hotel, I was amused to see that the soup was served in a porcelain bowl with the name Hotel Goha emblazoned across it. I was also tickled when I asked for some butter to spread on my bread and I was brought marmalade. On my way back to my room, I met two Voluntary International Service people who invited me for a beer, though there wasn't much need for strong persuasion, if the truth be known. The VIS run a number of schemes that send people all over the world to ply their different trades and it seemed like a good way to get out and about. I ordered a Dashen brew, which was becoming my favourite beer.

As the conversation went on, both Edith and Matt were shocked that I had not yet tried *tej*, and with a further bout of unnecessary arm-twisting, we were soon on our way to the local *tej beat*. *Tej* is a sort of mead flavoured with honey that used to be reserved only for consumption by kings. Luckily, since then the Commies have been in and decreed that the proletariat also ought to have an equal right to lengthy hang-overs, so now anyone can toddle down to their local *tej beat* (pronounced like gambling) and get *tejjed* up (my own expression, as far as I'm aware).

Indeed it did seem that one scoundrel had already drunk his fair quota, as he wobbled between the rough-hewn wooden tables playing his *masenko*, a single stringed fiddle which looked like a shoe-box, a stick and an elastic band, all cunningly cobbled together. He was quite amusing, both in his musical expertise and inability to stand upright, and he seemed to give the place the authentic air, but my companions were a bit miffed because he kept pinching their cigarettes. I could also see their point that the music could become rather annoying after a while: I think that perhaps listening to it once was enough... for a lifetime.

The *tej* is bought in a litre bottle and is poured into those spherical laboratory flasks that scientists would recognise as rounded-bottomed. The stuff tastes okay, a bit like cheap wine, but it has a kick that makes you wonder if someone is conducting an explosive experiment in your brain. After the first litre bottle had disappeared I was feeling quite sloshed, but two more VIS guys arrived and another bottle was ordered, and then another, and it turned into quite a lively evening.

The two new members of our group were working with street children and offered to send a boy round to my hotel to act in a guide capacity the next morning. I agreed but unfortunately, owing to the combination of four days with little sleep and the dastardly *tej* I slept right through the prearranged meeting time. I woke up feeling as rough as a badger's posterior, two hours after the meeting time but found that he was still loitering about and introduced myself to Habtomu. He was a nice kid of about 13 years, with thin limbs, a ready smile and who absolutely could not do enough for me.

We set off for the Royal Enclosure, a walled area roughly the size of Wembley Stadium in which successive monarchs had erected palaces and buildings to flaunt their power between 1640 and 1861. This World Heritage site has the feel of a misplaced fairytale setting of stone buildings harking to a possibly Byzantine romance. This is possible. Though the Byzantine Empire had expired 200 years before the first buildings were erected in Gondar there had been cultural and religious links between Byzantium and ancient Abyssinia, who shared the Orthodox faith.

The building work started shortly after the consolidation of power between the Amharans and Tigreans in the highlands, leaving the lower plateau to the Oromo sometime in the late-16th/early 17th century. Gondar was constructed as a show of force to both the Oromo and the constant and increasing threat of Muslim invasion. The Empress Helena had applied to Portugal for support in the early 16th century which had arrived in the shape of de Gama, who defeated Gran the left handed, a Muslim warlord who had overthrown most of Ethiopia. A later Emperor Susenyos converted to Catholicism, perhaps due to a relationship with Portugal, but he was forced to abdicate by an enraged populace who didn't want Catholicism any more than Islam, and his son Fasiladas was installed on the throne, bringing back Orthodoxy to his people.

We climbed the chancellery building and went past the old library to Fasiladas' palace. It was a two-storey, square building with a domed tower on each corner and an off-central keep rising above the crenellated curtain walls. Ethiopia had long been a cross-roads for world cultures and the architectural style of the palace reflects this: the domed towers reflect an Indian influence; the arched doorways onto wooden balconies a Moorish one, while Portugese and Axumite trends are also noted. It is an impressive building, but sadly I wasn't allowed inside as it was closed for renovation.

The next palace was that of Iyasu the Great, who was variously described by the French physician Poncet, who visited his court, as "intelligent, handsome, a lover of war in which he was always at the forefront of the army, a reformer of administration and deliverer of justice." An all-round great dude! His palace, with its arched ceilings, gold leaf and sumptuous paintings, was supposed to be a magnificent sight, before an earthquake and a 'liberating' British bomb hit it. It is still a very impressive building, both inside and out, though I felt at the time that there was no real need to build it when Iyasu already had his grandad's palace. Perhaps he was trying to outdo grandad?

Emperor Dawit built my favourite building, the lion house,

which used to cage Abyssinian lions. It is not so much that I agree with the caging of these beasties, but it seems to give the right feel to the royal court. When I was there the cages were being used to house great piles of gravel that were being stored for use in the renovation, and were not quite as imposing as a king of the beasts. At the time I was at Gondar, Abyssinian lions were assumed extinct, but this belief was proved unfounded. First a genetic test on the lions at the rundown Addis Ababa zoo in 2012 showed that they were Abyssinian, differentiated by their smaller but stockier stature and for the blackness of the males' manes. Then in 2016, conservationists announced the discovery of a wild population of between 50-200 Abyssinian lions in the northwestern Alatash national park.

Upon Dawit's poisoning, his successor, Bakaffa, built a banqueting hall in which you can almost hear the echoes of the revelry that would have gone on, and opposite that a large stable for his cavalry and guests. He also built a Turkish bath that was used in the belief it cured syphilis, which I suppose was just the job after a session on the *tej*, chasing the local ladies around your banqueting hall. The tiny doors in this building only came up to my navel, and suggested that Bakaffa was not as tall as our friend Lalibela.

The enclosure, sometimes described as Africa's Camelot, has a wonderful magical aura about it. You sit in the shade of it's palace walls and imagine the finely dressed royals partying, plotting, charming and politicking, while the azmari minstrels played and joked, and the lions roared from their cages nearby. Today the place is empty, but for the tourists, and if you sit and listen you can hear the beeping cars outside and the kites' cries for days gone by carrying on the wind.

From there Habtomu took me to Fasiladas' baths, some kilometer or so from the main group and I can only say that this guy had style. Not only did he have a cracking castle, but these baths were grand. Encircled by a stone wall, the rectangular pool had a two-storey tower with wooden balconies standing in the middle which was accessed by a stone bridge. The trees gave a cooling shade and this would have been just the place for a king to bring his kids for a splash about in the relentless African sun, before they grew old enough to poison him. Today it takes on a more religious significance, as the setting for *Timkat*, or epiphany, celebrations when people get in the water to reenact J.C.'s baptism as a token renewal of their faith.

After indulging in a little lunch and a tasty guava juice, we got a horse and cart up the hill to Debre Berhan Selassie church. The carts, or *garis* as they were known, were ramshackle contraptions with wobbly wheels and bits of wood nailed together for a frame that looked a bit like the work of a bored child. The driver screamed abuse at the poor nag and whacked him with his whip to maintain high levels of motivation. The horse, looking close to death, had its own back though, as it let out an almost constant stream of wind. Since we were sitting directly behind it's behind, we had a pretty smelly journey!

The church, whose name means "Trinity at the Mount of Light", is a very pretty building: stone-built and surrounded by columns outside, and festooned with stunning paintings of Biblical scenes, saints and other story telling images inside. Eighty smiling cherubs greet you (or freak you out) from the ceiling as you enter, but I particularly enjoyed playing "spot the saint' from the pictures painted on the walls and panels.

There was George, astride his steed, spear dipped into the dragon. Mary's assumption was depicted amidst a host of winged cherub faces. The rather nutty St. Tekla Haimanot, who stood and prayed on one leg for seven years, complete with an angel carrying the unused leg that fell off when it withered away. Abuna Arewagi was up there, doing something with a snake that animal rights activists might object to. St. Manfus Kiddus is surrounded by lions and leopards, fingers tightly, and amusingly, crossed.

On the opposite wall are scenes from the crucifixion and resurrection and the prophet Mohammed seated on a donkey that is being led by the devil. I suppose the Ethiopians did't feel the need for religious political correctness when they were fighting a war against the forces of Islam from Sudan. It is for this reason that the church is surrounded by a defensive wall with towers, though according to legend the Dervishes were sent packing by a swarm of bees, suggesting that the walls were unnecessary.

Gondar is a fabulous little town with lots to see and do. I ranked its castles, baths and churches as the highlight of my Ethiopian trip. I got my taxi to the airport and was hit with a bit of a shock. The airport charged a 10 Birr departure tax, which I hadn't budgeted for. In fact, I hadn't really budgeted at all, I had just brought a very small amount of money, of which I was soon to run out. During a very thorough bag search, I began to wonder if there would be a departure tax at the Addis Ababa airport for my onward flight to Nairobi. This could cause problems as I had calculated that after taxis and hotels were accounted for, I would only be left with 20 Birr for dinner.

I was distracted on the flight by the enormous Lake Tana and the Blue Nile river, which provided 85% of the nutrients that sustain Egyptian agriculture through annual silt deposits. I could not work out how this was still possible, in view of the Aswan Dam blocking the watercourse at the border with Sudan. I had now seen both sources of the Nile, having viewed Lake Victoria running into the Victoria Nile (which in turn runs into the White Nile) while in Uganda three months earlier. We landed without hiccup and I took a taxi to the Ethiopia Airways office in the middle of town. There, a smartly dressed gentleman greeted me with a forebodingly serious face.

"Do I have to pay a departure tax for my flight to Nairobi tomorrow?" I asked.

"Yes," was the reply I wasn't hoping for. İt will cost 20.... US dollars."

A bit of a shiver ran through me. My remaining 20 Birr equated to around US$2.50 and it seemed that once again I was up a certain famous waterway without a certain vital piece of boating equipment.

"And what happens if I don't have the departure tax money?" I enquired.

"You will not be allowed to board the flight," was the reply, delivered with chilling indifference.

This caused a degree of consternation, as one might imagine. I wracked my brains in the taxi on the way to my hotel and then oiled the grey matter with an Ethiopian Castle beer in readiness to wriggle my way out of this one. About half way down the bottle the magic set in and I remembered that I had secreted one of every Ethiopian note as a numismatic momento. This cash came to almost exactly US$20. Hurrah!

I asked at the hotel about my missing camera and was slightly disheartened, though not perhaps surprised, that no one knew anything about it. One way or another, it had been nicked! This was more disappointing because I knew that on my Kenyan wage it would be quite a while before I could afford a comparable replacement. The people at the hotel were genuinely concerned for my predicament and applied themselves to some amateur sleuthing to try to work out who dunnit.

As I was talking to the hotel concierge a random punter approached me and asked if he could buy me dinner. He was a camera salesman and though he apologised for his English, he had overheard my conversation and had been so frustrated that he couldn't read his book. Shango wanted to buy me dinner (and a couple of beers to wash it down with, I'll add) in order to make amends to a *faranji*, or foreigner, for a wrong done to him by a fellow countryman.

It is this impression that I remember of Ethiopia, and not the loss of my camera. I felt really humbled because I could not say in honesty that I would have definitely done the same if the situation had been reversed. Despite the handful of frustrations I had encountered that day, I went to bed at peace thanks to that warm act of humanity.

The next day I took a taxi to the airport (being somewhat alarmed when the driver suddenly broke the silence to declare that he loved me!) and, following some chicanery to secure the proper exchange value for my airport tax, I was flying on to Kenya, late, as every Ethiopian Airways flight had been.

I had thoroughly enjoyed Ethiopia for its beautiful scenery, awe-inspiring historical sights and genuine, friendly people. My only regret was that I didn't have a month there (with the funds to match!), so that I could have seen Axum and Bahar Dar, and walked in the Simien and Bale mountains.

MT. KENYA

The school I worked at ran an annual trip to Mt. Kenya during the February half term holiday. It was a part of the leaving activity schedule for those students who were graduating the preparatory school to join senior schools in the UK, South Africa and beyond at 13 years old. February was the best time to run this as it was in the middle of the dry season, which meant there was a reduced risk of rain, which makes the ascent more tricky, or snow on the top, which can get dangerous.

It sometimes felt a bit incongruous to find snow in Africa. Indeed, when the kids got to the permanent snow cap at the top, it was often their first experience of snow. However, Mt. Kenya, or Kirinyaga to give it its local name, is the second highest peak in the continent, after Mt. Kilimanjaro in Tanzania, and several tropical mountains have a high enough altitude to have snow on their tops at least for part of the year.

The two highest peaks of the mountain, Bation and Nelion at 5,199m and 5,188m above sea level, are only accessible by a day-long rock climb up their near vertical faces. This was considered a bit much for 13 year old kids (not to mention their 25 year old teachers!), so we aimed instead to go to Point Lenana, the third highest peak at 4,985m, which could be gained by walking and scrambling onto the rock that forms the pinnacle.

As with the rest of the highlands of Kenya and northern Tanzania, Mt. Kenya is formed by the tectonic plate movement of the Horn of Africa splitting slightly eastward of the main drift of the African continent. This causes a section in the middle to drop and form the Rift Valley where the African Great Lakes are found, whilst the boundaries to the west and east experienced the volcanic activity that produced a mountain chain from the Ethiopian highlands and Ruwenzoris in the north, through the Kenyan highlands to the Malawian ranges of Nyika and Mulanji in the south.

Mt. Kenya is potentially a very dangerous place due to altitude sickness, which can cause injury or even death. Altitude sickness is caused by reduced air pressure and lower oxygen levels at higher altitudes. Its effects include headaches, vomiting, tiredness, inability to sleep and dizziness. It is said to more commonly affect fitter people because they tend to ascend more quickly. You are also supposed to be more at risk if you live at sea level, have suffered the problem before, you fail to acclimatise on the way up, alcohol or other drugs have interfered with your acclimatisation and if you have pre-existing problems with the health of your heart, lungs or nervous system. I read at the time a claim that 4/5 of deaths on mountains around the world occurred on Mt. Kenya, because people underestimated its dangers. It was therefore necessary to take precautions when planning such a venture, particularly with children.

I had been on this trip the year before, when I had been one of its leaders, but with a larger team this time around I wasn't needed to lead. As I had the year before, I invited my uncle Nigel, my dad's brother and a keen mountaineer - nay, Monroe collector, no less! He had accepted the invite the first year and, I have to admit that when I asked him the second time around I did so a bit more tongue in cheek, as I wasn't as keen to go again. However, he eagerly accepted the invitation and so the chips had fallen, so to speak.

When we climbed the first time, we had gone both up and down the Sirimon route, to the north-west of the summit. This year I wanted to go up the Chogoria route to the east and come down the Naro Moru route to the south west, meaning that I would have walked all 3 main routes. However, logistically this was going to be almost impossible given our time constraints and with a large group it was inadvisable to ascend and descend on different routes in case you had to get injured people off the mountain.

As we weren't needed to lead the group, Nigel and I were going to accompany the school party to the summit via the Sirimon route but then take our leave, going 'up and over' and come down the Naro Moru side. We would spend a night of luxury at the Naro Moru lodge and meet up with the school bus to get a lift back. What could possibly go wrong?

"**D**on't underestimate this mountain. Mt. Kenya is big and the whole exercise is hard work! Probably harder exercise than anything you've done since you left school or were in one of the armed services. You will almost certainly be cold at times. Worse, you may get soaking wet in rain or sleet. At the higher altitudes (4,000m+), 50% of your group will suffer a headache. Some may well feel sick/ vomit. You will discover muscles you didn't know you even had, and at times you will consider yourself a prime candidate for the lunatic asylum. But don't worry this is quite normal for such a mountain."

Mark Savage and Andrew Wielochowski, Map of Mount Kenya, 1987

And so, with these cheery words ringing in my consciousness, I was going to attempt the climb to Point Lenana for the second time in as many years. In all honesty I wasn't intending to go up again. I had reached Lenana on my first attempt the year before and had ever since retained a healthy respect for the cold that had prevented me from sleeping and the mild but 2 day long headache that I had enjoyed. However, when I asked Nigel if he wanted another crack at it, he readily agreed and so I was going to climb again. Oddly enough, I then started to forget about the cold and look forward to the beautiful views that unavoidably make up the bulk of the experience. By the time I met up with him at the Fairview Hotel in Nairobi, I was eager for another ascent.

It is probably fair to say that my build up to the second climb was not as positive as it could have been. I had been suffering from a cold for about two weeks leading up to the climb, as well as a dodgy stomach that recurred every two weeks or so for the majority of my time in Africa. Only one week before, I had been thrown from a galloping horse and deprived of most of a tooth, among other minor injuries. The night before we set off I made dinner for Nigel, and for Rob and Sean who regularly allowed me to borrow their cars, which were vastly superior to the old, broken-down duffer that a teacher from a Nairobi school had fleeced me for. With dinner we imbibed perhaps a drink or two too many, considering the physical challenge that lay ahead. And so it was that with a thick head preventing an appetite for breakfast, I boarded the bus wondering if this was such a good idea after all.

I slept for most of the journey to the park gate, despite the tumultuous cacophony produced by 19 excited children about to embark on their first mountain experience. Such questions as, "Is this Nanyuki?" (the town we were heading towards), asked as we sped through some of the remotest African bush you could imagine, jarred a little given my semi-fragile state, but were to be born with humour.

The mountain appears as you round the northern end of the Aberdares mountain range and the children, seeming to have no clue of perspective and distance, ridiculed its minute size. Nigel and I exchanged wry smiles, and wondered how long this opinion would last once the walking started.

This second highest mountain in Africa was formed 3.5 million years ago by volcanic activity, but its last eruption is estimated at 2.6 to 3.1 million years ago. Interestingly, a rare type of rock named Kenyte has been found on Mount Kenya and also on Mount Erebus in Antarctica (there are also claims that it is found on Kilimanjaro), which stumped geologists for a while. The current theory is that it might have originated as a meteor that split up upon entry into the earth's atmosphere, with one part hitting modern Kenya and the other modern Antarctica. It is black coloured and glassy like obsidian and I didn't find any while I was there.

Arriving below the park gate, the track is surrounded by second generation forest, which means forest that has been cut down for human purposes and has grown back since these people were evicted by the authorities. This seems to be the norm for jungles worldwide, where population pressure is leading to the destruction of forest for timber and farmland. At about the time I was on the mountain I heard the pessimistic forecast that the Amazon rainforest would be extinct in 25 years. Happily, at the time of writing, 20 years on, this doesn't seem to be in imminent danger of coming true, but it seemed outrageous at the time to think that at the time of my dad's birth, the area was largely unmapped, but by the time my grandchildren would be born it wouldn't exist.

The world's rainforests are home to millions of species of animals and plants, many of them undiscovered. Every day new species are being found and their value in their ecosystems are being better understood, their medicinal use is being put to the test and their behaviour studied. All this is extinguished if the rainforests are cut down. Also the vegetation in these places are the lungs of the earth, producing oxygen for living beings to breathe. If we cut them down it will be like stripping ourselves of our own lungs. 25 years…

The vegetation on the mountain is referred to in terms of layers, as they look like concentric rings around the peak. This is due to the weather conditions changing with the altitude. As you get higher, rainfall increases as temperature decreases. At the lower reaches, the temperature is still suitably warm and the rainfall high enough for perfect rainforest conditions. Rainforest is supposed to receive 100 inches (254cm) of rain a year on average to qualify for the moniker.

We reached the gate, passing through virgin forest (it had never been cut down), and unloaded the bus to sit down for a big lunch. Following the meal we set off at a slow pace. The year before we had been fortunate enough to have our bags taken up by car to the first hut, Old Moses. This year however, there was to be no respite and we lugged our own packs up the jungle trail. I struggled on this first day, feeling like I was going to throw up on about three or four occasions. I was teased relentlessly that this was the after-effects of the beer I had consumed the night before, but it was more to do with the weeks of illness I had experienced in the build up.

Between the trees on the forest track there is almost no wind at all. The sun directly overhead beats down on your head and even heats up the track so much that you feel like you're being warmed from underneath. Naturally this didn't aid my ill health and I began to ail badly. Following two trips to the trees with the lavvy paper, I was offered a lift by one of the parents who was taking food and water in a 4WD. I gratefully accepted. Passing Nigel and the children earned me many complaints about cheating, but I really was struggling and I don't know how long it would've taken me to complete the three hour walk without this help. I recalled from the previous year that this section of the route was an extremely pleasant walk. The massive trees look like learned elders and a rainbow of butterflies and birds flit about among the trees and bamboo. This time around I wasn't getting much of the benefit.

The stone and timber built hut, Old Moses, is constructed in the giant heather vegetation layer of the mountain and is just above the rainforest layer. The heather here can grow to 10 feet

(3 meters) in height, though most of it is around my height. It is possible to walk through gaps in the enormous heather that have been made by animals passing through, and for someone who is more accustomed to the shin high heather of the UK, it feels a bit like you have been shrunk to the size of a mouse.

A hot cup of tea gave me a boost and then I was able to take in the views and enjoy the peace and quiet. The scenery was fantastic, with an eagle-eye vantage of the surrounding plains that stretch out to the distant horizon. One of my most lasting impressions of Africa is the scale of it. Everything in the continent seems larger than life and this view to a far flung vanishing point was an example of this. The peace was disturbed a bit by a group of our porters whose voices vied with the volume on their radio set for supremacy, but otherwise the evening stillness was serene.

I drank an Alka-Seltzer and turned in early to try to sleep off the dodgy stomach. Despite the excitable kids being noisy all night in the dorm around me, I slept pretty soundly and awoke refreshed after 13 hours of rest. During my time in Africa I suffered for about a year from what was cheerfully referred to as the "Gilgil Gallops", for the name of the town we lived in and the effects of the stomach condition. It was only towards the end of my time there that I got this checked out properly, diagnosed as an amoeba and was given a pill to cure it.

"Do you mean to tell me that if I had taken this pill when I first got the illness, I could have been spared a year of diarrhea?" I asked upon receiving this medication. The reply was in the affirmative. This trip occurred before this diagnosis.

I was able to eat a bit better at breakfast and we set off with the wind seeming to want to blow us off the mountain. This weather kept the second days' climb much cooler than I had remembered from the previous year, but once the sun came up the wind provided a welcome relief and made walking conditions more comfortable.

We were now into the moorland vegetation zone, which is home to a number of indigenous plants. Giant groundsel is like a 4-5 foot high phallic symbol growing from a large leaf base on the floor. It feeds a range of birds including the scarlet tufted sunbird, an iridescent green bird with a red patch on its shoulder and two long wisps of feathers that protrude from its tail. Dendrosenecio plants proliferate across the hillsides and give the landscape an alien planet feel. There were also similarly shaped giant lobelias, whose leaves are white on the underside, and numerous, delicate mountain flowers, which sprinkled colour across the golden tussock grass. Another interesting feature of these plants is that they have evolved to survive a daily thaw and freeze at an altitude and tropical latitude that provides both subzero night-time temperatures and blistering midday heat respectively.

We stopped for a rest by a clear, singing stream of water that originates from the melting glaciers and snow of the peaks. This was a handy source from which to refill water bottles, as drinking helps avoid the effects of both dehydration and mountain sickness. The path led up steeply at first before leveling out a bit as it set off across the shoulder of the hill and over a few undulating ridges. It then drops down into the valley of the Liki North stream before climbing quite a steep hill.

I had named this section "Two Step Hill" after the efforts of one of the parents who had accompanied us the year before. I was on what we called tail-end duty to ensure that no-one got left behind and had to keep everyone in front of me throughout the day. This means that you spend quite a bit of time walking with slow movers and gently coaxing them along. The idea of this is to have someone who is reasonably fit and mountain savvy in a position to help stragglers, rather than getting to your destination and discovering the weaker walkers are missing and potentially have to go back out again looking for them.

When we came to this ridge I found that this parent could take only two steps at a time before having to stop and recover her breath, owing to a combined lack of fitness and oxygen in the air. That year only 4 of the 9 adults who set out made it to the top. Though I found this parent vexing at the time, I am convinced that this helped me to be one of those four, as I couldn't get up the mountain fast enough to get altitude sickness.

At the top of this ridge was a most welcome boost to morale. The twin summits of the mountain, Nelion and Bation, which had remained elusive behind the surrounding hills, were suddenly presented in all their glory and seemingly so close you could reach out and touch them. With ice capped glaciers and dark volcanic rock set against the azure sky, this makes an almost fairytale picture of beauty and, when I turned around to look back down the mountain, I saw a magnificent panoramic view of the surrounding countryside.

One of the kids, Lily, had slipped and fallen onto a small bush, grazing her leg but escaped serious injury. Nigel and I spent a short while wiping up the blood on her leg and applying savlon to prevent infection. This completed, we set off again into MacKinders valley, which we followed to Shipton's Camp.

I found it odd that, despite my illness on the previous day, I was feeling stronger and stronger the further up we went, contrary to the normal feeling of climbing high altitude mountains. I think there is a significant psychological advantage to knowing where you are going and setting achievable objectives for rest stops. Shortly after the ridge we stopped for lunch beneath a rock overhang. The ground looked like a small rock garden, of the sort my granddad, Fred, used to plant in his yard. The ice from the overhanging icicles added melt water to the rich volcanic soil giving the beautiful clumps of miniature flowers all they required to prosper. Surely man's hand could not have arranged them as perfectly as nature's random one? Not even my granddad's.

The children, having lived their entire lives in tropical Africa, were fascinated by the ice. They would proclaim the great beauty of the icicles, then kick them over to melt the ice in their hands. Perhaps it was this innate destructive tendency in humans that was spelling the end for the rainforests.

Lunch itself was a bit of an anticlimax to the setting, but it was heavily reinforced from the enormous treasure trove of sweets that Mia, another student, had brought along. Soon we were on our way again and there were times when I got some distance between myself and the main groups of chattering kids and was able to really enjoy the quiet isolation of the mountain. It occurred to me that if you could bottle and sell this feeling of solitude and tranquility, you could make your fortune. It felt wonderfully relaxing.

Around the trail there were moss covered stones ranging from small rocks to enormous boulders and upon them hyrax sunbathed. The hyrax is like a cuddly looking, tailless rat, about the size of a house cat, and is supposed to be the closest living relative of the elephant. Traits they share include tusks that grow from incisors (most tusks grow from canines), flattened nails on the tips of their digits and similarities in their reproductive organs. Despite this they look very little like each other and the fact that a hyrax would have trouble climbing out of an elephant's footprint makes the whole idea of being closely related seem a bit funny.

Red winged starlings darted between the giant groundsel. This plant looks a lot like a cactus, which is not as daft as it sounds, as the air is extremely dry at that altitude, so both would have to be adapted to life with short water supplies. The huge, jagged cliff towers stuck up into the sky like teeth and the looming ridges on either side of the trail made me feel as if I was being folded into a gift card.

The last few kilometers before the camp proved exceedingly hard work for me, as I had exhausted my energy in the six hours beforehand. My thighs felt like they were devoid of muscles and I could barely put one foot in front of the other. The effects of the dodgy tummy and being unable to hold much food were catching up with me. I wondered what this would mean for the final ascent, but looked forward to the day off at Shipton's to recover and acclimatise before trying for Lenana.

When I got to the camp, I found Martin, the person who had sold me my car, and towards whom I was not feeling so friendly. He was on a solo hike and heading out the next day. Conversation didn't really flow and I didn't have the energy left to slap him as he deserved to be, so our interaction was limited. I sat instead on the imposing volcanic basin, looking down the glacial valley that had forced its way out through the side of the crater and continued down the mountainside forming MacKinders valley, with the smell of the longdrop toilets occasionally wafting past.

The scree slope we had yet to climb looked pretty daunting. Scree is a hill walker's dream: loose stones and pebbles that fall away underneath your feet as you try to climb, seemingly causing you to slip down nearly as far as you step forward each time you place your foot. Nigel and I half-jokingly discussed the possibility of hiring porters to carry our bags to the top or to meet us at the other side. The main group would not be carrying their packs as they would return to the camp before descending the way they came.

There was much excitement when we thought we had found the elusive saw-toothed rat for which we had searched in vain the previous year. It was very small for a rat though, and I doubted it really was a rat. Though it had a rather attractive stripe running down its flank, I was unable to identify exactly what this was. This rodent was living on the refuse that the porters and camp cooks tipped on the other side of the rock I was sitting on. Further research into the saw-toothed rat proved a disappointing endeavour too, as there doesn't seem to be such a thing. A groove toothed rat exists, but it inhabits lowland forests or seasonally flooded grasslands. I'm not quite sure where the legend of the saw toothed rat began, but it joined the list of things I didn't find on the mountain.

I took some kids to climb a few hundred feet further up the gully, as sleeping at a lower altitude than you have achieved during the day is said to help against suffering from altitude sickness. I had thought that it worked the year before and was happy to give it a go just in case, even if my legs were screaming for mercy the whole way up. At this altitude (around 13,800 feet/4200m above sea level) it got cold very fast in the evening. As the sun retreated behind the other side of the mountain and cast me into shadow, I was left in the frigid, mountain air. At 5pm, I headed inside to put on another jumper.

We found more of the stripey mice running around on the wreckage of a helicopter that had been called upon to rescue a stranded mountaineer. Unfortunately, bad weather caused the crash but the fact that there are people skilled and brave enough to come up after you if you get in trouble gives a degree of comfort, even if their reported prices do not. Our group was armed with a radio set with which to call in help if necessary, though thankfully the need never did arise.

The cloud came in quickly to embrace the peak in a scarf of cotton and, before heading to bed (in a third jumper), I took the time to survey the beauty of the moonlight that illuminated the misty mountain. I sat there in the cold, my frosted breath matching the witches fingers of cloud curling round the ridge, the silvered moonlight lending an ethereal prettiness to this scene. I drank in the atmosphere and, with the optimistic naivety of youth, I wrote in my notebook that nothing could take this memory away. Of course, the intervening time has done just that!

I eventually tore myself away and got a cold night's sleep. The year before I had only brought my old Cub Scout sleeping bag which I had used as a child for summer camping in the UK. This proved to be of no use to me at high altitude, so I had brought a second bag to put the first in and, combined with the five layers I was wearing, I was able to sleep better this time around.

In the crystal morning air, the mountain looked stunning, so much so that after eating a hearty breakfast, I went back to bed again! I was working on the basis that by eating and sleeping a lot I could recharge my batteries for the final assault. I managed four hours rest before the kids moved into the dorm with me and brought with them a noise I couldn't sleep through.

The year before we had set out for the summit on this third day and only 12 members of the original group of 21 made it to the top - though, importantly, no fatalities occurred! This ratio is reasonably normal for Mount Kenya. We had planned this year to spend a day at the highest camp to acclimatise and rest, to maximise our chances of success on the final day. The children were given a degree of freedom to explore and spent the day wandering about in the surrounding rocks and ridges, discovering glaciers, snow, streams and scree. I tried to reserve my energy and enjoyed the quiet isolation, returning up the gully to get some additional height before bedtime.

The local Kukuyu tribe believe that their god Ngai lives on top of Mount Kenya, known to them as Kirinyaga or "mountain of brightness." According to tradition, Ngai created Kirinyaga as a place to observe his land and Gikuyu, the original Kikuyu man. He told Gikuyu to go to a valley with fig trees to build his homestead and when Gikuyu arrived there he found Mumbi (meaning "mould" or "creator"), a beautiful woman he took to wife. They had nine daughters together, so Gikuyu offered a sacrifice of goat and lamb towards the mountain of Ngai. When the offerings stopped burning, Gikuyu found that they had been replaced with nine handsome men who married his daughters and perpetuated the Kikuyu people.

Ngai could not have chosen a better location for his residence. With no outside influences to disturb you, it is the perfect place for the meditation and contemplation that the local shamans, including those from the smaller Meru and Embu tribes, came up here for. Indeed, I used the peace I found here to contemplate my own future. I climbed up onto a rock outcrop to ponder a conundrum in the mountain silence.

Ceri and I had met on Millennium Eve in our hometown. She was pretty, intelligent and had a good sense of humour. I was my usual bumbling, gargoyle self, but somehow we hit it off. We spent some time together over the Christmas holiday that year before starting a long distance relationship while I was in Kenya and she finished her degree. I visited her in the school holidays and she came to Kenya twice when university had finished. Having been together for a year, Ceri had issued the ultimatum that I ought to move back to the UK to see if our relationship could cope with us being in the same place together. I had been offered a teaching position in the US, a possible next stop on my international travel.

Musing in the crisp air, weighing the pros and cons of each option, I determined to give the relationship a go. I contacted her upon my return and we began planning to move in together as she began her teacher training. It seemed like a big step, but I felt positive about it. I let the momentous nature of this decision sink in.

As I sat on the slopes I could hear the stream babbling away down the valley, birds chattering as they swooped about in the thin air and felt the gentle caress of the softly blowing wind. It was still cloudy which kept the harsh midday sun at bay and thus made it much more comfortable. I enjoyed this nirvana of tranquility before wandering back down to camp to put on some more clothes. There I bumped into Troy, a boy who had invested valuable packing space and weight in bringing his hair gel. He told me that he was really looking forward to getting to the summit as he looked forward to seeing South America. We held a brief discussion on geography.

As we came into the dorm room, we were asked by an American girl whether the children would be up until late, in a manner that suggested she hoped not. This amused us because we knew from experience that they actually seemed to get noisier once we'd put them to bed! When I got into my sleeping bags that night I was wearing 6 layers: a thermal vest, two T-shirts, a shirt, and two jumpers. I had another jumper and a raincoat (which was more for keeping the wind out) to put on when I woke up at 2am.

Sleep was difficult. Apart from the cold, the air was so dry that your lips are constantly cracked and your mouth dries out so that you can't easily close it. The thin air also impacts your sleep. A good quality night's sleep is said to comprise falling asleep in no more than 30 minutes, staying asleep for at least 85% of the time, not waking up more than once and being awake for no more than 20 minutes when or if you do wake. At this altitude, few, if any, of these criteria are met.

The year before, I had been woken by the trip leader, Greg. "Matt, it's time to get up and you're leading. I've been throwing up all night." Greg had been struggling with the altitude and as second in charge it had been my responsibility to lead on the last day. I was quite nervous. I had read what I could regarding mountain sickness, and from this could recognised what Greg was suffering, but I had no previous experience of high altitude, let alone leading a group in that environment.

We got everyone up and emerged into the darkness of the middle of the night. A faint paleness of snow above us had the children excited to touch the stuff for the first time in their lives and we began the steep start of the route. The stars glistened overhead like diamonds on a velvet abyss and I kept the kids distracted by talking about the constellations I recognised and their associated myths. Lucy, another student who was perhaps getting bored with my ramblings, contributed some pretty shabby jokes to the distraction cause, but they kept everyone from thinking about the lack of oxygen and worrying about whether they would make it up.

We passed the rock where Duncan had slumped the year before, having succumbed to the altitude. Due to the long line of walkers and insufficient communication, I had had no idea he had been struggling until a gap student, Tony, had asked me to make a decision on 'this.' I went to where 'this' was and was surprised to see Duncan sprawled unconscious across a boulder. The porters were in full panic, crowding him so that I couldn't get in and one of them had started taking his shirt off. This had once been thought to be a cure for altitude sickness but was now recognised as adding the problem of exposure to the existing condition. I quickly covered him back up and organised a porter to carry him back down to camp. I walked with Duncan and the porter, trying to get a verbal response and, once Duncan was able to grunt at me, I returned to the group. Duncan made a full recovery upon getting to lower altitude at the camp.

Someone had noted the landmark, but the response to this information caused the sort of reaction that convinced me to try to hush up any similar remarks. The ensuing conversation had not been overwhelmingly positive.

Lily had begun to feel a bit odd and vomited a very small amount. Her dad, who was also helping on the trip, asked me to keep her going as he feared that he would be viewed as a softer option for her to focus her complaints on. I could see his point and spent the rest of the climb encouraging her, cajoling her and it felt at times like just plain bullying her to keep her going. A place like that requires a certain amount of mental toughness to keep going but this has to be balanced with knowing limitations. Lily didn't have any other of the other signs of altitude sickness, like stumbling, slurring speech, headache or dizziness, so it could have been a reaction to something she had eaten at altitude, where your digestive system isn't tip top, or perhaps a very mild case of altitude sickness.

I was looking forward to reaching a ridge from where I had taken a photo of the molten sky as the sun rose the year before. I kept saying to the kids to keep going, that the ridge wasn't far and the view from it would be amazing, but it occurred to me that I had miscalculated its proximity, so I stopped using this to encourage the kids. I find it annoying when I'm told of a goal that's not as close as I'm told it is and I didn't want to demoralise the kids in what was an already tough situation.

Owing in part to my weaker than normal condition, I was absolutely shattered by the time we did reach the ridge. It had taken us about three hours on unforgiving scree to get to this position, but now we were there we were able to look forward to a slightly easier climb during which the sun would come up to illuminate our final destination. Things looked positive as we started our final ascent.

It was a good scramble for the summit. We climbed up and around huge boulders, some more scree and steep slopes until having to climb onto an eight foot high, tennis court sized block that is Point Lenana. On this occasion everyone had made it, which was both pretty incredible for a group of 29 people and the first time the school had managed a 100% success record on this trip. The views across the top of the grey, blue cloud went on for miles and miles in every direction and we were able to see the peak of Kilimanjaro to the south west (but not, of course, South America).

Unfortunately, the sun was unable to counteract the icy winds and this encouraged us to get a move along. Nigel and I bade our farewells to the school group and Lily gave me a death stare, for relentlessly pushing her to the top. The main group were going to return the same way we had all just come but Nigel and I set off via the Naro Moru route. However, as we climbed off Point Lenana, Nigel's rucksack caught on the boulder and he fell awkwardly, collapsing onto the rocks. He banged his thumb and, more crucially, twisted his knee painfully. This was quite a worry as we were going to be on our own without the radio to call for help if needed and with a full day's walk through what is known as the 'vertical bog' in order to get to the bottom of the trail.

He had a hobble about and declared himself okay to continue with the plan to part ways. I could see he was uncomfortable and offered to carry his pack for him, but he politely declined and we set off. We balanced precariously along a rocky spur before walking more easily down to the Austrian hut, the camp built in thanks to the Kenyan rescue services by the Austrian Climbers Association for saving one of its number. This is the usual starting point for the day-long rock climb to the twin peaks, Nelion and Bation, and the feat certainly looked challenging from this vantage.

From here we started down the scree on this southwesterly side. It was much worse than the Sirimon side scree, which had boulders to hang onto for balance. I nearly ended up on my arse on a number of occasions and I don't know how bad it was for Nigel on his dickey knee. As we climbed down this obstacle, we turned to view the beauty of the peak from this side and were astounded. The summit appears more striking from this angle, as it had an emerald tarn before a sapphire glacier arranged perfectly just below it. Sadly, the glaciers on the mountain are in retreat in the face of the global warming onslaught and will not be around for much longer. Recent reports state that only 6 or 7 of the 18 glaciers recorded a century ago still exist and are all much smaller than they once were, because winter snowfall is failing to keep pace with glacial melt. At the time we were there, there were quite a few picturesque tarns on the Naro Moru side compared to only one on the Sirimon route. Nigel and I agreed we liked the scenery better on this side.

We had passed MacKinder's camp where the valley looked very similar to the route we had taken on our ascent, when a bank of cloud rolled eerily up the cwm, like something out of a horror film. I was reminded of the foreboding in the Sherlock Holmes story The Hound of the Baskervilles. The cloud also meant that the temperature dropped again and we had to put back on all the clothes we had stripped while enjoying the sunshine earlier. Beneath the cloud, the path was very attractive with pockets of flowers and grasses tucked amongst the rocks. We sat down to enjoy a chocolate break when two American girls passed like blonde Heidis in the Alps. Or were they mountain mermaids, tempting us to our doom?

Shortly after we were in the world-renowned 'vertical bog', which, as its name suggests, is generally steep and waterlogged. We were fortunate that it hadn't rained for quite some time when we were there and, contrary to its notoriety, it was quite pleasant. The two things going in our favour were that we were going downhill and we didn't have to wade through deep mud. It actually reminded me a lot of UK moorland with its fog and tussock grass, though the giant lobelia and groundsel were a bit alien.

It wasn't all plain sailing in the vertical bog though. There were parts where we had to clamber over clumps of grass to stay dry and others where we had to enter and exit small ravines, neither of which were easy for Nigel on his dodgy leg. As navigator, I had to find our way through a monotonous landscape in the fog. However, between us we managed to do okay.

We stopped for lunch and sat down on a comfortable tuft of grass apiece. We were approached by a porter who had lost a woman and asked us if we had seen her? We recalled the two American girls but this lady had apparently been on her own. Though we found the nonchalance with which the porter conducted the conversation quite amusing at the time, this could have been a serious concern and we never found out if he discovered her. In any case, with Nigel already injured as he was, we were not in the ideal condition to help with a search mission.

With the fog starting to clear we were more confident she would be found and we were able to appreciate the fantastic views of the forest before us as we resumed our descent. There were some interesting rocky outcrops across the mountainside that brought to mind Hemmingway's leopard. Different mountain of course, but leopards had been recorded at high altitudes on Mount Kenya too. One of the tarns had even been named after a lion supposedly seen at a greater altitude than normal.

Nigel was making slower progress by the early afternoon and as we got into the giant heather zone, he injured his knee further, climbing down the clumps of grass and rocks. He had been carrying his rucksack for six hours since his fall and he asked if my offer for help was still available. I confirmed it was and took his rucksack the rest of the way.

It was interesting to note our differing psychological outlook on this downward journey. Nigel had shot off like a rocket early on, fearing getting stuck on top without access to assistance and I had struggled to keep up with him at points, but he had slowed down towards the end of the walk as we reached comparative safety. I was slower at the top, thinking we had a long way to go to reach the bottom, conserving energy and knowing we could stay in a mountain hut if we needed to, but sped up with the motivation of the end in sight.

The last leg of the journey was along a jungle path that wound its way through the bamboo forest. It was beautiful and we passed gnarled old trees covered in moss and epiphytes that had such character you wondered how anyone could cut them down. We had been walking for 14 hours when we arrived at the Naro Moru Meteorological station. We had spoken to a porter who overtook us carrying luggage for a group who were coming down and he had offered to get his uncle, a local taxi driver, to come and meet us here. We relaxed with a soda each and enjoyed watching the Kenyatta University bus perform a 362 point turn to get off the mountain having dropped off a large group of students.

Benson, the taxi driver, was very friendly and talkative and gave us a tour of Naro Moru, which might have actually been a pretext for dropping off a group of his free-loading mates who had jumped in with us. He dropped us off at the luxury river lodge we were booked into. A shower and a Tusker *baridi* were the perfect end to the trip and we slept soundly in soft beds for the first time in days.

When Nigel visited the hospital in Nairobi, he was diagnosed with a torn ligament in his knee. The fact that he carried on walking for 10 hours afterwards and carried his own pack for most of that was a testament to the determined and experienced mountaineer that he was.

Six years later, Lily of the death stare worked as a gap year student in a school I worked at in the UK. She thanked me for pushing her and confessed she wouldn't have made it without my encouragement. She also told me of the sad passing of Mia, the sweet horder, who had died of malaria shortly after I left Africa.

LAKE TURKANA

For the first part of my Easter holiday I had planned to travel with colleagues to the northern part of Kenya. Lake Turkana, formerly known as Lake Rudolf, is one of the chain of lakes in the Rift Valley that includes Victoria, Tanganyika and Malawi among others. It is situated in the middle of the desert on the border with Ethiopia and Sudan (now South Sudan), and is one of the hottest driest parts of Kenya. The lake shore is home to the El Molo and Turkana people, who survive the harsh climate by fishing, hunting crocodiles for meat and by herding the ubiquitous goats.

The area had been a no-go zone for some time as it had been filled with displaced guerrilla fighters from the neighbouring country of Somalia. They had exacted a toll on the wildlife by using their high-tech weaponry for poaching, and had held up a number of tourist vehicles, causing a few deaths. The authorities, needing the foreign revenue from the tourists, had fought and won a war with these shiftas about a year or two before, but it was still a relatively unstable area to travel in.

Being largely desert, the area was extremely lowly populated and so there was also the risk of being stranded if the car broke down (a near certainty with my vehicle!) and careful planning had to take place about, among other things, how much water to take. Basically, the rule of thumb was that you couldn't take too much! We had therefore taken the easier planning route by paying to go with an overland company. This wasn't as adventurous as we would normally be and we would probably be travelling with random people who we didn't know. But on the plus side, someone else would be doing all the driving and cooking, so we could just relax and enjoy the trip.

I made my own way down to meet up with Rob, Sean and Angus, a former employee at the school, all three of whom had just arrived back from Lamu, a Swahili town on the coast.

I arrived in Nairobi ahead of the rest of our group to do some paperwork and banking before embarking on the trips I would undertake over Easter. As I rushed about in the busy city I reflected that this was the polar opposite of what I expected from the trip we were about to undertake. The yin, as it were, to the yang. Here was city life: hustle and bustle, mobile phones like scraping nails down a window pane, barely a jambo to be heard. It is true that cities, in spite of their populations, are the loneliest places.

There was nowhere to escape. The roads were full of beeping cars, salesmen and beggars, the parks full of assemblies listening to the pretences of dubious preachers. Cities are like a temple to pretence. People congregate in the trendy cafes, they swagger in their Nike baseball caps, swinging their Coca-Cola cups the cool way. Yet where was the real world? Why couldn't I hear the birds singing, insects rattling, the low rumble of pachyderm wind? It was drowned out and choked to death by peoples' voices, the cars' exhausts and the infernal executioner of quiet solitude, the mobile phone.

I had the afternoon to wile away waiting to meet up with Rob, Sean and Angus. These three were all amusing company in their own way and represented a sliding scale of ostentatiousness: Angus was a full blown clown, happy in the limelight and kept everyone going with his never ending slapstick; Rob was more reserved but happy to contribute his good humour at every given opportunity; Angus was the quiet member of the group, ready with a dry observation.

I amused myself with the things I like about towns: I watched a film and browsed a bookshop. However, I was dreaming of an endless horizon of sand, elephants grazing under the motherly gaze of Kilimanjaro and dhows drifting on the Indian Ocean. When I met up with the others, we went for dinner and then, at Angus's behest, visited a casino, where he won the equivalent of £ 100 and the rest of us drank for free while we watched.

Next morning we were up bright and early to attack a substantial breakfast before heading out. We waited for about an hour in a hotel car park, where Rob and Sean could leave their cars safely, for the transport to arrive. When it did arrive we had a pleasant surprise. We had been expecting two other travellers (anticipation was high for Swedish nymphomaniacs, in the best possible silly boys way) and that we would be travelling in a lorry. However, the vehicle was a comfortable looking 4WD Toyota Land Cruiser and we were to be the only passengers. We were all pleased by this turn of events. We even completed the remaining paperwork in high spirits before wading back into the Nairobi traffic and finally getting on our way north.

I fell asleep for a while, lulled by the combination of moving transport and stuffy midday heat, and woke up at a stop in a village called Kirinyaga, after the mountain I had recently been on. A drunken bloke approached the car and introduced himself as Karaoke. He shook all of our hands and told us that he loved us, as drunks must do the world over. I pointed to a large advertisement for Tusker beer and asked him if we could get any in Kirinyaga? He replied that we couldn't, and I secretly suspected it was because he had already drunk it all.

We carried on along a decent road, watching the well-watered bush sprouting from the red volcanic soil. We passed a *shamba* where someone had used old rusted car parts to bolster his hedge against ill-intentioned passers-by. The *shamba* began life as a form of shifting cultivation, but as the population has become increasingly sedentary, this has evolved into forest gardening in its better version and single or few crop vegetable gardening, which exhausts soils quickly, in its less preferable form. The red volcanic soil of central Kenya is incredibly fertile and is ideally suited for growing cash crops such as tea and coffee.

As we got to Naro Moru the benefactor of the lushness made an appearance and it began to rain. I fell asleep again shortly after and yet it was still raining when we reached Isiolo. This was unusual for Kenya, where even the wet season normally produced only swift afternoon downpours before clearing up in the evening. This weather was in stark contrast to my last visit to this area, when the dust and heat were almost unbearable. We crossed the Samburu river, which is normally only a trickle, but was now a gushing orange/brown torrent of water.

It was still raining when we paid KSh1000 for park entry, which was far higher than I had expected and set against my flimsy budget rather alarmingly. We also picked up a chap who had a nervous cough that drove us all mad. Our first port of call was the triplet parks Samburu, Saba and Buffalo Springs, three parks that border each other and gather close to the Samburu river, which gives the wildlife the much needed lifegiver in dry times. I had come here on my first safari camping expedition a year and a half before and was looking forward to exploring the large and varied wildlife populations found here again.

We drove towards our camp and found an overland truck (of the type we had expected to be travelling on) at a 60 degree angle, with its wheel stuck in the mud. Its occupants were working against the clock to get it out before dark. It is an odd phenomenon of the human psyche that it lifts the spirits to see someone less well off than oneself. Perhaps it serves as a reminder that things aren't so bad. We offered our help, but were assured that matters were in hand, and it was with great relief that we arrived safe and sound at the ready pitched campsite for dinner and an early night.

In Samburu it was especially important to take precautions against insect bites, as the park was at a sufficiently low altitude for mosquitoes to be carrying malaria. Some of the boys were taking prophylactics, preventive medicines against contracting malaria. The short term side effects of these drugs were pretty interesting, including stomach pains and vomiting, headaches, dizziness and weakness, nightmares, itching and coughing. The long term effects had still not been thoroughly studied. I didn't fancy these risks any more than malaria itself, so I used to take a garlic tablet every day, which mosquitoes are supposed to dislike the taste of (I could sympathise with them), and vitamin B12 supplement, to boost my immune system. In the evenings, I would cover as much of my body with clothing as the temperature would sensibly allow and then put mosquito repellent on the remaining exposed bits of skin.

I had taken my usual steps to prevent being bitten just before the sun went down and the malarial mozzies came out. Just before dinner I answered the call of nature and, as I was about to eat, rinsed my hands. I was bitten on one of the interdigital folds, the bits of skin between the fingers that suggest we were once water dwellers, and, as malaria takes 10 days to incubate, began to wonder how I'd feel after those 10 days.

At 6:30 the next morning, we set off for the adjoining Buffalo Springs park for our first game drive. We found a martial eagle with its crest and dappled chest in the trees overhead and tiny dikdik, the second smallest species of antelopes that are about the size of newborn lambs, dashing into cover. The dikdik, who get their name from their alarm call, do not live in herds like other antelope but with their lifetime partners.

We headed for the ridge, passing the impressive oryx, a gazelle with the painted face of a Maori and the spear-like antlers of a warrior, making it look quite the force to be reckoned with. But, as with the rest of the antelope species, he understands that discretion is the better part of valour and legs it when you get too close. The view from the top of the ridge was truly one of Africa as one imagines it. A vast plain dotted with flat-topped acacia thorn trees rolled towards the slate blue volcanic hills and ridges where the horizon met the azure sky, all beginning to dance as the heat increased. As we set off again, we saw a pair of black-backed jackals picking their way through the bushes and gerenuk, whose name means 'giraffe neck', standing on its hind legs to reach fodder their impala cousins find unobtainable.

We came across another vehicle that had stopped to watch something - normally a sign that something good is about! It turned out to be a family of cheetahs, 2 adults and 3 young, who were trying to keep in the shade of the bushes as the harsh African sun slowly rose to its punishing zenith. The cheetah is a beautifully sleek animal: the well-toned Olympic athlete of the wild. They slunk between cover, interrupted only by the loud honking of a male Grevy's zebra who was copulating raucously with his equine floozy. Grevy's zebra differs from its more southerly relative the Burchills in its thinner stripes, larger ears and stockier frame. I haven't read any comparative study on genitalia but this male was huge.

We carried on and found a herd of reticulated giraffe. It is interesting to find these different variations of familiar species in the north. The reticulated giraffe has larger, more square-ish patches in its pattern with paler beige in between than the Rothschild and Maasai giraffe of the central, western region I resided in.

A troop of baboons was out foraging for its breakfast by the river as we returned for ours: a filling matter of fruit, toast and pancakes cooked on the campfire, washed down with some very good coffee. In this regard Mwangi, our chef, had endeared himself to me the most. An extremely friendly fellow, who talked almost without pause for breath on the way up, he echoed my own sentiments when he exclaimed that he didn't hold with freeze-dried instant *kahawa*. Instead, every morning was accompanied with the light, sharp flavours of freshly ground Kenyan roasted coffee beans. Bless this man!

After breakfast we went out again and added to the broad spectrum of game birds we had seen: bruised blue and black vulturine guinea fowl, dun shades of yellow necked spurfowl and little brown sand grouses, vermillion brilliance of the red necked spurfowl. We saw more of the white flower that must have sprouted in response to the rains. It was a palm-sized explosion of virgin white, with six slender tendrils, like the trails of jet planes, shooting off in hexagonal opposition.

We passed a couple of buffaloes who had buried themselves under a large bush to escape the midday heat. Only their heads showed from beneath the luxuriant leaves as they masticated their morning's foraging thoughtfully. A Grant's stag snorted defensively as we passed through his hareem of elegant does. We watched ground squirrels sprinting from us, with their tails trailing behind them motionless, as their paws went at a blur of action. A warthog, perhaps the most robust looking character of the African bush, dug his gnarled snout into the red earth to construct a wallow, coughing up clouds of blood-coloured dust. The warthog, with a reputation amongst the locals for being the most stupid animal in Africa, stands stock still watching you, trying to figure out if you pose a threat, before it turns quickly and bolts for safety, its tail held high behind it as a comical flag of warning to its fellows.

On our return to camp we passed the poor sods in the lorry who were bathed in mud having worked for 20 hours to try to dislodge their vehicle and get it moving. An oil tanker and a tractor had been drafted in to attempt to heave it out the day before, but had only managed to collide into each other without budging the truck. Now they were resigned to digging out the mud from under the wheels, whilst supporting the weight on jacks, and filling the gap with stone so that they could drive out. The scene resembled a rabbit's warren as everyone mucked in to climb underneath and dig. We left them to it, ascertaining that they had plenty of folk to do the job. Besides which, there was a whiff of lunch on the air.

Our camp was made up of ten tents arranged in a horseshoe around a large campfire and eating area. It was situated close to the river, which was convenient for sitting in the cool shade of the trees during the midday, and commanded a view of the nearby hills, two of which were quite, shall we say, womanly?

Relaxing in the afternoon sun, one was placated by a chorus of honeyed tones from the birds, who were awaiting their next opportunity to raid the crumbs you threw from your meals. It seemed like a fair trade to me. As Mwangi busily prepared our lunch, I found myself eyeing the fruits of his labours as greedily as the feathered choir around us.

After lunch we spent a lazy afternoon doing bugger all. I wandered down to the river, having heard a troop of baboons come down to the opposite bank to drink. I took off my shoes and waded in up to my ankles to cool down in the roiling midday heat and watched the activities of the troop on the other side of the river. Sentries hunched down on their ankles to keep watch as members of the troop took turns to go to the water's edge and take cooling draughts. Suddenly, an enormous crocodile shot about 4 metres up the beach in the blink of an eye, sending the baboons scattering, screaming into the trees. It occurred to me that I wouldn't be able to move as fast as those baboons just had and that it was probably approaching time to get out of the river now.

After drinking some good coffee, we set out on another game drive at 4pm as the heat started to ebb. We began with a trip back to Buffalo Springs, which Rob rated as the poor relation to the other two parks. After seeing some different antelope species, a call came through on the radio, the only part of which I caught being *'kuja hapa'* ("come here"), to which our driver's reply was *'asante'* and some increased pressure on the right-most pedal. As we raced out of Buffalo Springs and into Samburu, we asked our driver, Justin, what we were going to see. *"Chui"* he replied, leopard.

As we approached, we saw at least a dozen tourist buses parked around some bushes, which Justin explained were hiding some lions. It was very difficult to see the lions, between the overhanging branches and the wall of vehicles, so we left them alone and carried on to the tree with the leopard. The leopard is a beautiful creature, its rosetted fur an almost breathtaking sight. It carries itself with typical feline grace and this one seemed unfazed by the arsenal of telescopic lenses and camcorders pointed at it.

Writing this 20 years later, the population figures for the three biggest cats in Africa make stark reading. In 2001, when I was travelling in Africa, populations of leopards, lions and cheetahs were 5 million, 1 million and 250,000 respectively. At the time I write these journals, the latest figures are 700,000, 80,000 and 7,000, a harrowing indictment of our ability to co-exist with our animal neighbours.

We then ventured over to the 'Green Bush Trail', which is unimaginatively but accurately named, and found the king of the jungle sprawled out, fast asleep. He raised a sleepy eyelid and then, with Tusker breath, told us he loved us and resumed his snooze. The state of the monarchy today! The camouflage of the animals is amazing too. The grey-brown colour of the dikdik is identical to the colour of the acacia bushes they live amongst, and this male lion blended in perfectly too.

At the time I was travelling, lions were split between into two subspecies, one of which was called the buffalo lion, so called because, with its heavier build and greater size, it was capable of taking down an adult buffalo single-handed. The male of this line has a reduced mane, so we were able to identify this one as a pride lion, so called because, being smaller, it took a pride of females or small group of batchelors to bring down the buffalo. More recently, a Cat Classification Task Force has defined two subspecies of lion based on their genetic distributions: *pantera leo leo*, which includes the rare Asiatic lion, Ethioapian lion and those lions inhabiting western and central Africa, and *pantera leo melanochaita* which lives in eastern and southern Africa. The buffalo and pride distinctions would have both been of the *melanochaita* subspecies and the differences that suggested subspecies criteria to early naturalists would have been down to isolated behavioural and genealogical differences within the same subspecies.

We left the lion to his kip and discovered another family of cheetah. The two furthest cubs got up to join mother and sister, just as our friends on the lorry pulled up, waving a celebratory beer at us. It must have been a tough day or two for those overlanders, but they would surely have gone home with a great story to tell. The cheetahs all sat huddled together and I couldn't help wondering why. Was it to share body warmth, or to share some family time together, or for comfort in the face of the tourist hordes? The cheetahs spent the whole time swatting flies away, something that lions don't bother to do. It's strange, the things that you notice!

One of the cubs got up and started to play-wrestle with mum, biting her ears. It was a touching moment of family bonding, but in light of the reports on population numbers, one has to feel concerned for the cheetah. It makes the black stripe below their eyes look like a tear winding its way into an uncertain future. The cheetahs were startled away by something (which could have been a lion, who will take young cheetahs) and we returned to our camp with a sense of privilege at being allowed to share such a moment of family intimacy with them.

During the night as we sat around a campfire drinking Tusker, we heard a lion growling from afar. As I lay in bed that night I was awoken by more loud animal noises, but they turned out to be Angus snoring in the tent next to mine.

We set off early again the next morning and were able to leave behind Moses, the camp hand with the nervous cough. Though afflicted, and he of course suffered more than we, he was a very helpful and considerate chap, who had the camp in good order at all times, meaning we had to do little to ensure our own comfort and for this we were very grateful. We were soon out of the national park gate and crossed a dried up riverbed which had gouged an impressive channel from the surrounding rock, giving it banks like red brick walls.

We stopped in a small town called Archer's Post, which had the distinctive African village smell: cow dung, dust (in this case wet dust) and sweaty armpits. This became such a familiar fragrance mixture that I almost looked forward to it upon arriving in a new location by the end of my time in Africa. It gave a measure of familiarity when you arrived somewhere new. As usual the car was surrounded by kids wanting pens, and adults wanting all sorts of things from cigarettes to magazines. One of them asked us each in turn if we were Cockney geezers, which caused us all a great deal of amusement. He seemed very knowledgeable on the topic, asking us if we had been born within earshot of the St. Mary-le-Bow church, which to his disappointment, none of us had. I love the random conversations you have with strangers.

We set off from there into the bush under a sky full of cloud from horizon to horizon. There was work going on on the roads to replace the old metal drains that ran under the road, funnelling the water underneath without sweeping the road away. They were being replaced with huge concrete cylinders and each time we had to take a detour off the road and into the mud to get round I thought about the poor sods on that lorry, wedged into the mire for the best part of two days. But each time, we made it through, with hearts recovering from their cessation of duty.

We passed a huge volcanic hill shrouded in cloud from which waterfalls tumbled down the rocky steps. We were going through a low pan soaked with water from the rains and full of green thorn bushes. The flats were surrounded by pointed volcanic mountains like the dragon's teeth sown by Cadmos in Greek mythology, but these *spartoi* would have grown into titans.

The local Samburu people lived in quite distinctive houses. They were made from long wooden poles bent into bread-loaf shaped frames and then covered with whatever junk could be obtained that might be waterproof: sheets of cardboard, corrugated metal, plastic sheeting. They reminded me of the sort of dens we made as kids with sticks we had cut out of trees and whatever we could pilfer from the adult world around us.

It was into a village of such buildings, surrounded as they were by a hedge of dead acacia thorn to keep lions from marauding their cattle, that we drove to attempt to cross the Seralevi river. There was a huge traffic jam of lorries and as we drove through I recognised Ethiopian traits in some of the faces, as this was the main road to that country from Kenya. The river had flooded due to overnight rain and there was a delay before we could attempt to ford it. This would hopefully not set us back more than a couple of hours, but it was mentioned that if it didn't subside we could either camp in the village there or miss out Marsibit altogether and go round to Maralal.

We wandered down to the river to take in the scene and I noticed that the guys sat on their ankles watching the water in exactly the same posture as the baboons, our close evolutionary cousins, had days earlier. Their attention was riveted on three lorries that had tried to cross and now, having failed, stood like ominous warnings in the middle of the river. The intensity and focus of the audience's stares could almost have willed them from their watery, stationary position.

We decided to try to carry the luggage over the uncompleted bridge (apparently four years in the making at the time - no rush), so that a less heavily laden wagon could have a go at crossing the span. We set off in the 4WD to get the luggage a bit closer before we started carrying it, but we got stuck in soft sand and it took us half an hour to dig and push our way back out again.

By this time, two lighter cars had managed to cross the ford by going down the sides of the lorries where the water was shallowest. We all disembarked to let the vehicle cross without our weight and it made it across. We donned flip flops and rolled up our trousers to cross on foot, regrouping on the other side. There, a soldier asked us for a lift, so he joined us as an armed escort. He wasn't particularly talkative, but he seemed cheerful enough, perhaps just happy to be on his way in spite of the weather conditions.

Vulturine guinea fowl, with their blue wimples wobbling, rushed from the path of the car in much the same way you would expect a nun to run, hands pressed together in a prayer for salvation.

The rivers, normally dry beds known as *luggas*, all seemed to be full, though at one roaring waterway there was evidence of a recent bushfire, as the tree trunks were charred and blackened to a height of about 15 feet. This is all part of the regeneration of the bush, a human custom dating back millennia that has helped to keep the grasslands as productive for cattle grazing as possible. The fires burn out the old vegetation at the end of the dry season, which completes the dual tasks of ridding the ground of competition for new growth while also providing nutrients to embellish it in time for the wet season.

The local tribes of Samburu and, further north, Rendille wore a quite unusual traditional costume that included beaded earplugs that came out from the tops of their ears, and red wrap-around blankets similar to the Maasai *shukas*. The women wore multiple layered bead necklaces that covered their necks and to which they attached their dress/blanket, exposing the breasts. It seemed quite an outrageous costume to a conservative western taste, but the women showed no shyness in what they wore. It did occur to me that there was a measure of hypocrisy at a time when toples sunbathing tourists were arrested at the coast, but this was an example of the broad-ranging cultural differences throughout Kenya, with the coast inhabited by more conservative muslim peoples.

Both men and women wore very ornate bead designs upon their foreheads and across their chins. A group of Rendille warriors, dressed in this way, also sported red body paint on their lithe shoulders and serious faces. They were armed with spears and short, stabbing swords.

We approached Laimasis, the home of our adopted guard, which was a collection of rocks, dust and small leafless thorn bushes. It made me wonder how this town could scratch a living from such a harsh environment. The rain started again as we pulled out of town, soaking the gravel road and filling the potholes with orange water. There were sections of road that the rain had washed away completely, enormous puddles of unguessable depth, parts that the overloaded lorries had churned into slush and every few miles we would be diverted into quagmire where they were conducting repairs to the drains. We adopted a frame of mind that we were expecting to get stuck and that we only wondered when rather than if the seemingly inevitable would happen.

The hills became more scattered and we passed a volcanic cone with a circle of cloud around its middle like a hula hoop. It felt a bit like being on a giant chessboard, with smaller pawn outcrops and more impressive looking rook, queen and king hills.

We saw a chap asleep in the shelter of one of the drainage sections before the hills disappeared, as we travelled through a flat, boulder-strewn scrubland called the Kaisut desert. And it was getting hotter... I think we were lucky to be going through this area during the rains, as I can only imagine how bad the dust from moving vehicles would be when it dried up. The cloud cover meant that we were at a comfortable temperature when the car was going and the wind passed through the gaps in the roll-down canvas blinds, though it did feel hot whenever we stopped.

Two lorries had got stuck and we picked up one of the drivers, who wanted to go to Marsibit to buy food for himself and his mates. He told us that he didn't think they would get out of their predicament until the end of the rains, and so they would be stuck there in the middle of nowhere for a few months.

As we approached the forested hills of Marsabit Park, we saw a couple of black-backed jackals on the road before we spotted two elephants silhouetted on the tree lined horizon. We skirted round the park, as the road formed it's western boundary, but the forest looked somewhat out of place amidst the barren wasteland that surrounded it. The park was on higher ground than its surroundings, so it probably got more rain, which would make it possible for the growth of the larger and more varied plant species.

Eventually, we arrived in Marsibit town, which looked horrible! I was immediately reminded of the scene in Monty Python's Holy Grail where the peasants are slopping about in the mud. It was everywhere! The road was reduced to a mud surface, as was the pavement; the football field had not a blade of grass; and the forecourt of the hotel we pulled up at was uniform mud. I don't think I've ever seen so much of the stuff in my life. And I grew up playing rugby in Wales!

We went for a wander around town - through the mud - and called in at the Mountain Bar for a Tusker *baridi*. As we entered the bar a sturdy looking server spat on the floor before taking our order. We folded our beer bottle labels into paper aeroplanes and flew them around the dimly lit room, which somewhat lightened the otherwise rather dark mood of the place. The tank-like bar stewardess kept passing me and fondling my hair, a level of forwardness that suggested she was interested in either the comparative softness of my hair (which was not an uncommon experience for me in Africa) or a bit of fun with the *mzungu*.

The hotel we were in was a concrete shell with nothing in the way of furniture or decoration save the beds we slept in. We had a fantastic meal cooked up outside the building by Mwangi, before retiring for an early night. During the night, we were deafened by the noise of thousands of frogs who had returned to the lake covering the football mud for breeding. These amphibious crooners were leaving nothing to chance when it came to finding a mate and sang lustily all night long. Eventually it became white noise and I fell asleep.

I was awake at six o'clock to the sound of rain tinkling onto the concrete roof. When I got up an hour later, it had gathered pace to a thorough downpour, bringing with it a thick fog. It was like a November morning in Britain and not quite what I'd been expecting from a trip to the desert. It was without any real regret that we left Marsabit once the rain had relinquished a little.

We climbed further up into the hills, where we saw a couple of kites circling in search of scant morsels to breakfast on. We stopped to take a walk up to a ridge and upon reaching the summit discovered it was the rim of the volcanic Golfredo crater. Thick puffs of cloud swooped over the escarpment but were unable to drop down to where the green trees grew on the floor of the bowl. From this ridge we could see our next destination, the Chalbi desert, stretched out below us. The small, brown hills on the flat, barren plain looked like molehills on a dry lawn beneath the blanket of grey cloud.

Listening to a voice like Donald Duck's on the radio, we drove past a group who had slept on the rock strewn ground and I couldn't think of a less comfortable place to have spent the night. We overtook a camel train, the animals showing their big, flapping feet as they ran from us.

It was 10 o'clock, we were beginning to descend from the cloud and it was 24 degrees Celsius. The rock-scattered landscape looked endless. Dead grasses, the odd knee-high thorn bush and otherwise an unbroken expanse of rocks. Apparently, only 15% of the world's deserts are the sandy terrain we romanticise them to be, and this wasn't one of them. The wind was blowing without any hills to oppose it, carrying dust into our eyes as we drove through a patch of sand, but then we were back into the rock as we reached the bottom of the pan. There were puddles on the road as a result of the rain, which were good for goat herders, but not so great for vehicular progress. It was 11:20am, 29°C and Justin, our driver, still had his shell suit on!

Justin was a tall, well-built chap with a high voice, the latter somehow feeling incongruous with the former. He was very smartly dressed and, with his immaculate glasses, looked like he might be more comfortable pushing paper about on a desk than pulling the wheel through a desert. However, he proved to be a very pleasant, knowledgeable guy who was good at his work.

The landscape was punctuated with mounds of dark rocks, piled on top of one another to make what I presumed were burial mounds. In a place where it was all but impossible to dig, rock mounds would stop jackals and other carrion feeders from making off with deceased loved ones. We stopped at noon (32°C in spite of the complete cloud cover) and I had a wander about, finding brown patches of wetter dust where fresh green shoots had begun to sprout.

The smooth, black, porous rocks were cleared to make paths, presumably between watering holes. There were low circles of stone which I thought could be windbreaks for herdsmen to shelter in or were possibly corals for keeping livestock in overnight, so they didn't wander off to be eaten by wild beasties who were perhaps too shy to approach humans and take them.

We set off again and found a tennis court sized pond, complete with ducks, dragonflies and butterflies. Angus, being a science teacher, informed us that dragonflies are very fussy and will only make a home around the very cleanest of water. This seemed a bit strange given the filthy brown colour of the pool, but perhaps Angus was referring to chemical pollutants, of which there were probably none here. The bright green grass around the pond looked like a splash of ink spilled on brown parcel paper.

We pulled up next to a bush in which a martial eagle was busily devouring a stork, while a smaller volux eagle hungrily looked on. They both fled the meal at our approach, fighting with each other at a safe distance from us, probably for right to first dibs when we'd left. The desert had certainly greened up after the rain. There were more patches of incredibly vivid green grass. A group of eleven ostriches were making the most of the vegetarian feast while it lasted and we saw herds of camels silhouetted on the horizon.

Looking south west, we thought we could see a lake. Then we thought it might be the marsh area in the central Chalbi that we were skirting to the north, but it turned out to be a mirage caused by light being refracted by the heat haze. The heat in the desert is so strong it can make light bend, causing the sight of objects to curl over obstacles and be seen from further away than one could normally see them from. What we were actually looking at might have been the waters of Lake Turkana, the image bent over the landscape by the shimmering heat to make it appear closer.

Having gone past some sunbleached animal bones, lying like a reminder to take care in the desert, we stopped for lunch in a small grove of acacias beneath a rocky outcrop. It looked almost as though there could have been a river flowing down the gully at some time and there were more of the stone circles, which I went off to explore.

On the way up to them I came across two local Gabbra girls, who were out collecting firewood, a bundle attached by string to each of their heads, with the weight carried across the shoulders. I asked them where they had come from and they replied that they were from the *manyatta*, a grouping of traditional houses, and that there were many houses there. I wondered where they could mean, as I couldn't see any sign of life anywhere. It was possible that they had foraged quite a distance to find their loads.

I pressed on to the circles. At the first one, I found a circular construction of stones placed on top of each other using only gravity to hold them together. The wall came to the height of my thigh and had an area that could perhaps seat around 12 people on the ground inside, which supported my theory of windbreaks for the herdsmen. However, if that were the case, why would they not build them around the acacias to give them some protection from the sun? Perhaps they were only for livestock?

Upon further exploration, it turned out that the first circle I arrived at was unusually large and that most of them were only big enough for one goat. Some were smaller still, with roofs, like the chicken coops made by the old inhabitants of Easter island. These people had no chickens, but could they be for keeping younger kids in before they learned not to stray from the camp?

Perhaps they were storing food inside, so they didn't have to carry it about? Or maybe they were way-markers? Or perhaps they were some sort of ancestral graves, the size indicating the social importance of the buried person? Or their age at death? I never did resolve the mystery of the stone circles.

I turned to go back, away from the noisy crickets who buzzed from rock to rock and the enormous flying locusts, and noticed the girls again. They were adding another bundle of sticks to their loads, wrapping it in a leather skin to pad the thorns from their backs. I was suddenly struck by their feminine, fragile beauty in this place of harshness. They had very dark skin and wore bracelets at their wrists and elbows which enhanced their slender frames. They wore colourful *kangas,* of dark blue and purple dappled with brilliant red and orange designs, wrapped around their bodies and headdresses the orange of the rising sun. They were two vibrant desert flowers. Ghosts in reverse: exuding unquenchable life in a land absent of the living.

After lunch we drove for two hours seeing nothing but rock and sand, with the occasional parched hill for interest's sake, before coming to the town of Kalachwa, a grouping of thatched domed huts and two big churches. Here we found the campsite we were to stay at. We had been covered in dust throughout the day and I asked Justin, feeling it was too optimistic to hope for, whether there was a shower available.

"Yes, and there is a swimming pool too," he replied, very matter-of-factly.

My immediate suspicion was that he was being facetious. After just driving through the desert for the whole day, I found it incredibly hard to credit. Even when I had gone in the direction he pointed us in and found a large concrete tub full of chlorinated water, it still seemed incredible that it was there. It felt like the light trick we had experienced in the middle of the wasteland.

However, the temperature had been 34 °C all afternoon and this treat was especially welcome. We had an hour cooling off in the pool and then drove, with wrinkly fingers, to the other side of town to an oasis where there was a lodge. We couldn't believe our luck - a swimming pool and a cold beer! But alas! It may as well have been a mirage, as they had nothing at all to drink, not even a soft drink.

As we returned we crossed a small stream that babbled over the worn-smooth rockbed. Angus, a well-fed fellow who had a richly deserved lack of faith in his own capacity for balance and coordination, gave me his video camera for safekeeping as we crossed the stream. He told me to video his crossing as he felt bound to fall in. I called out for him to stop, as I hadn't yet fathomed the advanced technology, but instead he began his adventure.

If Angus had planned to enter himself for a gymnastics competition, his gravity-defying elevation would have scored highly; his ability to widely spread arms and to lift his legs above the height of his falling torso would have also placed him well; the facial expression of surprise and consternation would have endeared him to any judges who owned even a shred of humanity; but sadly his landing let him down. Like a fish that gracefully leaps from the confines of his marine abode, sparkling in the sunshine, and realises too late that he has overshot the water only to discover a less forgiving reentry point of solidity and hardness, Angus landed with an unflattering crunch as jellied limbs collapsed around him with all the fluidity of a drunken hippopotamus.

We all laughed raucously, even Angus, in spite of his initial self-diagnosis of a broken spine. This hilarity was only slightly marred by the fact that I hadn't had the camera rolling so we could enjoy replays ad infinitum.

That night I decided to sleep outside, as the sky could not have been clearer, so I made up a camp bed from the collapsible stools and a couple of mattresses, in order to put some distance between myself and the terrestrial scorpions we had been warned of. It was a wonderful nights' sleep as the chairs' canvas molded to my body and the temperature never dropped below 24 °C. Each time I woke up I could see a new constellation of stars above, like guardian angels taking shifts to watch over me.

In the morning, I made use of the luxury long-drop (a bench with a hole to crap through instead of the usual hole in the ground) and showers, before cutting my ear open on an acacia thorn. Acacias are tough buzzards. They grow seemingly anywhere and are protected from being eaten by a fearsome array of vicious thorns, anything up to 2 or 3 inches long. They can quite happily puncture the soles of flip-flops or trainers and this one had made a nasty mess of my ear. Perhaps understandably, Angus was not exactly forthcoming with sympathy.

We set off into the desert at 8 o'clock with the temperature already at 28 °C and clear skies all around. There were countless tracks leading into the yellow sand and no obvious way to tell which was the correct road. Sure enough, we were soon going round in circles trying to find the right way, after the section we had been following suddenly stopped. The problem then was trying to find the correct direction, as there were no landmarks at all. No hills, no towns, no rivers, just sand, rock and acacias in a 360° arc, as far as the eye could see.

After wandering apparently aimlessly, we found the road we were looking for (which looked like all the others from my undiscerning point of view) and we proceeded along a dust track patched with muddy puddles. I was just thinking that the acacias were starting to thin out when the vehicle abruptly slowed to a halt. We were stuck!

Fortunately, we were able to push it out with little difficulty and we carried on, taking wider berths of the darker patches and surface water.

We approached a river, which had come to life following the thunderstorms we had witnessed the previous night over the northern, Ethiopian end of the Huri hills. This precipitation had already prompted flowers to spring up along the banks. There were large bell-shaped, pink blooms and delicate, yellow ones that looked like primroses. Unfortunately, we lacked a botanist sufficiently expert to identify these flowers exactly.

Justin rushed through the ford and we all got soaked, which was quite refreshing, if a little dirty! One of the strengths of the 4WD we were in were the roll-up canvas sides that allowed the wind to keep you cool(-er) in the desert heat. However, on this occasion, we should have perhaps had them rolled down. We got out to have a look at the river and snoop about, but there was nothing more to be seen than the moving water. There was nothing at all in front of us and when we turned around there was nothing at all behind us. It did beg the question: what are we doing here?

We set off again, racing two male ostriches, who appeared to enjoy the challenge, before turning off and heading into the surrounding emptiness. Not only can ostriches run at the incredible speed of around 70kmph, they can maintain their pace for long periods too. It is estimated that an ostrich is capable of running a marathon distance of 42km in 40 minutes. Every stride at full pace covers around 5m, or double their height.

This area of the desert was supposed to have been submerged by Lake Turkana many centuries ago. As we passed the potholes full of water, it was easy to see how the remaining soil could have been silt from an engorged lake. The same went for the shingle and rounded pebbles that lay in other areas. There were one or two fluffy clouds looking like lonely sheep that had wandered too far from the flock, but otherwise the penetrating blue of the vast sky pulsated overhead. The area we were driving through looked like mile upon mile of pebble beach interspersed with sand dunes.

As the temperature climbed, we reached North Horr, which was a surprisingly large town of thatched huts and a few western style buildings. There was an enormous church and World Health Organisation Land Rovers carrying people to their work in the fight against AIDS. We wandered about and I found a sign commemorating the planting of a tree by Mrs. Jackie Goldrick in 1995. Sadly, I could find no sign of any tree anywhere near the sign and it was only 6 years later, making the proliferation of the native doum palm even more impressive. The doum palm is related to mint, but grows successfully in desert areas where almost every part of the tree can be put to use by humans. The timber can be used for construction, the leaves for basket weaving, the nuts can be eaten and contain an impressive array of health benefits and the roots have medicinal uses.

We passed some huts that had been thatched with doum palm fronds, and had the psychedelically coloured local *kangas* hanging for sale, amongst other less interesting stock. There was also a small post office. I toyed with the idea of posting a letter from this station, as it was the most remote post office I have ever encountered, but the sobering reality of having no paper, no envelope and no stamp meant that I wasn't able to see this wish come to fruition.

When we returned to the car, we were mobbed by children who were very keen for us to buy their water. However, the liquid they held up for our close inspection was the colour of a toilet's contents after a dodgy stomach and certainly did not look like we should drink it. Eventually Sean gave them some pencils and they ran away happily.

We passed some graves marked with wooden crosses, before plunging into a forest of doum palms and sand dunes that was criss-crossed by rivulets of water. We drove past some more doum palm huts, outside which were thatched windbreaks and loaded camels, before I succumbed to the heat and fell asleep.

I woke up in a town called Gas, though it wasn't the most inspiring of mini metropolii. There were huge cracks forming in the ground, where the rain had expanded the volume of the dirt and the sun was now drying it out, reducing the volume and creating creases in the hard baked floor.

Shortly after Gas, we topped a ridge and got our first glimpse of our final destination: Lake Turkana. As we dropped down to the valley it became more and more obvious why it was also known as the Jade Sea, its green colour becoming more vivid as we dropped through the heat haze. The temperature was 37°C in any shade that could be found (it couldn't) and a sweltering breeze came up the gorge towards us. We passed some El Molo women with Mohican haircuts, red dresses that exposed their breasts and the vast stack of bead necklaces that were worn from an early age.

We pulled into the Turkana-El Molo Lodge, where the swimming pool had no water, but we were offered a hot shower. This didn't seem so appealing as the mercury in the thermometer pushed the 40°C mark, so we instead shared lunch with hundreds of flies that descended on our repast in plague-like clouds. At some juncture both Angus and Sean bought some fossilised fish and we headed into Loiyangalani to pick up some beer.

The usual gathering of kids instantly materialised around us: a young boy with tribal scarring around his left nipple; a girl of not more than 9 years old who was already weighed down by about a 6 inch depth of bead necklaces; a child with a broken shard of mirror, held like it was his most prized worldly possession; and a boy who was whistling 'Figaro' from Rossini's "the Barber of Seville". Though we lacked for an expert botanist on this trip, Rob, a music teacher, was able to quickly diagnose whistled tunes, and we all admired this worldly young fellow, wondering where he had heard the tune.

Loiyangalani comprised dozens of dome-shaped El Molo/ Turkana huts, about two thirds the size of the Gabbra ones we had seen before. They were made from the ubiquitous building material, the doum palm and featured openings for a door and a couple of windows as architectural features. Being a small town, we soon passed through to the other side where we found a surprisingly green pastureland around the lakeshore. Between the loose rock, bright green shoots of grass were beginning to appear, encouraged by the rain that had fallen recently. From here we had an excellent view of South Island National Park, which sits in the lake. This park has the continent's largest population of Nile crocodiles, and is famed for the breeding and rehabilitation of these beasties.

We parked next to a row of thatched El Molo/Turkana huts that would be our camp for the night, as the afternoon shimmered towards dusk.

The first job was to take a dip in the lake, as the temperature was still 36°C. However, before we could begin our aquatic activities we were advised to throw some pebbles into the water first to scare off any crocodiles that might be lurking nearby with thoughts of dinner. It seemed sensible to take precautions, but since the largest Nile crocodile ever found, at 28 feet long and 6 feet wide, had been pulled out of this same body of water, the distribution of a few tiny rocks didn't seem to match the potential threat of a giant predator. At the advertised size, this largest croc could have nearly swallowed me sideways, but we were reassured that this was all that was necessary, as the local tribes hunted crocodiles, making them a bit timid.

The swim was very relaxing and the remaining sun quickly dried me out afterwards. We relaxed on the black volcanic sand and watched a bloke bring a fish up for our dinner that looked big enough to pull him back into the lake. Angus, a keen angler, reckoned this fish was about a 40lb catch, but told us it wasn't even big enough to use as bait for the bigger Nile perch, which can grow to a tonne in weight. No wonder the crocodiles here were so big!

The wind, caused by a changing disparity in temperature between the lake water and desert ground, howled persistently all night. This did and didn't aid sleep. The noise was loud but it helped to keep off the mosquitoes, which only come out in very still air. We sat enjoying a couple of Tuskers in our palm thatch lodge, as the moonlight glinted off the lake and the stars shone like beacons, with no light pollution to compete with. It was a wonderfully tranquil evening.

When we got up the next morning, the wind was still blowing so strongly that we could not go on the boat trip we had planned. Instead, we just idled about in the camp all morning, swimming, sunbathing and reading. After lunch the wind had calmed down a little, so the boat was brought round and we set off for the tiny El Molo village.

The El Molo are Kenya's smallest tribe, with a population of around 3000, but with far fewer of unmixed blood. Their language is all but extinct and they are said to have historically constructed tombs in which they laid their dead near wells or water sources. This made me wonder if they were responsible for the stone domes I had seen earlier. When we arrived in the village, there were naked children playing in the water and they eagerly rushed up to greet us. They followed us all around the village like faithful puppies and, once they had plucked up the courage, held our hands. This was fine but for the fact that the boys were constantly playing with their genitals and you couldn't be quite sure what the hand you held had just been touching.

The guide took us to see a goat enclosure and chicken coup,

which were difficult to get excited about. We were told that sometimes Samburu and Turkana tribesmen came raiding and the El Molo had to run for their lives into the highlands. With this proclamation the tour was over and we were sped to the curio stalls, where we were welcome to pay over the odds for anything we saw and liked. I wondered if the trouble the El Molo had with the Samburu and Turkana was because these tribesmen had also parted with KSh300/= each for this 'guided tour' and knew how to ask for their money back more forcefully than we did.

In fairness, the stalls were full of interesting things, ranging from wooden dolls wearing leather clothes and brass bead jewellery, to stones and fossils, to the El Molo uniform necklaces, which were all the boys were wearing, to baskets, shells, calabashes, huge earrings (which might have been of use to me, thanks to the acacia!), and an interesting, carved wood device I had seen the day before which doubled up as a stool and sleeping head rest.

One teenage girl wore a full and elaborate dress, including a spectacular beaded headdress that looped around her eyes and shaved head. Further pendants and ornaments dangled from the bead structure and she completed the look with about 6 inches depth of bead necklaces, two wrap-around cloths that covered her torso and bracelets at the wrists and elbows. I was so fascinated with her dress that I sketched her to remember how ornately she was presented. The kids, who were pressing tightly around me and asking for my pen, were impressed with the drawing and they called her over for her to see it. She showed her approval of my perhaps unflattering and certainly hasty sketch with a shy, *"Iko mzuri,"* and a demure smile.

I had noticed that all the older women had warlike Mohican haircuts, whereas the youngest wore only shorts and a necklace (the boys of course wore only the necklace). I wondered if this girl's more exotic costume was indicative of her adolescence and availability for marriage. I found out later that I had not been far wrong: she was wearing the clothes of the engaged bride-to-be.

We left the El Molo and looked for crocodiles, but we could only find a small one of perhaps 5 feet in length. This could be because both the El Molo and Turkana hunt them for their delicious meat, which produced a direct population pressure from hunting and the knock-on behavioural change that the crocs kept a low profile. Having first tasted crocodile meat at a restaurant in Nairobi, I recalled that its texture and flavour tasted like a pleasing combination of pork and fish. I couldn't blame the locals for wanting to add it to their diet.

The journey back was quite rough, as the wind had picked up again to make some bigger waves for our small boat. I enjoyed visions of wrestling twenty-footers to get back to shore from a capsized craft, but it was alarmism and we returned without incident. That evening we went to a Turkana village, which I would have struggled to tell apart from the El Molo one, being almost identical. We were going to watch the traditional dancing of the Turkana tribe. Our vehicle had barely pulled up when the dancing began.

These people obviously had a close cultural link with the El Molo because, as well as the buildings, the clothing was very similar. The same naked youngsters (this time without necklaces, but an all-over covering of dust instead, perhaps due to being further from the water), Mohican cut women with the many layered, coloured bead necklaces and men naked from the head to the waist, where a blanket of red pattern was wrapped for modesty.

The male dancers, who were more numerous to begin with, also had white feathers on their headbands and cymbol-like metal discs attached to bands below their knees. This was to produce a rhythmic jangling as they stamped their feet and clapped their hands to the melodic chanting. The women's haircuts were probably derived through practicality, as long hair all round the head would be uncomfortably hot in the 40+°C heat of the dry season. It also combined with the necklaces to accentuate the slender line of their necks, giving them a very graceful beauty.

Some aspects of the women's dress were different to the El Molo. They tended to wear large circular earrings, which I hadn't noticed the El Molo wearing. The younger girls wore red ochre on the sides of their heads, where their hair had been shaved, perhaps also to signify unmarried adolescents again? Some of the older women wore black wraps and leather undergarments, which I speculated might have been the attire of bereavement.

The first dance involved the men standing in a circle bobbing and chanting, keeping rhythm with their hand claps and knee cymbals, while the women danced slowly, hand-in-hand, in single file around the outside in time to the chanting.

The next dance had a line of men facing the women, chanting and all leaping in time to the music. Slowly they got closer until they were paired together and doing a dance that would become familiar: holding hands and jumping so that their heads passed each others' alternate shoulders and their breasts nearly touched: the Turkana tango! A rolling, high-pitched scream, "rrrrrrr-ha!" stopped the dance and they took up new positions ready for the next set.

I noticed that the dancers were extremely tall. Two women were over six feet tall and many of the men were around six foot four.

A mixed gender jumping circle was formed and the women took turns to enter the middle and invite a man to Turkana Tango with them before returning to their separate positions to make way for the next invitation.

"Rrrrrrrr-ha!" and the sun sank below the skyline.

They all formed a circle hugging the person to either side around the shoulders, something like we used to do after an evening of beers in the student union bar to 'C'mon Eileen.' Then the group split into two and carried swaying and jumping, then into more groups until men and women were again paired off doing the Turkana Tango.

"Rrrrrrrr-ha!"

The older men retired to the sides to chant and clap, while the younger ones danced in a circle. The women danced around the outside holding hands and the men leapt after their chosen partner and danced the most frantic Turkana Tango yet.

By this time they were dancing by the light of the gibbous moon. They were leaping like the shadows cast by a flickering campfire, or by the fiery passion for and enjoyment of dancing that burned within them all. The white feathers in their headbands curled up into the night sky like sparks.

While mesmerised by the at times deeply moving, and at others overtly sexual, symbolism of their display, I found some amusing sidetracks. The dancers, both men and women, would periodically step back from the dancing area to evacuate the contents of their nostrils onto the dusty floor. A kiddy asked me for my pen, tried to pinch it when I said no, and then stood with his fists raised and punched me in the arm, despite only coming up to my waist!

The smaller children began to join in: the dancers of tomorrow learning their steps from their older peers.

This didn't have the feel of an empty show, put on just for money, like the contrived Maasai dances I had seen. Though we were paying to watch, these were more genuine people, the least touched by Western 'civilisation', really enjoying a dance. We quietly left them - moonlit figures still rising and falling in time to the primordial music - and made our way back to the camp fulfilled.

Next morning we awoke to a glorious sunrise: purple clouds crept over the Kalal mountains, as the sun tinged the sky radiant orange. During our stay at the lake, the temperature never dropped below 28°C, even in the early pre-dawn 'cool.' Fortunately, the wind kept it feeling bearable. We set off at 7:30am along the tyre tracks that were the only landmark through the scattered rock. I was sorry to leave the camp, a most relaxing spot kept fresh and mosquito free by a constant breeze.

The road led along the lakeside, offering a superb view of South Island and the hills that marked the western shore, and into a narrow gorge. Here we passed a truckload of people, one of whom was a Japanese tourist, clinging desperately to the side of the vehicle as it bounced along the rocky track, and no doubt dreaming of the safer transport options at home.

There were distant mountains on either side of us, whose peaks were obscured by cloud: the lofty Mount Nyiro and Mount Supuko, which I felt sounded like it more readily belonged in the tourist's home country of Japan. These mountains looked to be of the same vertical sided type as those in Ethiopia, which isn't so surprising since they are the southern end of the same range.

We stopped at the camp of another expedition from the same company, who had amongst its members the head teacher from the school up the road from ours. While the others chatted with him, I played with some local kids who enjoyed hanging from the jeep by my hands. One boy touched my hand and pulled his away so quickly he must have thought it would sting! I don't suppose they see many white people there.

We were in the acacia forest around South Horr, the evil thorns passing close by the open windows and keeping us on the lookout. We saw wattle and daub huts with mud roofs through breaks in the trees. The ride was not the most comfortable as the rain had washed away the road surface, leaving only uneven bedrock, but the other effect was much more pleasing. Millions of yellow star-petalled flowers had sprung up, as if the world's largest fruit cart had been upset and spilled all its lemons, or a vast army of chicks was marching through the greenery. It gave the woods a fresh look. There were pink pimpernels, orange pansies, red forget-me-nots. Lilac morning glory and tiny blue blooms like those on cow-parsley. It was a botanical delight.

We came out of the forest and into an area of plains between two mountain ridges. There were more yellow flowers, a group of ostriches and a Kori bustard, Africa's largest flight-capable bird. It could have been on its migration between southern Sudan and Tanzania on this course.

We arrived in Baragoi, where I wondered what the heavily advertised 'Good Morning Lung Troyc' was, while Justin and Mwangi disappeared to procure supplies for our homeward leg. The local children again crowded around the car and asked us for pens. I wondered if they were told stories about a *mzungu* pen-fairy, who came in Bic-abundance to rain writing implements on the well-behaved. One of the kids had a large catapult with which I assumed that he might hold us up for biros: a veritable Dick Tur-pen!

Having resumed our trip we stopped for lunch in Marsi, where we were supposed to pick up a trailer. I got talking to a Turkana guy called Lawrence, he told me that there was still a lot of inter-tribal conflict in the area. He said that not long ago a group of Samburu and Pokot had come to his village and killed 47 people. I was amazed that this was still going on and asked how frequently this happened. He replied that they had come in March, which was only a month before.

I fell asleep again and woke up to have a look at the Sukta valley, which was a series of interesting volcanic ridges. We were in the hills of the Ukeresha forest, where the lichen gave the tree bark an eerie silver/green tint that made it look metallic in a terrain low on human impact.

When we got into Maralal, there were many men dressed in the traditional Samburu warrior costume, which is similar to that of the Maasai: bright wrap around the waist, feathered headdress, a profusion of bead necklaces, red ochre face paint and short stabbing sword strapped into the belt. The Samburu have enormous earlobes with a huge gap cut into them to hang earrings from. One old chap had folded this hanging loop over the top of his ear, making it look rather strange, like a very bad case of the cauliflower ear that prop forwards are afflicted with.

The children again pestered us for our pens and some guys tried to sell us some carved wooden dolls made by the Turkana. They looked very confused as I took the dolls from the salesmen on one side of the car and tried to sell them to the hecklers on the other! I did buy a roughly carved ebony lady, with a big pregnant or beer belly and a lucky cowrie shell on the front of her skirt. I was told that this would ensure that I had plenty of babies - not a thing I was particularly looking for as a single young chap. I also discovered fairly quickly that the doll was covered in shoe polish to give it the ebony look. The Samburu hawkers won that one!

We arrived at our campsite and, having set up the tents, had a look around the souvenir pieces at a Samburu man's hut, which was within the grounds. Petri told us that he was a blacksmith, that his father was too, and that his grandfather had also been one. He came, if you like, from a long line of blacksmiths. Petri had a collection of well made weapons to sell and we had a go at shooting barbed fishing arrows at a tree trunk, from which I calculated that if I had to sustain myself in this way, I would go very hungry.

Petri showed us how his clay and goatskin bellows worked before placing a heated spearhead on his anvil and hammering the daylights out of it. He also had a Samburu musical instrument called a *nchamuka*, like an old fashioned madrigal (I was reliably informed by Rob, the music teacher), that was played a bit like a harp. He played this and sang for us as we ate dinner, which added to the atmosphere.

On the last morning of our trip, we saw zebra, bushbuck, Thomson's gazelle, great crested crane and grey heron by the roadside and stopped at Thomson's Falls, a 74 metre waterfall, interestingly named after the same Scottish geologist as the gazelle. This site juxtaposed the natural beauty of the falling water, roiling pool and miniature rainbow with the gimmicky claptrap on sale to tourists. Here, with only a couple of hours of our trip remaining and therefore perhaps not much left to write about, I finally gave in and donated my pen to a pestering child.

AMBOSELI AND
THE COAST

On the tenth day after my mosquito bite in Samburu park, and the day before friends were supposed to arrive from the UK, I lay in bed, one minute shivering with fever, the next minute sweating profusely, with one of the worst headaches I can ever remember having and with all my joints aching painfully. Having never had malaria before, and thus knowing only that it was supposed to make you feel really awful, I checked in the guidebook 'Bible' to see what it had to say on the matter. It read, 'symptoms include headaches, fever, chills and sweating which might subside and recur.' Well, that sounded like a good match.

I rang some of my colleagues at the school, who I knew had suffered malaria and was offered a lift to the hospital the next morning. I did start to feel a little better as the day went on, but I was glad to know that I'd get some medication fairly soon. When my colleague arrived the next day, I said how I was anxious that my illness would not interfere with the travel plans I had made for the next couple of weeks. Her sage, and typically colonial Kenyan, advice was to visit her local doctor in the village, get the medication from him to cure malaria, and if I still felt rough, then I knew it wasn't malaria. If it was malaria, then the medicine would be curing me. This felt sensible enough.

I have to admit that I wasn't sure of what to expect from the professional who was known only as the *daktari*. I had wild notions of a fellow with a bone through his nose shaking the ashes of his ancestors over me to cure all my ails. It wasn't quite this extreme, but it also wasn't quite the first world medical treatment I was used to. The *daktari* gave me no examination, asked me for my self-diagnosis and sold me three batches of Chinese herbal medicine, which all had more Zs in their names than seemed grammatically possible. He then showed me the fourth patient's room, which was full to the ceiling with crates of beer from which he made his more lucrative business, and asked if I'd like to purchase some while I was there.

It's always a good idea to have some beer handy, so I bought a couple of *Tusker baridi*, thanked him and got going to Nairobi. I picked up the hire car and drove it to the airport, where I got talking to Koinet, which he explained meant 'tall one' in Maasai. This was a pretty good description for Koinet, as he towered over me at perhaps 6 feet 4 inches tall. It turned out that he was from the town of Namanga, where we were heading that afternoon, so I followed up with an all-important line of inquiry.

"So, Koinet, are you a rugby fan?" I asked.

"Yes, I like lugby," he replied. Kenyans often confused rs and ls.

"Oh good," I continued. "Because I'm going to Namanga this afternoon and I want to watch the Wales/Italy rugby match. Do you know where I can watch it, please?"

Koinet thought about this carefully. He was clearly keen not to let me down by not knowing the answer and was therefore going to make one up.

"Yes, a friend of mine, Sironka, will almost certainly be watching the match. I will give you his address."

"Okay, thank you," I said, playing the game by the rules.

Tom and Carrie arrived and we set off immediately for Namanga, where we were planning to spend the night before heading on to Amboseli park the next morning. I always loved watching people's reactions to being in Africa for the first time. My first impressions had been the enormous African sky, going for coffee on the way out of the airport and being surrounded by Kaleshnikov-wielding security and seeing the hordes of people on the roadside, apparently not engaged in much. Although the stretch of road between Nairobi and Namanga wasn't particularly interesting, it was just grassland dotted with acacias, it was most certainly African. Other people's excitement about being there was like reliving the experience again for myself, and I always felt more appreciative of being where I was, as it got easy to take it for granted sometimes.

We got to Namanga, which isn't the most exciting of towns, but is the last dot of civilisation before the park. Here we found a hotel with a lawn on which to camp and got the canvas up. By this time we were hungry, so we ate before investigating our lead for the rugby match. We followed the directions we had been given to a small wooden hut with a TV in it. I asked for Sironka, but he was out. His friends were watching a football match and didn't want to turn over to watch any rugby and that was that.

We made an early start the next day and were on the road by 5:30, despite difficulties finding a petrol station that would open for us at that time. The first part of the trip was conducted in the dark, as we were intending to spend the early morning game-driving in the park before finding a suitable place to pitch our next camp on. Once it got light we saw some interesting beasties from the road including Maasai giraffe, dikdik, impala and gerenuk, the gazelle with a longer than normal neck that can gain additional elevation to access higher leaves by the unusual ability to raise itself up onto its two hind legs.

In that early morning light, we were treated to one of the classic sights of Africa. Above the morning mists, rising like a waking giant, towered Mount Kilimanjaro, the highest mountain in Africa and the highest 'stand alone' mountain in the world at 5895 metres above sea level.

The road to Amboseli's main gate also forms the park boundary and as we drove along we saw a group of spotted hyenas out hunting or scavenging in the cool of the morning. I always remembered the Swahili name, *Fisi,* because someone told me that they were "a bit sh*t" to other animals. Hyenas are given a bad reputation like this but are actually an integral part of the ecosystem, as are all scavengers, as by ridding the savannah of rotting carcasses they help control disease. This said, apparently only around 5% of their food comes from scavenging, as they are adept hunters, working in packs of up to 80 to hunt and kill their own prey. The laughter sound they are famous for is a form of communication to the rest of the pack that food has been found. When lying in bed at home, I could often hear the more common hyena call as I went to sleep, a rising "oo-wup!"

We entered the park and immediately found the weakness in its administration: there were no signposts to help you find your way around. Well, there had been once, but in their infinite wisdom, the park officials had removed them all to boost map sales. All that remained were the stone obelisks upon which the signposts used to sit, with the screw holes for hanging the wooden information plaques staring back at you like the eye sockets in a skull. We had to make do instead with the imperfect map from the guidebook and used Kilimanjaro as a point of reference.

We plunged further into the park, in the rough direction of where we thought the campsite was. The vegetation in Amboseli was mainly grass, with a smaller area of acacia woods towards the Kilimanjaro side. However, this being April and the rainy season, there were tracts of reedy marsh and the infamous 'black cotton' mud from which the reeds thrive and vehicles never return.

We saw the odd wildebeest, or as they are alternatively known, bearded gnu (I love the word gnu!) looking a bit lost without his thousands of mates, who were probably grazing happily across the border in Tanzania. The gnu herds follow the north/south movement of the rains as they pass the equator twice a year in what is known as the inter-tropical convergence zone. The famous pictures of the mass migration of gnu are between the twin parks of Maasai Mara in Kenya and Serengeti in Tanzania. There are smaller populations in many parks throughout east Africa, and this chap was one of those in the smaller population. In fact, he constituted a population of one, from what we could see.

However, the main attractions of Amboseli park are the elephants, and perhaps more so the image of the elephant with the background of Kilimanjaro behind it: two African giants of the popular imagination. There were loads of elephants and we saw them at almost every step of our journey. Of course, they are difficult animals to hide in open grassland, but it was great to see such large herds.

We had just passed a hippo, wallowing about in a pool of mud, when we saw a lone male elephant heading towards the road we were on. We backed up so that he would pass in front of us, as I wanted Tom and Carrie to get a really good view of him. He kept bashfully trying to circle behind us, so I kept edging a little further back in the car. In the end he saw that the only way to get to the other side of the road would be to cross in front of us and so he crossed the track fifty yards in front of us. It was peculiar to see these behemoths so dwarfed by the mountain behind them. The elephants were to Kili what an ant might be to an ellie. It was an odd perspective.

We carried on past a large herd of buffalo, who were looking quite content to lie around chewing the cud and watched a pair of giraffe pulling leaves from an acacia. Giraffes are able to loop their tongue over acacia branches and twigs to pull the leaves and this was a skill that had always impressed me, as the thorns on these branches were little short of deadly, as my ear injury in Turkana was testament. Giraffes have evolved especially tough skin along their 20 inch tongue and the inside of their mouth, which enables them to withstand the onslaught of the spines. On another trip to a giraffe sanctuary I was able to experience the toughness of the giraffe's tongue when I fed them from my hand. It felt like being licked by a dampened sandpaper.

We stopped for a quick stretch of the legs (a bit naughty that, according to the strict interpretation of the park rules, but it always seemed a bit daft in light of the fact that you can camp in the park and must get out of your vehicle to get into your tent) overlooking a large herd of elephants, all watering in a marshy pool. We counted roughly eighty pachyderms refreshing themselves in that swamp, which made it the largest group we had seen so far, although it was more probably several groups who had all converged on the same watering hole. Elephants have a wide range of vocal sounds, many of which they produce at a decibel level that is subsonic, too low for humans to hear. The low frequency makes this communication travel for many miles and they often coordinate between herds to meet up at popular spots as humans communicate to meet friends at the pub.

We decided to go and set up our camp, which we found without too much trouble and began pitching our tents. A Maasai man approached us and asked if we would require a guard for the night, to which we replied politely in the negative. He continued to tell us the gruesome fates that awaited us if we didn't have a guard for the night: elephants might trample us, lions might gobble us, hyenas might nibble us but, having heard these sorts of fable before, and noticing that we were near enough to a settlement to be fairly safe from all this, we again politely declined. The guy refused to leave the camp and watched as we finished setting our tents up. He simply wouldn't take no for an answer and, even though we told him very clearly we wouldn't be paying him for any services, he stayed in the camp silently. It felt like we hadn't seen the last of him.

We met up with Angus and Rob, who were also staying in Amboseli, and we enjoyed a tasty lunch at their lodge, followed by a wash up and a cooling swim in the pool. It was a very relaxing afternoon after which we prepared for another game drive.

We proceeded towards a wooded area in the hopes of catching a glimpse of a leopard, who prefer the cover of trees or rocks as opposed to more grassy areas. We crawled along the road, inspecting every tree closely, but leopards are extremely well camouflaged and if there were any in those trees, we never found them. We had seen some interesting birds of prey though and undeterred we turned towards the marshy area, where we found more elephants, buffalo and gazelles of different species.

At 6 o'clock I suggested that we return to the campsite as the park rules state that you are not allowed to drive at night. With an hour of daylight left, this gave us a comfortable amount of time to get back, barring difficulty. We headed in the direction of the camp, relying to the greater extent on sense of direction as neither the shoddy map or the lack of signposts were any help, and came across a roadblock in the form of a flooded section of the track. There appeared to be a track that might lead around the obstacle and so we followed this, but after a short distance it simply disappeared into the grass. We repeated this several times.

As the last vestiges of daylight slipped into inky darkness, we found a road that appeared to lead back in the direction of camp. We followed this until we came to a crossroads at which we took the right turn that we felt most confident led us back to camp. I was just telling Tom and Carrie that it would be a good idea to put some insect repellent on now that it was dark when we came across a huge, lone, bull elephant who stood in the road blocking our way. Or maybe that should have been a huge, lone, *curious,* bull elephant because as I seized an opportunity to take my own advice and administer the 'Doom' (another great name, this time for the brand of insect repellent I used in Africa), the bull turned towards us and started heading right to us.

This is not uncommon, but as he got closer, Carrie asked if we could put a bit more distance between us and I started to reverse up the road we had come down. This only seemed to make the ellie more curious and he picked up his pace in order to continue his investigation. It wasn't until we had reversed over a quarter of a mile that the bull got either tired or bored and returned to his foraging. We retraced our route to the crossroads and took the other direction that we thought could lead us back.

By now it was starting to get a bit late and I began to wonder how vigorously they would enforce the rule about nighttime driving if they found us. After all, it shouldn't be too difficult to spot a vehicle wandering about in the near total darkness with their headlights on. Consequently, I was driving a bit quicker than normal in order to get back before we were spotted (though still only 40kph). The roads in the park were crisscrossed by drainage ditches and where they run beneath the road, there were small humps in the road to bridge the pipes.

We bounced over one of these only to nearly crash into two of the biggest lions I have ever seen, who were out hunting in the moonlight. They were muscled and maned males, who often form small groups when they reach sexual maturity and are ousted from their pride. They were following the road in the same direction we were and so we tagged along at a safe distance, enjoying this chance encounter. Eventually they loped off into the dark and we continued towards camp.

By this time we had seen enough familiar landmarks to be confident that we were heading in the correct direction, when we encountered two adult elephants and a baby who were grazing just next to the road. They didn't seem ready to move and I wondered what their reaction might be to having a vehicle almost brush against their trunks as we passed. We really did have to be getting back though, and so we hugged the furthest side of the road and crept past, eager not to arouse fear for the young elephant.

As we got back to the campsite, we saw a civet dash in front of us in the headlights. These are extremely difficult animals to see as they combine beautiful camouflaged patches with being nocturnal. Perhaps we had been quite lucky to be caught out in the dark in terms of what we had seen, even if we had experienced a couple of hair-raising adventures as a result. We bought a couple of Tuskers from a little shop on the campsite and sat by the light of a fire, chatting about the wildlife of the African plains before retiring for the night.

Next morning as we packed up the camp, the Maasai bloke returned to ask for his money. He claimed that he had kept guard of the camp all night, though we hadn't seen any sign of him. He also claimed that an elephant had come into our camp and he had chased it off. We had heard none of the telltale gastric rumblings that I had heard on my first African camp when I incorrectly thought that lions were prowling for a bite to eat. (It turned out that, even more incredibly, a herd of elephants had come tiptoeing between our guylines to eat the potato peelings we had carelessly scattered around our campfire. We began collecting peelings and throwing them a good distance from the tents from the next meal onwards). There were no enormous footprints, the size of serving trays in the moist earth or the longer grass anywhere near our camp. He was trying it on.

One of the things I never felt comfortable with in Africa were the conmen of great and small designs that one encountered, mostly it seemed in southern Kenya and Northern Tanzania, where the tourist droves were thickest. Early in my time there, I gratefully accepted help from people who then asked for what seemed like a large amount of money. I still don't know if I was being mean on the occasions where I refused to pay for made up services. I was earning very little by European standards as a teacher in Africa and so I didn't have much to lavish on probably very deserving charity candidates, as many tourists who come in from other countries do. At the same time it seemed a bit cheeky to ask for the equivalent of a month's local wage for holding a spanner while I changed a tire (someone once did this and asked me for money), when there were certainly more genuine ways to gain employment.

This is set against the fact that when I arrived in Kenya, my first impression was of thousands of people who apparently had little to do. Unemployment was extremely high - figures that did get floated were almost certainly made up, but the idle people lining the sides of the main highway told their own silent tale. I recall looking at these people and being aware that the people of places like Africa were poor SO THAT people in more developed countries could be rich - it doesn't work any other way in a capitalist system. This made me feel guilty.

At the same time, I didn't have the budget to reduce African national debt on my own. Even if I could have given a percentage of my wage to demonstrably deserving causes, that didn't mean that anyone else would and didn't seem fair either. I worked with a colleague to try to bring football uniforms over from the UK to be used by the local teams, which brought me a meeting with the richest dressed person in town, the local priest. I wondered how he was so well dressed, bejewelled and travelling the globe, when his flock lived in the streets. This made me feel cross.

In the end, I tried to spend the money I did have on people who had a genuine cause and who were working their way towards improving their lives. It didn't do much, but I could at least feel that I was helping people who were genuinely working their way towards a better future. I tried to buy trinkets from hawkers, buy from roadside vendors and either bought drinks or snacks, or paid a reasonable tip, for people who offered genuine help. This Maasai chap wasn't one of those deserving causes. We were quite firm with him so that eventually he got the message and disappeared into the bush he hadn't spent the night in.

We had offered Angus a lift back to Nairobi and, after picking him up from his lodge, we set off on an early morning game drive. Again we saw lots of elephants, buffalo and gazelle, but were disappointed to see no big cats. We drove up to a low hill that never-the-less gave a grand vista of the savannah, marshes and woodland around us. From there we could see the head of a lonely bull elephant in a pool below us. He had obviously reserved his spot for cooling down in the midday heat, and he was enjoying a good bath.

We passed another lake with pink flamingos dotted on it. Flamingoes are migratory in East Africa and tend to descend upon a given lake for long periods of time during which the waters are ringed in a candyfloss pink band. They must have been at a different lake at the time, because there were only a few birds sifting the shallows for algae, crustaceans and aquatic plants, their strangely curved beaks ideally evolved for a life with their head upside down.

Shortly after that, we got stuck in the dreaded black cotton and we emptied the vehicle to swerve and skid our way free without the added weight of passengers. Fortunately, we were not needed to push, as the mud spraying from the back axle would have covered us completely, but we nevertheless kept a watchful eye out for any lurking beasties in the vicinity.

We passed through the gates and headed for Namanga and on

to Nairobi. We stopped for a drink in a village full of Maasai in full traditional dress: red wrap-around blankets, colourful beads, spear, stabbing sword and shaved heads. We went up to the kiosk, ordered four colas and were handed glass bottles with the metal caps loosened for us. Carrie asked me where the bin was, to throw away the cap.

"There isn't one," I answered, having become accustomed to these tricky local customs. "Just throw it on the floor like everyone else.

"You can't do that!" she exclaimed. "There must be a bin somewhere."

"Ask the bloke in the kiosk," I suggested. So she did.

"No," he replied. "Just throw it on the floor."

Carrie gave me a somewhat dumbfounded look. It seems strange now that I accepted littering so easily, but there wasn't an alternative. Not only were there no recycling facilities, but there was no rubbish collection either. Instead, I often found people who had made draughts sets using a chequered board drawn onto an old bit of cardboard, and sets of soft drink caps in the green of one label against the red of another.

Upon arriving in Nairobi, we dropped Angus off at his top end hotel and went to look for a campsite for ourselves. We found just the spot: cheap rates, enough grass to pitch on, a marijuana-smoke filled bar and some seating outside the timber cafe to relax on. We got the tents set up and enjoyed some Tuskers, playing cards until Carrie got fed up with my cheating!

Next morning we set out bright and early for a game drive in Nairobi Park. This park sits right next door to the bustling modern capital city, and from the park you can look past the animals at a backdrop of glistening towers and industrial factories that is positively 21st century. It was only my third time in this park, but I had seen lions each of the previous times

I'd been there and was hoping that we might get a daytime viewing for my guests.

It was a funny thing, taking visitors to game parks. I always used to feel quite pressured to find some interesting beasties for whoever I was showing around. This normally meant lions, but also whatever the particular park's speciality beasty was: be it elephants in Amboseli, or rhinos in Nakuru, the nearest game park to where I lived. I always found Nigel's attitude towards the game drives most rewarding as he was just as intrigued by the ornithology as he was by the mammalia, and would be fascinated by flitting finch or dabbling duck. It was reassuring to know that he was enjoying himself.

On this trip we saw lots of gazelle and giraffe, and some hartebeest, hyrax and black-backed jackals, which were new animals for Tom and Carrie, but unfortunately we didn't see any more big cats. We had breakfast at Leopard Cliff lookout, where we had to defend our food from marauding baboons, who were just as intent on filling themselves as we were. They had been making a mess upsetting the bins to forage for food scraps too. So even when there were refuse facilities, the local fauna was scattering it anyway.

We dropped the car back at the hire company after leaving our baggage at the train depot and whiled away the afternoon searching for bargains among the *dukas* in the Westlands suburb. That evening we boarded the overnight train to Mombasa and heaved our luggage into the four-bunk second class dorm. The train departed Nairobi at about 6 o'clock in the evening and was scheduled to arrive in Mombasa at around 7 o'clock the next morning… when everything goes to plan.

The train was something of a relic from the colonial era and probably hadn't been maintained much since that time either. The train line was supposed to open up the interior of Kenya and Uganda to trade with Britain and the Empire, in addition helping to bring about the end of slavery as steam power replaced that of porters. But it was derided in parliament especially by Henry Labouchere, who wrote the now famous poem The Lunatic Line, which is now more commonly known as the Lunatic Express, highlighting its great cost and, at the time, unclear purpose.

The construction was beset by many obstacles among which was a pair of maneless, man eating lions who became the stuff of myth. In his book, 'The Man Eaters of Tsavo', Colonel Patterson describes the quest to rid the East Africa Company of these pests who dragged construction workers from their beds aboard the carriages in the night. His book gives a real insight into the attitude of Britons during the colonial period, and modern prints, I have found, come with a disclaimer about the views of the author. Two parts that struck me were Patterosn's ability to admire the beauty and majesty of the animals, before going on to kill them with what he repeatedly, and self-deprecatingly, describes as 'lucky shots.' The other, and perhaps more alarming, is that he reported the human loss as ""two people, 24 coolies and an uncounted number of natives." That the natives weren't counted at all has always felt rather chilling to me, and the fact that he counted the coolie workers was probably only due to the expense of having to replace them with new workers from India, at a time when recruitment there was held up by a plague.

At the time I was travelling the compartments came with signs advising you to lock the windows to prevent thieves breaking into your dorm, which struck me as a difficult task given my belief that the train would be moving. The 'silver service' dining carriage could have done with new silverware and some more enthusiastic staff if it were to relive its golden days. Everything was done on a reduced budget, though it was still a good experience, as the train grinds its way noisily and painstakingly slowly along the line, hopping like a rabbit from time to time. This last part meant that your dining experience included wearing more of your meal than you were able to eat, and breakfast would have been a particularly nasty trauma had the coffee they served been warmer than tepid.

As with all commercial establishments of the time in Kenya, the dining carriage had a framed picture of good old President Moi hanging on the wall. We were amused to hear a thickly accented *mzungu* tourist ask the waiter if it was a picture of him. The waiter, without breaking a smile, firmly corrected the man's ignorance and proceeded to his next call of misery. The train was eventually closed down after my time in Africa, which is a shame for it was a window into the lost past.

Of course, the same problem that causes your shirt to gain a few extra colours at dinner causes attempting to sleep to be a mostly futile effort. All through the night the train stopped and started, some of which was planned, and chugs ponderously to the coast, the humidity level rising as the altitude drops.

When we woke up in the morning, we were already sweating, even though the sun had barely risen, and the landscape outside was lush green, with palms replacing acacias and grass replacing dust. The train crawled its way through some of the poorer areas of Mombasa, which to tell the truth, is not a pretty port town, even as port towns go. The corrugated iron shanties billowed forth half dressed, waving kids, as the train puffed oily smoke, and one marvelled at their happy faces in spite of the crushing poverty that surrounded them.

The station at Mombasa has a very British looking platform, which shouldn't be too surprising as it was built during the colonial period, and we made our way towards the taxi rank outside. There a mass of taxi drivers assault you with bellowed prices that only tourists would consider, causing you to haggle for your life while being physically jostled by the throng. We decided to avoid the initial crush by throwing an American football for 10 minutes on the platform. I was about to suggest to Tom that we should be careful with the overhead striplight, but decided not to, as it was very high - surely we couldn't actually hit it? With the very next throw, Tom hit it and the shattered remains crashing to the platform silenced the station.

We were soon joined by a gentleman claiming to be a plain clothed police officer, who wanted to arrest us. Would we prefer to pay a small sum (the Swahili term for bribe is *chai*, for tea) to keep it quiet? We chased him off and went to the station master's office to confess our ineptitude and pay him for the light. It set us back about a hundred shillings but much further in Carrie's estimation, and she continued to wear the "I told you so" look of a teacher for the rest of the afternoon. This also shouldn't be surprising, as Carrie is, in fact, a teacher.

We set off for lunch at my favourite burger restaurant in Mombasa. They served delicious meaty fayre, but I began to notice that the food had a regrettable effect on my digestive system and soon after this trip I had to forgo tasty burgers for bowel health. After eating, we visited Fort Jesus, originally built between 1593-96 by Joao Batista Cairato, an Italian architect who worked for the Portuguese. The fort has a colourful history, changing hands between the Portuguese, Omani Arabs and British nine times: twice by trickery, twice by starvation, twice by assault, (both times when the defenders were insufficient to properly man the walls) twice by negotiation, and once by a bombardment of rockets and shells.

The building combines the Renaissance idea of the perfection of the human form with the military technology of the time. Standing on a spur of coral rock overlooking the entrance to the town, Fort Jesus has 5 limbs reaching from its centre, like the arms of a starfish, each of which could provide covering fire to another in times of attack. The walls were made higher by the Arabs after they successfully stormed it by placing ladders against the battlements to climb in. This, one feels, gave them an insight into the strategic weaknesses of the fort.

The building bears testimony to the first successful attempt by a western power to control the Indian Ocean trade routes. It was taken over by the Imperial East Africa Company and for most of the time East Africa was under British control, it was used as a gaol. These days it has an interesting museum, keeping displays on archaeological finds, treasures that have been donated by various persons whose families are connected with the fort and its history, and the culture of the local tribespeople.

While wandering the gardens, we found a stack of cannonballs, once used to defend the military installation, but also, we realised, effective as sports equipment. I accordingly challenged Tom to a shot put competition. I tucked mine under my chin, sank down onto my right leg before spinning and heaving the weight of the cannonball into the air, whereafter it landed with that satisfying dull thump into the manicured grass. Tom followed suit and his attempt landed 25cm further than mine.

I immediately filed a stewards enquiry into both the technique used (in my opinion, Tom hadn't had the shot at his chin at the launch point, making it a foul throw) and in his selection of what seemed to be a smaller lighter cannonball (which I confess I wished I'd thought of). The independent adjudicator, Tom's wife, ruled in his favour and Tom had won. Naturally for Tom, there was much joy, but for me, much woe. We quickly put the cannonballs back onto their respective piles before we were discovered. I quietly fostered a burning ambition to get even.

We went for a drink in the Mombasa Club, which is next door. As a member of the reciprocating Gilgil Club, I was supposed to be allowed entry, but the major domo on the door wasn't for it, as the club had quite a strict dress code that our shorts and T-shirts didn't pass. However, we successfully argued that, since no-one else was there, maybe we could have a quick refreshment and scarper before anyone else showed up. Tom and I briefly discussed the merits of using the men-only bar, but Carrie's icy stare convinced us that this wasn't sound policy.

We were fairly well oiled by the time we boarded the *matatu* for Malindi. I aped the bus driver by shouting out of the window to advertise our destination as the locals do, much to the amusement of four Asian girls sitting in front of us. Carrie rolled her eyes in disbelief. Eventually, this effort in the hot sun with a belly full of beer wore me out and I fell asleep with my head resting on the shoulder of an enormous lady I collapsed next to.

Malindi was one of the places that Vasco De Gama stopped at on his pioneering voyage around the Cape to India. It has a pretty chapel, in which some of the first Portuguese inhabitants are buried and it has beautiful beaches on which to soak up the sun. It is supposed to have a lively nightlife too, but if this is true, we could find no sign of it while we were there. After a night in Malindi, we turned south again and stayed in Watamu, another touristy village on the shores of the Indian Ocean. While we were there we attended a fund raising party for James Ashe, who runs a snake sanctuary, where he researches antidotes for snake venoms.

I had taken my class there on an educational trip and at the start of the visit he asked the children to raise their hands if they thought that snakes were bad animals. All the kids put their hands up. He then explained that snakes play a vital role in keeping the population of disease carrying vermin in check, and are vital middle order predators that help keep the entire ecosystem functioning. Most snakes try to avoid contact with humans at all costs and as such pose little or no threat to human life. His arguments won the day and by the end of the visit, all the children (and their teacher) were won round to how great snakes are.

We visited the Arobuko/Sekoke forest, home to the endangered golden rumped elephant shrew. The largest of its species, the golden rumped elephant shrew grows to around 20cm in length, has a long prehensile nose, with which it searches for invertebrates in the forest mulch and uses its dazzling orange flanks to tempt predators to bite it on the posterior where its skin is three times thicker and gives the beasty its best chance of surviving the attack. Once again, I regretted not bringing a sleeping bag with me, as there was a tree platform raised some 20m above the silvan floor which overlooked a watering hole frequented by the forest elephants. I always fancied staying overnight to see these incredibly invisible animals when they were in comparatively plain view in the clearing of the watering hole. On the other hand, there were some pretty huge ants crawling about on the platform, which might make an overnight stay less comfortable.

Afterwards, we visited the Gedi ruins, once known as Kilimani, Swahili for 'the town on the hill'. The town was renamed by the Galla people who overtook the town in the early 18th century and gave it the name Gedi, meaning 'precious.' Despite their apparent reverence for its value, the town declined and was abandoned shortly thereafter. Nowadays, the ruins look fantastic, with trees overgrowing the coral-rag walls. I have always had a fascination for this overgrown, jungle-clad ruin townscape. I had long been interested in the Maya civilisation of Central America and Angkor Wat in Cambodia, and poured over photos of ruins peeping out from beneath centuries of tree and plant growth. I enjoyed the simple, descriptive names they gave to the individual buildings in Gedi. The House of the Chinese Lamp, so-called because they found a Chinese lamp in it; the House of the Scissors because... well, you get the picture.

After Watamu, we went back through Mombasa, taking the rickety Likoni ferry to Tiwi, one of my favourite spots on the coast. This was cheap, laid-back Africa. You could camp on the beach beneath the palms for a quid a night, eat and drink at the bar and relax all day in the sun on the narrow beach. It was also one of the best places to buy *kikois*. *Kikois* are wrap around cloths which men wear around the waist at the coast. I had a good collection of them while I lived in Kenya, and all the friends who visited me there, ridiculed me for wearing them, before going home in possession of one. They seemed to have a hundred uses, being used as scarves up Mt. Kenya, as a wind shield on the beach, as bed wear or a sheet in hotter climes, and as a baby carrying vessel by the local women. They were very handy things and I never travelled without at least one.

Having returned to Gilgil, Tom and I again pitted our sporting talents in a round of golf on the 'browns' of the local golf course, where the low rainfall meant that you putted across a fine gravel surface instead of the manicured grass of a green. We imposed drinking penalties of a can of beer per lost hole to make things more interesting. For some reason, my usually pathetic golf form abandoned me and I stormed around the nine hole course, winning seven holes and losing only one, with one draw. This meant we were now 1 - 1 in our sporting endeavours which necessitated a tiebreaker challenge. We settled on chess, as it was getting dark, and this time the drinking penalties were shots of Kenya Cane, the local *aguardiente*, for the value of each lost piece. This had the effect of snowballing a poor opening. Fortunately, I got on the right side of this phenomenon and was able to take the series score to 2 - 1 in my favour. It got messy before we all went to bed.

Tom and Carrie returned to the UK shortly thereafter and I had really enjoyed sharing my experience of Africa with close friends.

TANZANIA

At the end of my two years in Kenya, I planned to go on my longest trip yet, through Tanzania and Malawi and back again to Kenya to get my flight home. Originally, I had wanted to get all the way to South Africa and fly home from Cape Town, but I had done more dreaming about this than saving for it, and so I had to put this plan off for another time (hopefully).

I was extremely fortunate that, in making friends with several of the parents of kids I taught at school, I had offers of places to stay along the way. I am greatly indebted to all of them for their fantastic hospitality, perhaps most particularly to Maggie, who had me thrust upon her by a generous sister.

I had looked into climbing Mt. Kilimanjaro, but decided against it, instead planning to go and stay with Shamba and Connie at its base in Moshi. From there I was headed to Zanzibar, then on to the Catt's, another family I hadn't really met, but whose son I had taught in my class that year. Then I was planning to go to Malawi to stay at Livingstonia, a missionary town above the lake, Nkhata Bay, Nkhotakota, on the shore of the lake and on to Lilongwe, the capital, before returning to Kenya.

I had hoped to go with Dan, a good friend with whom I taught at the school, to the Aberdare range, as we had done many times before. I loved the Aberdares: beautiful, lush forest perched atop a mountain range, which was once (thousands of years ago) higher than Mounts Kenya and KIlimanjaro. The waterfalls on the top, most particularly Karuru falls, are some of the most breath-taking sights in Kenya, almost unseen by tourists as they race between Nairobi, the Maasai

Mara and the coast.

Unfortunately, when I returned from this trip, I found a note from Dan saying that he couldn't make it up the Aberdares, as he was buying a boat in Mtwapa. I didn't mind, as he was always talking about the boat he wanted to retire to and I hoped he would soon be building the vessel in readiness for the day.

It was a strangely emotional trip. It was an enormous undertaking, which I was really looking forward to, but at the same time it signified the end of something almost too good to be true. After this trip I would return to Britain to face British weather, unsettled student debts, high pressure work in less pleasant schools and a whole host of things that I had become fond of not being used to. I would also be moving in with Ceri, with whom I had enjoyed a relationship in which we were mostly in different continents from the moment we met, and this was a big step.

By the same token, I was going to be returning to my friends and family, whom I had missed dearly for two years and I was looking forward to that. Even so, during this trip I experienced a somewhat empty feeling of the sort you sometimes get when you have finished an intriguing story and wish it hadn't ended, only more so because I had been living this story.

BADOOF! went the timeworn, wooden handled, rubber stamp. "Three months!" announced the roly-poly immigration officer as he turned his attention to the next in line. I was now a legal alien in Tanzania. I had travelled from Nairobi with Shamba and Connie, with whom I was going to stay a few nights in Moshi, in the north of the country beneath Mount Kilimanjaro. I had got to know my hosts when I took the children water skiing on Lake Naivasha. Shamba owned a small motor boat which he would bring up to the lake and he would take the kids out in turns to water ski, avoiding hippos and laser sailors in the warm sunshine, while Connie presided over picnics on the bank.

I had planned to attempt a climb on the highest peak in Africa, given as a gift by Queen Victoria to one of her German nephews causing the boundary to bow around the base of the massif, but having looked into the costs, even with the mates rate offered to me by one of the parents, it had become apparent that I could choose between the mountain or touring Africa, as my budget certainly didn't include the former in the latter.

There are many theories for the origin of the name Kilimanjaro. One says that it comes from the local word 'Kilimani' for road (though eagle-eyed readers will recognise that at Gedi, it meant "Town on the hill") and in full means 'mountain of the difficult roads' implying that it is damn hard to reach the top. However, in Swahili *kilima* means 'mountain' and *njaro* means 'hunger', perhaps suggesting that frequent and hearty meals are needed to accomplish its ascent. Another story claims that it was once called Kilijaro until the first human reached the top, whereupon the moniker 'man' was sneakily slipped into the middle while no one was watching, but this version is probably too far fetched.

Having left the border town of Namanga, the first mountain you come across is Longido, a stand alone mountain of some 2629m above sea level that overlooks the bush for miles around. In fact, the scenery changes very little as one crosses into Tanzania from Kenya: acacia scrub with sun-yellowed grass beneath, pock-marked by occasional low hills and full of Maasai overgrazing the land with their enormous, dust-spewing herds.

The Maasai traditional dress is very striking, composed of a predominantly red tartan blanket around the waist and another around the shoulders, with coloured beads suspended from every possible dangle. They have necklaces, belts, tiaras, bracelets, anklets, bandoleers, all with intricate and, in some instances, symbolic designs. The Maasai are unpopular with the surrounding tribes, perhaps particularly the Kikuyu who comprise the largest tribal group in Kenya. This is partly the antagonism between nomadic herders and sedentary farmers, but has evolved through warfare and distrust into quite a mutual loathing.

We came across a group of young *morani* (Maasai for 'warrior'), who were dressed in black robes and had their faces painted white. They were in attendance of a circumcision ceremony, which the Maasai take very seriously. If the young warrior's body flinches while the surgery is performed the warrior is branded a coward and the only way he can redeem himself is to kill a lion while armed only with his spear. This is particularly difficult these days as lions are not only protected by teeth and claws, but the law as well. It also occurred to me that the greater act of cowardice might be remaining still during the ceremony, as this would avoid having to pick a fight with a lion.

Another quirk of the Maasai is the closeness of their brotherhood bonding whilst in the *morani* training lodges during their adolescence. Thereafter, the warriors are allowed to share the wives of fellow graduates in a move that sounds like something from the swinging sixties and seems to offer little hope to women's rights. It is a custom that perhaps helps explain why AIDS was rife, infecting 25% of the Tanzanian population.

The Maasai are a very conservative tribe and Tanzania has had a history of communism that would naturally grate against those traditional values. For instance, the egalitarian government made the decision that all its citizens should look the same, and forced everyone to wear shirts and shorts. The Maasai grudgingly accepted this policy, but wore their bright, red *shuka* blankets over their shoulders in an act of defiance.

As we sped along the potholed highway, a tawny eagle nearly became roadkill, waiting until the last second to get out of our way. Directly ahead of us, Mount Meru was obscured from view by a heat haze that was to be the bane of my mountain view seeking. Meru is Tanzania's second highest mountain, being no tiddler at 4556m above sea level. It is covered in lush forest and has a sheer cliff face of over 1500m on its eastern side, said to be the largest of its kind in the world.

Meru gradually appeared as it shed some woolly clouds to stand as the perfect example of a volcanic mountain: exactly conical with a crater on top. The road navigated around the base of Meru to get to Arusha, giving it the impression of a giant sleeping sentinel that you had to creep around without waking.

We passed a deserted village, another remnant of the failed communist policy in the Maasai heartland. The government had wanted to establish communes on which to centralise education, religion, health and bureaucracy, but the semi-nomadic Maasai weren't interested in being settled and continued their lifestyle of moving between seasonal *manyattas* and their grazing grounds that followed the seasonal rains, meaning that the villages stood empty.

We saw crooked trees, smartly planted in rows, which were too twisted to be of value as timber and bore no visible fruit. They were another testimony to the failed political regime. These trees had originally been planted by white settlers to shade their coffee bushes. When independence came along, the white settlers were thrown out and the land was given to the locals, who were supposed to use it to grow their maize and bananas for subsistence, while selling the coffee surplus to government buyers for cash. However, the Third World problem of corruption stepped in the way, as the government buyers decided the money intended for buying coffee surplus was better in their own pockets. When the farmers discovered there was no market for the coffee, they just let it die off and with it died a potentially valuable export commodity. All that was left were the contorted, silvan corpses lined up amongst the withered crops on an exhausted soil.

Tanzania seemed to have made a good effort to make a go of communism in some respects, and took a brave stance against what it perceived as neo-colonial imperialism (which we would probably now call capitalism). They refused to have anything to do with the apartheid state of South Africa, which had a strong regional influence, and supported the Cubans in the Congo. President Julius Nyerere, known as *"Mwalimu"* ('teacher'), seemed to have some good left-wing ideas, which came to grief through a potent mix of corruption and the oil crisis of the 1970s. African leaders had a habit of assuming these sorts of nicknames: Kenyan President Jomo Kenyatta was known as "Mzee", or 'respected elder', but my favourite had to be President Mboto Sese Soko of Zaire (which periodically changes its name to and from the Democratic Republic of Congo), who interrupted wasting his country's vast mineral wealth on Parisian shopping sprees to give himself such titles as "The Pacifier", "The Unifier" and "The Guide", but steered clear of more accurate epitaphs, such as "Embezzling Crook" or "Despotic Megalomaniac."

Rounding the mountain, the countryside looked much greener to the southern side, on account of its higher annual rainfall. The prevailing weather moves from the south and deposits its precipitation on the southern slopes, causing a rain shadow of dryness on the northern side. We passed through a town called Bomang'ombe, meaning 'cattle pen', possibly due to its foundation as a dipping facility to prevent the spread of foot and mouth between herds on the foothills to the north and those from the Maasai Steppe to the south. We then drove through the town of Kwasadella, from which the Tanzanian equivalent of the *matatu*, the *dalla dalla*, (a dangerously overcrowded minibus owned privately and acting as public transport) got its name.

I enjoyed the fact that Kilimanjaro, dominating the area so imposingly, was used as a navigation tool, and so, keeping Kili to our left, we arrived in Moshi. Shamba and Connie lived in a large house in a suburb known as Shanty Town. Despite the connotations implicit with such a name, Connie assured me that it was, "where all the really smart people live." They gave me a tourist guide to Moshi as an introductory read and I was amused to find a Golden Shower Restaurant. I wondered what sort of refreshment was served there.

The next day we went to have a look at the house that Shamba and Connie were doing up to move into. It was a project that was still very much underway when I saw it, but it promised to be a great house with balconies commanding spectacular views of the mountain.

We then went to look at a smallholder coffee factory, passing many African *shamba* plots on the way. These were really quite picturesque, as they grew alternate patches of maize bordered by sunflowers, and bananas shading coffee bushes. These patches were delineated and shaded by the larger mango trees, with their pendulum fruit, hanging pale against dark, waxy leaves.

We met the manager, Henry, a tall dark haired chap, sporting a black eye won through an altercation with his drunken neighbour, who also happened to be a sort of business partner of his. The neighbour also seemed to have been the former manager of the coffee factory, which was what had led to the difference of opinion. This altercation was shrugged off as horseplay and we began a tour of the coffee producing process which took place there.

In the factory, they used only Arabica beans, which are the better quality coffee, producing a more bitter, variable taste than their Robusta cousins. The coffee berries, which grew so thick on the bushes that they weighed the branches almost to the ground, were picked by hand when they had ripened to a bright red colour. These were then fed into a mechanical process that separates the red flesh from the twin beans within.

This done, there is still a slimy juice on the beans, which needs to come off. They are put in water to soak for a day, in which time the slime ferments before disappearing. The beans are then put into a wood burner dryer for another day before being placed on 40m long cloth tables for a week to dry out thoroughly in the sun. The coffee bean is now a pale beige colour, which needs the parchment layer rubbed off before the silver layer beneath is shined off to leave a dull grey coloured bean. Once this bean is roasted to taste it can be ground and served in boiling water for a tasty beverage.

Coffee is the world's second largest export commodity after oil and, as countries in the tropical zone have rushed to plant this valuable commodity, prices have been driven down through a glut of supply, which is not so pleasing for the original coffee producing nations. Unfortunately, attempts to create an OPEC-type organisation, similar to the oil producing nations, have stumbled at every attempt, meaning that these developing nations cannot fix prices for their further economic benefit.

We went out for dinner to a steakhouse called the Saltzburger, which was a restaurant-come-pub with an Austrian theme. It was also the base for the local Volkswagen enthusiasts club, and was something of a haven for a Beetle fan such as myself. The manager had used Beetle hubcaps for the backs of the barstools. He had also used a lot of advertising for Steigl lager, which I presumed was an Austrian brew. When I asked if there was any, I was told that there was not. However, far from leaving me disappointed, it gave me an inspiration: to take a Beetle loaded with Steigl lager from Austria to Moshi to re-supply the Saltzburger! It sounded like a plan with no obvious drawbacks at the time, but, of course, all plans seem bulletproof following an afternoon drinking strong beer, and this ambition has remained unrealised to date.

Next morning Kilimanjaro was obscured by the cloud blown in from the Indian Ocean; water carrying air gets forced upwards by the mountain so that it coalesces into rain cloud, rendering the mountain invisible. Occasionally, the cloud would part a fraction, offering you a tantalising glimpse of Africa's highest peak, Kibo, but invariably the view would be brief before it was again concealed behind its watery veil.

Shamba and I went to play golf at the Moshi club that morning, with perfect weather for losing balls, digging divots and generally frustrating oneself. Even for me I played a shocker that morning and was 17 over par... after only three holes. I tried to explain it away using such excuses as different clubs, playing on greens instead of the browns I was used to, the deafening roar of butterflies as I was on my backswing, but the real reason for my abject score was that I am awful at golf. I managed to find a late run of form to bring the scores to a more respectable 3½ holes to 5½, but I still retained the honour of buying the beers. I selected an Ndovu which means 'elephant', though despite the name, it had a crisp light taste.

The beleaguered group of Indians who had followed us round the course came in shortly afterwards and were throwing money around like it was going out of fashion. They noisily settled their gambling debts from the round they had just played, which I thought would be for social prestige gains, but Shamba leaned across towards me and whispered that it could all just be a money laundering show for some dodgy money they had come into.

We went for a picnic lunch at Shamba's new house and a walk down the gorge to the river. It was quite a steep climb, but the huge trees and vibrant greenery were well worth it. The riverside was a very tranquil place, with the water bubbling and spilling its way over the rocks from pool to pool. The kids enjoyed a swim, but it was too cold for us older, wiser heads. Sunday dinner was another of those "only in Africa" moments, as the roast joint was a leg of impala. Connie had cooked it to perfection and it had a deliciously tender, gamey flavour.

Next day I left Moshi for Dar Es Salaam. Connie dropped me at the petrol station, from where I took the 1st class bus to my next destination. Shortly after setting off, a small convoy of public transport vehicles came rushing past, hooting madly, with hysterical people hanging from the windows, shouting wildly. I have no idea why. Tanzanians certainly know how to travel in their enormous country, as almost everyone on the bus was asleep. I followed their sage example for much of the nine hour journey, whilst hoping that the driver wasn't doing the same thing.

We were travelling with the flat Maasai Steppe to our right and the Pare, then the Usambara mountains reaching up vertically to our left. I felt like I was a mouse running along a skirting board. It was a pleasant journey, as sodas were handed out and, after a stop for lunch, the bus conductor came round with serviettes for everyone. We passed enormous sisal plantations with row upon row of the chest high, blade leafed plants used to make rope. Sisal, being of the same agave family that gives us tequila, is native to Central America and Mexico, but following the mechanisation of the rope-making process, was planted in the Bahamas and Tanganyika, the former name for Tanzania, in the late 19th century. The plant grew in rows of aging punk rockers, with explosions of silver green hair.

There were a plethora of baobab trees with their trunks so wide that an African proverb says that, "Wisdom is like the baobab tree; no one person can fully embrace it." They get their name 'upside-down tree' from the fact that their branches look like roots, which inspired the myth of its creation in this position. The first baobab grew next to a small lake, and in the lake it could see its own reflection. The baobab complained to God that He had made it so ugly. Why couldn't it have the slender body of the palm, or the beautiful flowers of the flame tree, or the abundant fruit of the fig? God grew angry, pulled up the first baobab and replanted it upside down, so that the tree could neither see its own reflection or moan about its lot. Since then the baobab has repaid its discretion by being one of the most useful trees to humans and animals. The baobab's bark, fruit and leaves have traditionally been used for the treatment of malaria, tuberculosis, fever, microbial infections, diarrhea, anemia, toothache and dysentery, and modern science is supporting some of these uses. Its fruit has high levels of vitamin C, potassium, phosphorus and antioxidants and is being used in commercial powders and tinctures across the globe.

The village farmers grew a lot of maize, but also lemon and mango trees became more common as we descended towards the coast and the temperature and humidity rose. We passed round huts made of wattle and daub walls and thatched roofs, all nestled together like batches of eggs. A sign read, "Dar Es Salaam, 284km." We were getting closer.

The concept of staring too long at someone doesn't really exist in Africa. The bus stopped to let a guy off and two people, who had sat nowhere near him, stood up to stare at him as he left and walked away along the road. A boy in front of me spent the whole journey turning around to look at me, sometimes for as long as 15 minutes at a time, and I wondered if he realised I could see him through my sunglasses.

Finally, just before dark, we arrived in Dar. A suspicious stain on my rucksack proved to have been caused by the explosion of my shampoo bottle, which in turn had been caused by the heavy crate that had been slung on top of it. I trundled off to find somewhere to stay for the night before heading to Zanzibar on a ferry in the morning. I checked out the Jambo and Safari hotels, but they were both full. I was accosted by a friendly knave who insisted on taking me to another hotel. I grudgingly agreed based on his advertised price (one has to be careful that one doesn't get led somewhere to be mugged) and followed him down the main road, then along a side road that smelled overpoweringly of urine, to the Simba Hotel. We had now checked off just about all the Swahili words most tourists could list, and I was introduced to Naira, the hotel manageress. Naira was an aging Indian lady, whose face was creased by time but not by humour. I inspected the room, which was uninspiring, but had a cold shower and clean toilet, so I took it.

I slipped out for food and, being a bit of a connoisseur of local delicacies, I took some trouble to find the Chick King fast food restaurant, where I ate a burger that tasted like it might have some unfortunate repercussions. After this nutritious supper I went looking for a beer. At the first cafe I turned up at, I couldn't see anyone else drinking beer, so I asked the chap in the booth if they had any.

"Oh no, thank you!" came the reply, in equal measures of alarm and campness.

I tried next door, which was an even bigger dive than the hotel, but I was rewarded for my pluck with a cold Kilimanjaro beer. Kili became my favourite Tanzanian brew. It wasn't too strong at 4.5%, didn't have a chemical taste and was light and refreshing. Kibo Gold was similar, a little stronger, but not as widespread. Safari lager once had a reputation that no two ever tasted the same, but they had been taken over by a South African brewery, which had improved the consistency of the flavour. Safari was the strongest of the four main national beers at 5.5% and tasted like it with quite a powerful chemical tang, of which I was not overly fond.

I sat down at a plastic table and met a local guy called David, who was fluent in the 'f' word, or at least used it as if it was an entire language of its own. He told me a long and complicated story about four Germans who had just left, and had been charged for nine drinks when they had only drunk seven. David was most upset by their treatment.

The waiter who was accused of overcharging was just resting his haunches at the table next to mine and, as I sat sipping my Kili,

David got up and started a fight with him. It was only the usual African style pushing contest, sometimes punctuated with the odd-misdirected karate-style kick (every local youth seemed to fancy himself a bit of a Bruce Lee), but it filled the vacuum for entertainment. It was also interesting that the waiter, who was a kid about half the size of David, was able to hold his own quite capably, suggesting that maybe David was well oiled.

David, exhausted, gave up his fight and flopped down in the chair opposite mine.

"Buy me a beer," he barked.

I declined politely, wondering whether he was where the other two beers had gone, and returned to my hotel. There I found that hard-faced Naira was actually rather a sweetie, who was very helpful and gave me lots of advice for my travels. I wondered if she felt that she couldn't let her guard down in front of the employee or representative who had brought me to her hotel. Asking for a seven thirty wake up call, I retired for the night.

I had a self-inflicted cold night's sleep (I had left the fan on too high a setting) and was woken early by the market that was right outside the hotel, but which sounded like it was in the bed with me. I got up for an icy shower and was already packed when my wake up call arrived at 8 o'clock. Though this was half an hour later than I had requested, this was the best wake up call I had ever received in Africa, where normally they don't bother at all.

I took my heavy rucksack and walked to the seafront to buy my ticket for the catamaran. There I met two men in the street who asked me if I wanted to buy a ticket for Zanzibar. I replied that I did, and they led me past all the ticket booths and tried to get me to follow them down a dark side alley. I refused to go and they told me that if I gave them $25, they would go and get the ticket for me. I remonstrated towards the ticket offices we had just passed and asked why I shouldn't just get my ticket from one of them. They became very persistent, but eventually, as my patience with them started to wear thin, I resorted to threatening them with violence and they slipped away. I wondered afterwards if I should have given them the thick ear they so richly deserved, to deter them from trying it on with the next tourist who passed through, but by then it was too late.

Having bought my ticket from the more reputable vendor in his wooden cabin at the port, changed some more money and dropped my baggage off in the company office, I spent the morning relaxing with my book in cafes along the seafront. The sun shone brightly, sparkling off the rippling water of the Zanzibar Channel and all seemed right with the world.

I boarded the Flying Horse at 12:30 and was ushered up to the top deck, which was not blessed with the most comfortable seating, but offered the best views. As the catamaran loaded up, I watched a group of kids playing on the beach, running down the sand and using an old tractor tyre as a springboard from which they performed cart wheels and Arab springs. I could see on the seafront the enormous Gothic Catholic cathedral and the smaller, Lutheran church, snugly tucked away between the office buildings and hotels that made up the rest of the front. The view to my left was not as inspiring, as it was just a docking yard which looked similar to any port town anywhere in the world.

At this time, I considered Dar to be a friendly town, which felt safer than Nairobi and where the people took no for an answer. It was a bit shabby looking, in a sea-grimed way rather than a sea glammed way, but there were some interesting looking buildings that could look quite spectacular with a little investment.

The ferry to Zanzibar took three hours, of which the only event of any note, indeed the only relief from an uninteresting crossing, was when we approached the Stone Town and it swung into view. The Stone Town is the name given to the older traditional part of the town and there was certainly something majestic about it, tinged with a sense of fantasy.

Upon arrival there, I discovered that the Zanzibaris clung to their former independent status quite longingly, meaning I had to fill in some pointless forms and get another stamp in my passport. The baggage check was an even bigger farce: the two policemen, who to their credit were extremely friendly, stopped me struggling to get my rucksack off and, having confirmed that it was indeed baggage, marked it with a bit of chalk and bade me farewell. I found the whole process a bit silly really.

As soon as I had legally entered Zanzibar, I was jumped on by a tout who offered to show me to my hotel. Having read the guidebook, the brilliantly named Hotel Bottoms Up sounded like it would fit the bill my budget could afford, so I asked him to take me there. He agreed and said that if I didn't like it, he would take me to see the ubiquitously named Hotel Jambo instead, a plan to which I consented. He then took me on a dizzying tour of the back streets and alleys of Zanzibar to... the Hotel Jambo. In the process I had become thoroughly lost.

In view of the morning's antics with the ferry ticket fraudsters, I have to confess that I suffered a bit of a sense of humour failure at this point and berated the poor guy for his trickery. Oddly, he thanked me profusely for telling him off and then redeemed himself by taking me to the hotel of my choice, which looked fine, included a bar, and I took one of the available rooms.

I went to the Africa House hotel for a beer at sundown, but it must have been undergoing repairs, as the whole place looked like a building site. However, the bar on the first floor was open and gave a great view of the sun dropping through pink and purple clouds into the Indian Ocean and mainland Tanzania. This place used to be the club for the Europeans in colonial times, and its clientele didn't seem to have changed much in the intervening years. There were a few young lads hanging around to see if any tourists would get tipsy and buy them a drink, which for an African coastal town, seemed about the norm.

Zanzibar is the biggest of a series of Swahili towns that dot the Eastern coast of Africa from southern Somalia in the north to northern Mozambique and Madagascar in the south. From the 8th century onwards, Arab traders used the monsoon winds to bring such items as glassware, porcelain from as far away as China, silks and fine cloths and jewellery down the coast to trade for animal products, metals, incense, perfumes and slaves before returning with their loads when the monsoon winds changed. Though the Arabs never militarily conquered the locals, they intermingled, bringing about the adoption of Islam among the African coastal dwellers and producing the Swahili language that combined Bantu African and Arabic, before European words began to pepper the lexicon after contact beginning with Vasco de Gama.

These towns shared similar characteristics: narrow streets between white-painted, boxy buildings evoking a romantic aura of times gone by. I had visited Lamu, in Kenya, which is described as "Kathmandu in Africa" and had thoroughly enjoyed its otherworldly charm. There was certainly something enigmatic about the dhow boats drifting on the water and the spice plantations in the hinterlands, that adds to the architectural beauty of the towns themselves.

My first impression of Zanzibar was that it was of a similar ilk to Lamu, only on a larger scale, with more tourists in town. Lamu was sleepy and seemingly unprepared for visitors, while Zanzibar was clearly well set up in that regard. There were more tourist shops and options for trips, making it a lot easier to be active but at the expense of its undiscovered charm. There were a plethora of intriguing buildings though, and I enjoyed trying to find my way around the maze of the old town.

After grabbing some dinner while out, I returned to the Bottoms

Up for a cold Kili and tried to work out what the freakish decoration in the bar represented. The walls were painted in a sort of giraffe pattern using white patches on crimson background, making me feel almost as if I was trapped in some sort of membrane. I didn't want to have too much to drink there - it might terrify me! I met a few fellow travellers, one of whom, John, suggested we play beach rugby sometime. However, it sounded like his group were all heading to the north coast of the island, something I didn't plan to do, so it didn't seem likely we'd be able to see that plan through. I also noticed a locally made gin, *konyagi*, in the bar and made a mental note to try some before I left the island. I could scarcely have made a more ominous plan.

The next morning, I took a beer-enforced lie-in until 9 o'clock and found that it was raining quite heavily. Since I had come in the wet season, I suppose I should have expected the weather to be slightly less than perfect, but, even when the rain stopped, the clouds persisted, scuppering my plans to spend the day sunbathing on the beach.

I wandered upstairs for breakfast, where from a room I had accidentally blundered into, I enjoyed the view of a hodgepodge of white-washed buildings, narrow, rain-soaked alleyways, old rickety tin roofs and an enormous satellite dish, proving the 21st century had arrived in Zanzibar. From this vantage point, the town looked a bit like a scrapyard, with buildings thrown up apparently at random and the tin roofs arrayed in a rusty, metallic patchwork like a decaying, robotic quilt. Unlike Lamu, some of the streets were wide enough to permit cars to travel, but in the narrow streets of the Stone Town, it was more common to hear bicycle bells, or the tooting and high revving of mopeds, which are the most convenient mode of transport after your own two legs. I listened to the harmony of these sounds drifting up to the rooftop dining room and noticed that, although the walls were crumbling just about everywhere, there were the unmistakable sounds of repair work being carried out.

A grey blanket hung over the town suggesting that my sunbathing would be out indefinitely. Planes laden with tourists flew to and from the nearby airport, as I sipped at my coffee and read my book. I passed most of the morning this way, before striking out for an exploratory walk. I planned to make a circular tour past the Arab fort, along the seafront, down Malawi Road (the Stone Town's northern limit), down Creek Road (its eastern boundary), before plunging back in to loop back to the hotel.

The Arab Fort is a boxish structure built from peach-hued stone, with a crenelated roof. It was built by the Busaidi Omanis, who took the island from the Portuguese in 1698 after two centuries of European rule. The Omanis referred to this area as 'The Land of Black People', the land of *Zenj*, from which it is believed that Zanzibar got its name. The Busaidis were quick to get their defences built as they were not only cautious of a Portuguese counter-attack, but also invasion from the rival Mazrui Omanis, who controlled Mombasa at the time. The town developed as a cosmopolitan market town, drawing Arabs, Indians, Africans and Europeans to a trade based on spices and slaves.

After the Arab Fort, came the *Beit-el-Ajaib*, or House of Wonders, which used to be the Sultan's residence, but was at that time the headquarters for the Chama Cha Mapinduzi party, ruling in both mainland Tanzania and the island of Zanzibar. Built by Sultan Barghash bin Said in 1883, it contained such wonders as an extra large door that allowed the Sultan to enter on elephant-back, a two storey clock tower, painted brilliant white and the first electric lift in East Africa. The Palace Museum next door, housed a collection of exhibits that demonstrate the combined Portuguese, English, Omani and Swahili culture of the town and island, including local garments, wooden doors carved with passages from the Quran and David Livingstone's medical chest.

When you include various hotels and the Cultural Centre, the seafront was an aesthetically pleasing vista, combining Arabic architectural features with the African boats bobbing in the water in front. The buildings all had crenellated walls, sturdy mangrove timber and whitewashed walls, large windows and doors and front-facing balconies supported by carved posts in the Swahili style. The balconies were a clever, but simple, piece of engineering, throwing the walls into shade, so that the sun was unable to directly heat the building.

I went past the police station on the corner of Malawi and Creek roads, and stopped to ask a friendly copper why some of them wore all white uniforms and some khaki. He explained that the traffic police wore the white and the khaki was reserved for the maritime police, which made sense, as camouflaged traffic police perhaps wouldn't survive as long. All the police wore colourful belts in a stylised pattern of the Tanzanian flag, which I thought looked particularly striking against the reflective white traffic cops' get-up.

Looking away from Stone Town, there was some kind of swamp to the north and a football pitch to the east, which was in constant use throughout my stay. I turned right along Creek Road, which was lined with market stalls. It was a colourful place, full of bustle, that smelled alternately of fish, fruit, exhaust fumes, dust and old wood. All the time there were people calling, cars hooting, mopeds revving and rubbish floating past on the sea breeze.

Just then, a police motorcycle came past with lights flashing and siren wailing, and the traffic, both motorised and foot, came to a standstill. Behind the policeman came the ambassador of the People's Republic of China in a stretched Mercedes, workers' party flags in lucky crimson and gold flapping at its extremities. China had been very supportive of the Tanzanian communists, the greatest evidence of which was the TANZARA railway line, which linked the Zambian copperbelt to the Tanzanian coast and meant that these two left leaning countries no longer had to transport the ore through an uncooperative Zimbabwe (then

South Rhodesia) or apartheid South Africa. This was for a long time China's biggest overseas investment and they perhaps retained close diplomatic ties on its account.

I then decided to take the plunge into the winding alleyways and narrow streets of the Stone Town, where every corner is said to present something new. I wasn't disappointed. I passed a building full of giggling schoolgirls in white head scarves and brown *buibuis*, like a gang of hysterical iced buns. The UNCA cathedral was followed by a building bearing the interesting moniker "Moo Centre', and I wondered if this was a bovine meeting house.

A chap was mashing sugar cane for its juice on what appeared to be an instrument of torture, with an attendent cloud of wasps drunkenly buzzing around him for the fruits of his labour. I stopped to try some and he cranked the handle, producing a jarring mechanical grating as the cane stalks were fed into the workings, to half fill a plastic cup. It was, perhaps unsurprisingly, sweet, but I was impressed with the effort the guy was putting into his work. The sturdy juicer was about the same size as him, and seemingly much older. He put a fair amount of elbow grease into making the drinks for a negligible profit.

I saw a kid on a bike give a fellow pedestrian ahead of me a high five and held out my hand to receive the same. However, he didn't let go of my hand and I inadvertently pulled him off his bike! There were no tears and my heartfelt *"Pole sana"* was greeted with a toothy grin, as he remounted and sped off again on his clanking steed.

I was starting to get more lost, but even more worryingly noticed the trend that the bars all seemed to have closed down! As I looked for one such, a local hollered, "Hey, white man!" at me, but I suspected a ruse and carried on, wondering at the comparative political correctness of Africa. I sat down in a narrow alleyway to figure out where I was. An *askari* approached me and I thought I was about to be helped with my dilemma, but he told me firmly that I couldn't sit on the steps to the bank.

Everywhere I went I saw the beautifully carved Swahili doors. These large, double-doored portals had intricately carved frames and doors, stained in a deep, rich brown shade. Some were studded with brass spikes, a spear point embedded within a flower the size of fists, which were supposed to have originated in India, where they were invented to repel elephant attack. I couldn't imagine any pachyderms possibly fitting down the narrow Swahili streets.

The initials of the opposition political party, the CUF, were daubed on many of the walls, whereas the CCM campaign seemed to centre on a distribution of garish yellow print posters and equally eye-catching T-shirts. There was a German consular building, which seemed to owe its architectural heritage to Teutonic rather than Arabic origins and over the road I was amused to find a No Parking sign, rendered completely invisible by the parked cars surrounding it.

I found a nice restaurant by a sea full of bobbing dhows and tooth-white sandbanks, and I sat down to relax with my book. The price of my beverage was relatively steep and I reflected that perhaps there were too many tourists here, driving up prices. When I walked back behind the fort, I found gift shop central, though I did look into the price for incense, as I thought Zanzibar would be an authentic place to buy the stuff for the burner in my Ethiopian coffee set.

That afternoon I returned to the Palace Museum, which, in addition to being a former abode of one of the Sultan's, had some interesting exhibits on the history of Zanzibar. Said bin Sultan was the sultan who moved his capital from Oman to the booming port town of Zanzibar, from where he ruled both lands between 1806 and his death in 1856. Upon his demise, and with pressure from the British government, his sons split the two provinces again, with Thwain taking Muscat and Majid, Zanzibar. Barghash, the fort builder, took over from his brother, Majid, in 1870 and his nephew, Hamed, became sultan indirectly from Barghash in 1893. Hamed was at the centre of an unfortunate claim to fame, as the leader of the defeated nation in the world's shortest ever 'war.' His anti-British stance was challenged by a bombardment from the Royal Navy lasting less than 40 minutes, upon which he surrendered and was replaced by a more anglophile cousin, Hamud.

A shabby family tree was displayed with photos of the Sultan family, and it was interesting to note that, while Said bin Sultan was very much Arab-looking, a few of his sons seemed to have African features. In a later display it was explained that his wives were from Persia and Arabia, while his concubines were from Circassia (a region on the east coast of the Black Sea, world famous for its beauties at that time) and Ethiopia, the latter perhaps lending the more African features to the Said line. Further down the family tree, there were more and more African features, suggesting a continued intermarriage with women from the interior.

Zanzibar grew in prosperity as a clove exporter, following the plant's introduction to the island in 1818. Fuelled by slave labour, Zanzibar soon grew to be the world's biggest exporter of this spice and, by the middle of the century, was also the largest slaving entrepot in the region, sending as many as 50,000 people a year from the interior of Africa (from as far away as lakes Tanganyika and Malawi) to eastern destinations including the Middle East and India.

Another interesting story from this dynasty was that of Sayyida Sulme, one of the daughters of Sultan Seyyid Said. She fell in love with a German bureaucrat and, throwing all the perks of princess-ship to the winds, eloped with her husband-to-be to Germany, where she took the name Emily Ruete. However, her tale became one of tragedy when her husband was run over by a tram, leaving Ruete with three children and struggling with loneliness in a foreign culture, far from home.

In an interview with an elderly doctor, said to be the only living person of the time to remember Emily Ruete, the doctor took great pains to describe the enormity of her moustache. This tickled me all afternoon, as I thought that a person of greater discretion could have possibly omitted this detail without anyone contradicting him to the tune of, "Wait, don't you recall the ruddy great caterpillar on her top lip?" But instead, this unfortunate lady must be remembered as, not only the Arab princess who absconded but, the Arabic princess with the moustache.

I was interested in the choices of interior decoration in the rooms. In one of the sitting rooms, the furniture was an eclectic mix of beautifully carved rosewood imported from India and 1960s tack. Another sitting room had been given half each to the Sultan's two wives: Bibi Matuka had purchased Indian rosewood and Chinese porcelain along an Eastern theme, while across the room, Bibi Numu had bought in from the English home counties for a Victorian theme. I have heard that the Chinese pictogram for 'trouble' is a stylisation of two women under one roof, and I wonder if these two had been exemplars of this theory.

I noticed that clocks were another popular item of furniture. These were everywhere and it was only years after that I realised the probable explanation for this, that Muslims, who pray five times daily at set hours, would have probably welcomed the opportunity to accurately plan their daily activities through the use of an accurate timepiece, and that this might explain why there were so many of them in the house.

I returned to my hotel, my opinion of the museum riding high. I relaxed on the rooftop plaza reading, enjoying an ice cold juice and listening to the sounds of Islam, as the faithful were called to prayer at the mosque next door. There was a caged African Grey parrot who I could hear from all the way upstairs, who gurgled noisily and spoke phrases in Swahili, ushering in a Swahili themed evening. I ate calamari masala curry from the Swahili dishes section of the menu before returning to the Bottoms Up bar where I met Troy, an American living in Abu Dhabi who was on holiday, and Amani, a Pemba islander who was looking for work in Zanzibar. Amani, a well-dressed, athletic gentleman, spent most of the evening fine-tuning my Swahili language skills, which were graded not-so-*safi*. The Swahili of central Kenya is renowned as being a bit *shenzi*, or of poorer quality than that of coastal Kenya and the whole of Tanzania, where it is the official language. Zanzibar holds itself as the centre for the language, so it was good to take tips from someone who hailed from the island next door.

The next day I met Willis, who organised the spice tour of the island's plantations. He led me through a maze of back alleys to 'the baobab tree', which had a trunk about 10 feet wide making it a local landmark, and a bus waiting to pick up some more people. The vehicle was gaudily decorated in pale blue paint with four teddy bears playing football across its panels. It was always fun to discover these cultural gems. The group that assembled for the tour included a Ugandan guy who was working in Cameroon, two French Canadian girls, a Dutch doctor, an Isreali couple, an Italian lady travelling with her German friend and two Eastern European men. As is often the case in a group as diverse as this, the lingua franca immediately became English which is both useful for, and interesting to, me. And of course, Willis, who had traded Swahili pleasantries with me in the morning, dropped straight into English as he kicked proceedings off.

The tour started at the Kisimbani plantation, where we were given a guided walking tour with comprehensive information about all the spices and tropical fruits we encountered as we ambled around.

Lemongrass, originally from Sri Lanka and South India, can be grown to keep mosquitoes away but has many benefits when drunk as a tea. These include relieving anxiety, lowering cholesterol, preventing infections, boosting oral health, relieving pain and bloating and boosting red blood cell production. The plant looks exactly like a long grass and has a sharp edge to it that doesn't invite too much handling.

Cacao, which was first used by the ancient cultures in Central America, grows as a knobbly fruit about the size of a mango. Inside, the dark coloured beans are covered in a sweet-tasting goo, but it is the bean itself that is used to produce chocolate. Using cocoa powder or eating good quality dark chocolate of over 70% cacao can have an incredible range of health benefits which include, but are by no means limited to, reducing inflammation, improving blood flow, lowering blood pressure and improving levels of blood sugar and cholesterol. Cacao and its derivatives are brain food too. Polyphenols improve blood flow to the brain and general brain function, and early research suggests that it may also help prevent age-related brain degeneration. Though the exact causes are not well understood yet, flavanol in cacao has been shown to improve mood and reduce symptoms of depression.

The clove trees, upon which the island's spice fame was originally built, can provide leaves to make spice for cooking and fruit which can be dried for a week before being pressed into oil. The health benefits of cloves include being a rich source of manganese, which improves brain function, killing bacteria, preventing cancer, improving liver and bone health and treating stomach ulcers.

Cardamom, another spice that originates in India, sends a primary root straight downwards to lock itself into position against storms, while sending secondary roots horizontally along the top of the ground. From these the flowers and seeds are produced which provide benefits such as lowering blood pressure, fighting cancer, anti-inflammation, digestive health, antibacterial properties that help in oral hygiene, cavities and treatment of infections, improved breathing and oxygen use, and lowering blood sugar levels.

Anato is used as a food colouring in tandoori dishes and gives a red dye like lipstick. This property was demonstrated on the group by marking our wrists, giving us the look of a group who had recently attempted a mass suicide. Our guide, Mohammad, a tall, lean African in a full length thawb dress and the flattened cap of his faith, could have perhaps prescribed us more chocolate to reduce the depressive impact. It was fun to listen to the group's synchronised "aaah!" responses to his bequeathing of further knowledge, as if explaining something that had long vexed us. How Mohammad could remember such detail about such a wide range of different plants is lost on me. I am someone who generally has to write down everything if I am to have any chance of remembering it. He certainly knew his stuff.

The leaves of the cinnamon tree can be used to make a weaker spice, but for the stronger flavour, it is necessary to strip chunks of bark. The inner part of the bark is removed and curls up into what are called sticks (but aren't sticks in the strict sense) when it dries out. Along with a lot of other properties that are common to spices already mentioned, cinnamon seems to be very useful for preventing and treating diabetes, as it improves sensitivity to the naturally occurring hormone insulin, which regulates sugar in the body, and lowers blood sugar levels. Cinnamon also inhibits the build-up of a protein called tau, which is one of the causes of Alzheimer's.

I was interested to find that the pepper plant is actually a vine, which is usually trained to climb up trees that don't grow very tall, meaning that the ascent to harvest them isn't so death-defying. All forms of pepper are produced from this same vine, differing only in the processing of the seed (this doesn't include the capsicum family, which includes chilis). Red pepper is ground from the ripe seeds; green pepper from unripe ones; black pepper from unripe dried ones; and white pepper from unripe ones that are boiled before they are dried.

The ilanglang flower seemed to have myriad uses including being used as a perfume, soap, cream, being added to coconut oil for a Vaseline-like jelly and to keep clothes smelling good in the cupboard. But my personal favourite was when Mohammad whispered conspiratorially that Swahili women wore the fragrance of the ilanglang to let their husbands know that they might be in luck that night! The group had leaned in to listen and at this announcement leaned back again, let out a knowing, "aaah!", and fell into fits of giggling.

Turmeric is a bright orange root, the colour and size of a carrot, which is ground into a yellow powder to be used in foods. This spice, which again comes originally from India, contains the compound curcumin, which is another incredible health tonic. Its many benefits include, but again are not limited to, reducing risk of heart disease and cancer, improved brain function, preventing and treating Alzheimer's, arthritis and depression, as well as being a strong anti-aging chemical, due to its antioxidants.

Nutmeg, a natural pain reliever from Indonesia, is medically proven to help with insomnia, digestion, skin health, blood pressure and brain function. It seemed that if you took all these spices in just the right quantities, you might be able to live forever!

After the tour we were shown into the spice shop, where the spices we had just seen were bagged up with descriptions of their healing properties printed in suspect English on the labels. For instance, nutmeg had a label which read, "for women that given up strong desire for making or fulfilling their men," from which I assumed that it was intended as an aphrodisiac.

I bought some more incense for the burner in my Ethiopian coffee set. We were given jackfruit, coffee and doughnuts, and washed our hands in coconut oil before we were herded back onto the bus to go to the Persian baths at Kidichi. These were built on the highest point of the island at 153m above sea level to catch any cooling breeze that might pass, but were not particularly well preserved. From outside they looked like a shower block, and inside the crumbling plaster and mold belied the beauty of the Persian stucco and former stained glass windows that would have cast a rainbow light onto the white walls in their heyday. The building was erected by Sultan Seyyid Said for his second wife, Schesade, who was the daughter of the Shah of Persia. This little home comfort was offered for when they were on trips to the plantation to inspect work progress and hunt, and stood the test of time as a romantic gesture.

We stopped off for lunch in a village, where we enjoyed spicy rice, green vegetable goop and a flavoursome sauce that looked like, but thankfully didn't taste like, baby poo. This was washed down with lemongrass tea. We clambered back on board the bus and headed to our next destination, the Mangapwani slave caves.

Though a sign at the gate says that no slaves were kept in these caves, there are other versions of the story that seem to question the accuracy of this proclamation. Supposedly discovered by a goatherd, who was also a slave, looking for a missing beasty, on land belonging to Hamed bin Salim el Harthy, a wealthy slave trader, he stumbled across a cave entrance that held fresh water inside. A chamber was cut from the rock in which to store human cargo waiting to board the boats to their new destinations, mostly in the Middle East. Upon the abolition of slavery in 1873, the underground cavern became a perfect place to hide these human chattel from the eyes of the authorities, a smuggling activity that continued into the twentieth century.

Zanzibar, a former centre for the trade of slaves, tries very hard to distance itself from this dark history.

We stopped off at the beach in Makoba, whereupon the sun, having spent the day until now behind cloud, obligingly made an appearance. I was able to sit in the shade of a palm tree on the white sand, as the clear blue Indian Ocean lapped at the beach. On the bus going back to Stone Town, I discovered that I had lost my sunglasses, but reflected on how clever I had been to make this pair last a whole eight days without losing or breaking them. This was something of a personal best, but things were about to get even better. We pulled up for drinks in the same village that we had eaten lunch in and a fine fellow named Samuel handed me my sunglasses back, so that they could continue their incredible run. This was an occasion to be celebrated.

I got sat in the Bottoms Up bar, and was just enjoying a celebratory beer when I recognised someone who came in.

"Hello, you were at the dock yesterday and I think you were the first person I've met carrying a bigger rucksack than me! I'm Matt!"

Derek was from Texas, shorter than me with an athletic build and a retreating hairline that threatened to run away altogether. He was a gregarious and likeable bloke, who was travelling the world. He had made his money in computer sales, bought a house by the age of 30 and took off for a year travelling financed by the rental income from his house, which he claimed ran to US $1000 a month. This was about as much as I had brought for my planned 6 week journey, and seemed a fortune at the time. His year travelling was seven years when I met him, and he didn't seem in a hurry to return home. I felt like this was about as idyllic a lifestyle as I could imagine.

However, he explained that he wasn't having such a good day. Apparently, his house had been blown down by a hurricane. He flippantly claimed that this happened all the time, then thought about it and corrected himself. This had happened once before.

"But it's always getting flooded."

Having recognised someone with a refreshingly philosophical attitude towards life, it wasn't long before the *konyagi* bottle stood empty on the table before us and we staggered out from the membranous confines of the Bottoms Up to find out what treats Zanzibar held after dark. The rest of the night became a bit of a beery blur as we visited a couple more bars, drank a few cold cans on the harbour, visited a night club and avoided the amorous attentions of the local girls.

The result of the *konyagi* binge was a totally wasted day the day after. I finally got out of bed at 1:30pm to go and have some lunch, but came back straight away to further sleep off the unwanted aftereffects.

Derek called round again at 5pm, and told me that he had been held up at knife point by two teenagers trying their luck. He said that he had roared and run at them, chasing them away, but that he hadn't any money anyway. We resigned to take things a bit easier that night, borrowed a chess set from a shop owner, who may have thought we were interested in buying, and played while sitting on his shop step, sipping recovery beers from cans bought at the local store.

We had arranged to meet so that he could take me to the food market at the seafront (of course, I hadn't remembered this at all, and I'm surprised he did). I'm really glad he did remember though, as the experience entirely lived up to the high acclaim he gave it. There were about a dozen stalls, mostly just barbecue grills with the boats arriving a few metres behind them from where the catch was being loaded straight onto the coals. There was a huge range of seafood available, not all of which I recognised. I tried lobster for the first time, enjoying the whole tail, barbecued for under £2. I had the obligatory paper bag of chips for the Brit and also a marlin kebab. The whole meal cost less than £4. We wandered around and saw prawns of every size, crab claws as big as your fist, tuna kebabs, kingfish steaks and sailfish with salad. If only I had a fathomless appetite, I think I would have encountered a few culinary firsts there, but alas! the flesh is weak and the stomach limited. We were a bit more sensible with our beers, mostly through not attacking *konyagi* again, but still managed to stay out until about 4am.

Waking up at 11am the next day, I was determined to make something a bit more constructive of my day than the previous one. Having relaxed on the beach for a couple of hours, I had a look round a bookshop where a poster on the wall reminded me that this was the birthplace of an idol from my teenage years.

On 5th September 1946, Jer and Bomi Bulsara, he an officer with the British consul in Zanzibar, were blessed with the birth of their first son, Farroukh. The family left Zanzibar when Farroukh was nine years old and he studied at an Indian boarding school where, among other skills, he learned to box. Having graduated from his private school in India, he moved to London to study art and there met up with Brian and Roger to form a band. He changed his name to Freddie Mercury, they renamed the band Queen and the rest, as they say...

I used to have a 40 minute bus ride to and from secondary school every day and for about 4 years, every second of those journeys was taken up by listening to Queen albums on my walkman cassette player. We even passed the Rockfield recording studios where the famous A Night at the Opera album was recorded, including the record selling Bohemian Rhapsody. I recall the devastation I felt on the day Freddie's death was announced over the radio on the bus on the way to school (funny I wasn't listening to my walkman that day - dead batteries?) and I listened to their albums over and over until I was word perfect, though not always pitch perfect, when I took my bath of an evening.

The poster had some information on where I might find the house in which Freddie had been born: in a small square behind the Post Office on Kenyatta Road. These instructions seemed a little vague but I felt confident that I could manage it. However, having looked at several small squares behind the Post Office, I was unable to find any marker that confirmed the location of his birthplace. Having looked at every house in the vicinity, I am happy that I have seen the house I was looking for, just without knowing which one it was exactly.

After this search I went to look for the Universities Mission in Central Africa cathedral, built upon the former slave market site. The cathedral was pointedly built here, but the holding cells, in which many thousand unlucky people awaited their sale, were still intact. I couldn't find anyone at the ticket booth, so I followed the signs and crept into the inky cells with my mag light illuminating the way. The rooms were incredibly dark and musty, with only only four small barred windows between the two holding rooms. There were stone slab shelves on which the slaves would have slept, squashed together, unable to move from their own excrement.

They reminded me a little bit of the Ethiopian chat dens, only with the opposite atmosphere. The chat dens were relaxed places for men to meet and talk and laugh off the day's comparative hardships. It was awful to think of the fear, deprivation and suffering that would have been the experience of those spending their last nights in their home continents in these chambers.

I met Derek again in the Bottoms Up bar for a sun-downer beer, before we set off again to the seafront for more seafood indulgence. This time I enjoyed lobster, crab, kingfish steak and chips, which again came in at less than £4. Though we had intended to call it an early night, once the beer and conversation started flowing, we ended up staying out until 2am. As we sat outdoors enjoying the night breezes, a couple of guys came up to talk, but quickly turned the conversation to a request for beer. A few girls followed, but they seemed to be selling something we weren't interested in.

By the end of the night, we were stuck with two very drunk girls who we struggled to shake. I was talking to one who looked a lot like Janet Jackson, a teenage crush of mine, though it could have been beer goggles that were distorting the view a little. Nevertheless, I felt proud of myself for declining her advances, before she keeled over and fell asleep. We felt this was as good a juncture as any to bid goodnight to the still conscious one, who proceeded to ask Derek for money. When he refused and turned away, the girl picked up an empty beer bottle in a manner that suggested she wanted to make some decorative improvements to the back of Derek's head with it. I quietly disarmed her, replaced the bottle on the table and we disappeared while she looked about herself in confusion.

Next day I was set for a dolphin watching day trip and then a ferry back to the mainland. I packed my rucksack and stashed it with the tour company for safe-keeping and we set off. The bus did a tour of Stone Town seemingly picking up every tourist on the island. It turned out that we were passing a village that was hosting some kind of music festival and that this was a very popular event. The only snag with this was that we got stopped by police roadblocks about every ten minutes, as they wanted to make sure that there were no drugs or bad guys on board. The funny thing was that once we had picked everyone up in Stone Town, we were the same people being stopped six or seven times, for which one road block would have done the trick.

The bloke sitting behind me had an annoying habit of opening and shutting the slide window so that it cracked me in the shoulder every time. But Bob Marley was telling me that every little thing was going to be alright over the stereo system, so I sat back and enjoyed the views of banana palms, mud huts and policemen.

I decided that we really were on the clown bus. Coco, sat behind me, was chewing something so loudly that it almost deafened me and he must have beaned me with the window about 15 times before I started leaning on the American girl to my left to get out of his way. His stage mate, on the other side of the bus, was blowing kisses out of the window to everyone we passed. In Zanzibar, they make this noise to attract people's attention in the same way that people in Nairobi hiss and people in Britain whistle, but I had not seen it performed with quite so much filthy gusto as this particular clown was putting in.

There was a long argument at one roadblock with a policeman who didn't understand why the driver had picked up passengers of such a varied racial background. When I suggested to the passenger next to me that we should just offer the policeman some *chai* (literally translated as tea, but meaning a bribe or tip), it was met with laughter. He explained to me that bribery didn't happen on the island of Zanzibar. I was genuinely impressed by this, as corruption is such a massive detriment to any form of progress, though I quietly wondered if the policeman would have his price.

When I arrived at the beach, disorganisation reigned. I was told that I had to sort out my own snorkel, mask and fins, so I approached some guys who had their *palapa* shelters set up on the beach. I got fitted out with the works and tried to haggle the price, which is the standard for most of Africa in my experience, but the guy wasn't budging. I later found out that those who waited until getting on the boat paid a higher rate, so perhaps I had done well enough. There is a certain amount of competitiveness that creeps in when haggling and it sometimes feels a bit like a game. The key was to not take it too seriously as no-one wants a confrontation. It was difficult to judge exactly how much higher than their real price hawkers were pitching to begin with. After a couple of years of haggling in Nairobi and

Nakuru, I had a good idea of where to start there, but every location had its flexibility on prices. The other thing was that the more desperate you are, the more power the seller has. At the beach, there were a couple of snorkel hire guys set up beneath their banana palm shelters, so there could have been some give and take on prices, but once on the boat, they knew that if you really wanted to snorkel, you either paid their price or you didn't snorkel.

We drifted towards the open topped canoes and the outboard motors sputtered into life to take us to the dolphins. However, it seemed to take a long time before we saw any pods. Though there are ten species of dolphin native to the western Indian Ocean, only three are found off Zanzibar, the bottle nose, the Indo-Pacific humpback, which can sometimes have a pink or white colour, and the smaller spinner dolphin, so named because it can spin itself in midair when it jumps. I had been interested in dolphins for some time, as it was said that you could see them from the seafront in Aberystwyth, where I attended university. I never saw one there though.

The idea of this trip was that we should get into the warm Indian Ocean and swim with the wild dolphins. The only problem with this was that the dolphins clearly didn't care for the noise of the motorised boats or the humans on board. Consequently, when ten motor boats whizzed up close to them and spilled fifty odd people over the side, they weren't inclined to hang about. It reminded me of chasing chimpanzees in Uganda. Those chimps didn't want to be seen and they were jungle-dwellers, who could move through the vegetation pretty damn fast. Therefore we didn't see any chimps until we came across another group who didn't mind us being there.

Without wanting to overstate my athletic prowess, I reckon I could've caught one of these dolphins if we'd been on the beach, but in the ocean they had millenia of evolution in their favour, even though dolphins are mammals too. I couldn't help but feel like we were part of a practical joke and it did make me laugh watching how daft we all looked, zooming up in the boats, all swimming about with our goggle-clad heads pressed into the water in search of them before climbing back onto the boats and waiting to catch a glimpse of them, perhaps quarter of a mile away.

No time was this more true than when we arrived late to a circle of boats around a large group of people swimming vainly in the centre. Just then, from outside the circle, but right next to our boat, a graceful dolphin leapt clear out of the water, gave a swish of its tail in mid air and then landed with a crash before swimming away again. It was then that I knew for certain they were teasing us. I'm not even sure I didn't see him wink.

I did eventually get my mask underwater in time to make eye contact with a dolphin. He gave me a confused look, as if to say, "What are you doing here, land-lubber?" Then with a twitch of his muscular tail, he disappeared into the blue-green hue of his home. It was beautiful.

These bottlenose dolphins are listed by the International Union for Conservation of Nature Red List for endangered species with a status of least concern, meaning there are loads of them and they shouldn't go extinct any time soon. They can grow up to 14 feet in length and weigh up to 1,100lbs, which is a fair old size. Dolphins are carnivores, working in groups to locate fish, squid, and shrimp using echolocation, in which they emit a series of clicks that bounce back from their potential prey and can give information regarding the location, size and shape of the prospective meal. They also communicate with others in their group using a mind-bendingly diverse array of communication methods which include vocalisations (including whistles, chirps, screams and other continuous sounds), tail slaps, jaw claps, chuffs (quick bursts of breath that create a rushing sound in or from the water), bubbles, postures (there is evidence that dolphins may adopt an S-shape similar to that of a shark to communicate that sharks are nearby), gestures, aerial displays, object carrying and tactile cues.

Having enjoyed our time near, but perhaps not with, the dolphins we headed to shallower water to do some snorkelling along the reef. I had only ever snorkeled once before, in the Africa pool (so named because it is the shape of Africa including Madagascar) at Tiwi in Kenya. The snorkelling in Zanzibar was superb: all the colours of the rainbow in various stripes and patterns, darting through the water. I hadn't realised how many different colours starfish could be, as I saw red, white and blue ones, like an American national rally. It felt like being caught in an explosion at a paint factory with so many vivid shades of every colour all around you.

We returned to the shore where I noticed a baobab tree, with a trunk that was perhaps 5 metres across, and a small sign that read, "Most scenic dolphin view, 1km walk, but most worth it." You can readily imagine my delight to discover that this was where we were heading for our lunch and as we followed the signs they gave a countdown of the distance remaining every so often in case we became exasperated with our unending journey.

As we approached the restaurant, I noticed an animal I at first dismissed as a goat, because it was standing on all fours. However, this monkey had a white bushy face, blue-grey shoulders and forearms, with a rusty red back and tail. I thought it was a blue monkey, but it turned out to be the rare Zanzibar red colobus. I felt really pleased to have found this, partly because I was considering paying to enter the Jozani forest, which is where it is normally found. It was most obliging of him to come down to meet me instead.

The colobus genus of monkey is named for the Greek meaning "cut short", which describes their shorter than usual thumbs. However, the locals call these monkeys *kima punju*, meaning poison monkey, referring to their horrible smell, thought to be a by-product of their diet of young leaves. Zanzibar red colobus monkeys play by burping this noxious gas into each others' faces, which reminded me of the sort of asinine behaviour I used to enjoy at rugby clubhouses. There are only around 6000 of this endangered species left, as they are restricted to their island home where their habitat is threatened by timber cutting, bush clearing and charcoal burning.

We relaxed at this tropical beach idyll, taking in the postcard perfect white sand beach, palm fringed and lapped by the gentle blue waters of the Indian Ocean. Our lunch was a delicious curried tuna with coconut rice. I spotted a poster advertising the Jambiani festival and asked one of the locals what it was about. He told me that it had a Persian origin and involved setting fire to some houses and fighting each other with sticks.

"Ah, yes," I replied. "We have this tradition in Britain. We call it a riot."

As I got onto the bus, I applied some more suncream and my friend Coco asked if he could have some. I shared some with him, uncertain of whether he actually needed it or not. He proceeded to daub it onto his skin and rubbed it like mad until he was white all over. He tapped his stage mate and said, "Hey look at me. I look like a *mzungu*," which was pretty funny, as it goes.

The trip back, without the constant stoppages at police roadblocks was more leisurely and I spent the evening relaxing and talking to some of the locals. A teenager called Ibrahim introduced me to the Swahili expression, *"Poa, kichezi kama ndizi,"* meaning 'cool, crazy like bananas,' which he assured me was the way young Zanzibaris greeted each other. I soon discovered that when a *mzungu* uses the term, it inspires instant hilarity.

Another quirk of Tanzanian Swahili is the use of the term *Shikamoo* when you greet someone older than yourself, to which the appropriate reply is *marahaba*. Loosely translated this means "I recognise you are better than me,' to which the reply is, 'I know I am better than you.' The literal translation has something to do with stepping on heads, which I never fully understood. No one in central Kenya understood me when I used the *shikamoo* greeting upon arriving in Africa. Tanzanians are generally more polite than their upcountry Kenyan counterparts. They also use a more polite form of attracting your attention. In Tanzania they say *"semahani"*, meaning 'excuse me', in Kenya people just call out *"wewe"*, or 'you!'

I went back to the seafront food market where I had lobster for the third night in a row. I was really getting used to this budget luxury eating. I wolfed it down with crab claw and prawns, watching the sun set on my time in Zanzibar.

That evening I boarded the ferry for Dar Es Salaam, which for some reason was going to take eight hours instead of the three the crossing to the island had taken. This meant an overnight trip sleeping in the seated area onboard. I settled down and noticed that they were playing the soundtrack to the film 'Titanic.' I wondered if they knew that the Titanic had sunk? This reminded me of a story a friend told me about how he was flying somewhere and the aeroplane had the song 'Ironic' by Alannis Morrisette playing. The clever airline had crudely cut the verse about the plane crashing so as not to unnerve their passengers.

I met two British girls on the ferry, Cara and Alice, who had thrown in their jobs and were travelling the world for fifteen months. Their planned itinerary included a Nairobi to Cape Town leg, which I had hoped to do, then South East Asia, on to Australia and from there, the Americas. It sounded fantastic! Our conversation was interrupted by someone who sat down close to us with an electronic keyboard, which had a full repertoire of Christmas tunes in the African, rather beepy, style. Not only was it July, but the damn thing didn't work properly, so the keyboard kept playing back over the same part, again and again. I made a note in my notebook, "Tempted to force feed him it… anally," but in the end I managed to sleep instead.

The ferry crossing was much rougher than the first and I only slept sparingly, as I was thrown off the couch a few times. Once back in Tanzania, I took a Dalla Dalla with the girls to the Ubungu, which was a big new bus station. Unfortunately, the new station was very poorly planned. All three of us were set upon by rabid ticket touts in a noisy hurly-burly that buffeted us about in a similar way to the storm of the previous night. There was a narrow corridor outside the ticket offices where touts were crammed tightly together and were literally fighting each other for our custom. I was pulled bodily in every direction and I was only unhanded when I put a guy in an arm lock.

Eventually, I had my ticket and, having said farewell to Cara and Alice who were heading off to a different destination, sat down on the bus that would take me to Iringa. I was exhausted. A poor nights' sleep followed by a rugby scrum to get my ticket and it was still only 6:15am. I had just shut my eyes to get some much-needed, when a guy sat down next to me and asked to see my ticket. I had just shown my ticket to the driver as I climbed aboard, but I gave it to him anyway. He took it from me and wrote on it, "one big bag. 5000 shillings", and signed it.

"You must pay extra for your baggage," he explained. He gave him a less than pleasant reply and he sportingly gave up his scam. I was beginning to see a downside to Dar Es Salaam.

As we waited for the journey to begin, lots of hawkers climbed aboard to offer us their wares: water, loaves of bread, biscuits, samosas and one had what appeared to be cartoon pornography, judging by the fairly graphic illustration on the front cover.

Once we got going, the bus absolutely flew along the roads. Fortunately, they were in better condition than the Kenyan ones I was used to, but we still hit some potholes, which threw the bus and its passengers all over the place. As I peered out through the window, I was reminded of an appropriate expression I had been taught by a school colleague, Sarah: MMBA, standing for miles and miles of bloody Africa, a euphemism to describe the vast distances that seperate locations in this continent and the similar or same scenery that you encounter between them. This was a view that perhaps came with a tiredness of the continent which I hadn't yet developed. I still felt the privilege of being able to see the continent, and its vast scale was part of what made it interestingly different to the UK that I was familiar with. Yes, the journeys were pretty long, but they were worthwhile and I maintained my passion for African exploration throughout my time there and to this day.

We picked up some more passengers in Morogoro, a crossroads town with not much more than a couple of factories to distinguish it. The bus was filled with the zesty aroma of oranges, which had been bought by passengers from the street sellers who approached the bus windows, holding their wares high over their heads. The smell made a welcome change to that of body odour.

We drove through the Udzungwa forest, which was a pretty, silvan landscape with grey/brown trees growing on the ridges and verdant green ones by the river. It reminded me a bit of the Wye valley around Monmouth and Symonds Yat, where I grew up. The Udzungwa mountain is one of a chain called the Eastern Arc Mountains, that soar above the plateau and are a trove of endemic species including the Iringa red colobus and the endangered Sanje Crested mangabey, a grey, rather nondescript monkey that numbers only just over a thousand. The road wound its way round the ridges and the driver floored the bus all the way, despite the serious deterioration of the road surface. A child wailed.

The mud huts here were rectangular and I was able to get an idea of how they were built thanks to the view of a half-completed abode. A structural frame of upright posts was placed into the ground and then sticks were tied horizontally to this frame, both on the inside and outside to create a wall cavity between. This cavity was then filled with carefully balanced stones before both the inside and outside of the wall were plastered with mud. These houses had wattle and daub roofs but elsewhere they had grass thatch, *makuti* palm frond or corrugated metal, depending on what material was readily available.

We had been climbing the Urungua hills for some time when I spotted two contradictory signs. The first read: Iringa 111kms; the second, 20m further along the road, read: Welcome to Iringa. I think the first was referring to the town that was my destination, while the second meant the district. As confusing as this was, I was thinking how I hadn't showered in what felt like an eternity, that my body was covered in seawater, sun oil, mosquito repellent and sweat, and how therefore, I was probably not smelling my best.

We pulled into Ilula for lunch where I indulged in that cornerstone of any nutritious diet, the chocolate biscuit dunked into yoghurt. In actual fact, this meal was half self-preservation, as my stomach had not been feeling so well and I wasn't sure how much longer I'd be on the bus and without a toilet for. This was also the first food I'd eaten since I left Zanzibar. Sometimes it doesn't help to load the cannon. The rock-strewn, craggy hills looked beautiful from here, only partially marred by the lines of pylons that marched up them. Swahili rap music blared from the speakers as the bus roared to life, rocketed up the hill and our last leg began.

I arrived at the bus station on the main road and was accosted by an army of taxi drivers who all wanted to drive me somewhere, but in their bluster to attract my custom, were not much help in telling me where Iringa was. I eventually ascertained that Iringa was a 4km walk up a hill, which was fine by me, as all I'd done for the last day or so was sit on my arse. I duly shrugged on my rucksack and got started.

When I reached the top of the hill where the town was, I had some fun and games trying to find a peanut seller called Kiswaga, who was a friend of the Catt family with whom I was going to stay at Ruaha National Park. I was pointed in the direction of a gentleman standing in the shade of a canvas roof, with wooden crates of peanuts around him.

"Good afternoon, are you Kiswaga?" I asked, feeling confident.

"Yes," replied Kiswaga, and things seemed to be going swimmingly.

"Do you know what time the Catts will be arriving?" I went on.

"Excuse me?" he answered, a worrying frown starting to cloud his visage.

I explained that I was hoping to meet the Catt family and that I had been told to go to Kiswaga the peanut seller to await a ride to their place.

"Ah!" Kiswaga said, a measure of understanding beginning to dawn upon him. "Maybe they mean the other Kiswaga the peanut seller?"

"Are there two?" I enquired, I felt not unreasonably.

"Yes, the other one is up the road over there. *Karibu sana.*"

Ignoring my slight wariness of the term *karibu sana*, which doesn't always translate to the "very near" of its literal translation, I set off in the direction indicated. Exchanged pleasantries with another peanut seller confirmed that I had found the correct one and I sat down next to Kiswaga's market stall to wait for Philip to arrive. I had never met Philip, or his wife Sally, but I had taught their son in my class for the last year, and they had kindly offered to let me stay at their camp for three nights.

I therefore didn't have a clue what Philip would look like, but soon enough the only other *mzungu* in town showed up in a Land Cruiser with two caracals painted on its doors, little known members of the big cat family. I am no Poirot, but it seemed reasonable to assume in this instance. Although Philip may not thank me for this pigeon-holing (Tanzanian whites have a curious grudge against the Kenyan ones), he was a typical East African white guy: reserved in speech, but extremely friendly and an absolute expert on all matters bush.

He told me that he took hunting expeditions in the park, which I didn't realise still went on. It is still possible to shoot lion, leopard and elephant in Tanzania, but the endangered species such as rhino and hunting dog were strictly off-limits. However, you must come with the readies to cover it, as the license for shooting a lion costs $60,000. This policy is part of a holistic conservation practice, where the funds from hunting, which also helps to cull overpopulated species, are then plowed back into further conservation projects, improving the lot of all animals and the biosphere as a whole.

In small parks, elephants alone can wreak massive damage to the environment if their populations get too large. Because of the encroachment of human populations on former wildlife domains, these populations get boxed in and are unable to move freely between the increasingly isolated pockets that are preserved for their benefit. The counter argument is that all killing of endangered species is wrong, and I did feel this side of the argument a little more strongly, but as someone later pointed out to me, no wildlife are living in a natural state any more, so all wildlife populations need managing to some degree. It is a thorny issue and one that will probably not be easily resolved.

As we crested an acacia covered ridge, Philip expressed an equal dislike for killing lions as I had, especially when they were baited, where meat is laid out to attract the animals, saving the hunter from having to wander into the bush to find the trophy beasty. Though native people who have lost loved ones would disagree, Philip and I discussed how even lions are generally docile and amiable towards humans. He had been taught by his father to only kill animals he was going to eat afterwards, and had had this strictly enforced. He went on to say how disgusted he felt by the trophy hunting attitude, to which I wholeheartedly agreed, adding that it was much more pleasurable to see something alive than dead. I then recounted to him my brief career as a lepidopterist.

Walking the mile home from the school in the afternoon, I loved seeing the butterflies drifting past me in thick, lively clouds. Having seen my great uncle Cecil's collection of butterflies and moths in the museum at Keighley, Yorkshire, and spurred on by my uncle Mike, who shared a similar interest, I decided to give butterfly collecting a try. After all, how difficult could it be? Some of the kids at the school were keen butterfly collectors, even to the point of building their own butterfly house on the school grounds.

I returned to Kenya with a 'killing jar' of ethyl acetate, which I should imagine would now be heavily questioned by airport authorities, and began netting and mounting the insects. The netting part was quite good fun, chasing around with hoop in hand trying to catch the butties before they flopped away into the ether in a curiously evasive manner. This seemed like quite good sport. However, seeing them still wriggling with a pin through them on a setting board, despite the effects of the ethyl acetate and the perforation of their vital organs in the surprisingly long-lasting death throes (it could go on for literally days), deprived them of their vivid, delicate energy that had most attracted me to them and so I stopped.

Philip laughed.

The conversation wound its way to the local tribe, the Wahale. During the colonial period, the Wahale had refused to back down in the face of German advances and had carried out a withering guerrilla campaign for many years before the Germans could finally corner them. Faced with defeat, their chief committed suicide, whereupon the Germans beheaded his corpse and displayed the trophy like that of a wild animal in a museum in Munich.

We came across a flock of vulturine guinea fowl and I nonchalantly asked Philip what it tasted like, as I had not had the chance to try it. When we came across the next flock, he stopped the car, pulled out a handgun from under his seat, leaned out of the window and, resting the firearm on the wing mirror, bagged one for the pot.

"We'll try it tomorrow," he said, picking it up from the road where it had fallen. Vulturine guinea fowl are not an endangered species.

As the sun began to set, we sped through the dense bush towards the camp, seeing a herd of lesser kudu, some buffalo, a few Maasai giraffes, a couple of spotted hyenas and a genet cat, on our way. The 'cat' suffix of the latter animal is a bit of a misnomer. The genet is actually not a cat, but is of its own genus *genetta*. It is a secretive nocturnal animal about the size of a fox, with a tail that is as long as the rest of its body, which it uses, along with retractable claws, for tree climbing. As I got out of the car at the lodge, an elephant trumpeted from what seemed to be very close by and I thought to myself that I was going to enjoy it here. After dinner, I was shown to a very comfortable, stone built *banda* that overlooked the river where I slept soundly until I was awoken by the hippos honking at each other in the water.

I had been asked if I would like to go on a safari trip with some other guests who were being taken out by Ted, a resident biologist from Cumbria in the UK who was working as a manager. I joined four other people, two middle aged American ladies and a young Dutch couple. We set off into the thick woodland of low, leafless trees, which looked a bit like silver birches. A copper carpet lay thickly below. It was somehow eerie that despite the heat, which in Britain we associate with good growing conditions, these deciduous trees had shed their leaves owing to a lack of water during the dry season.

We saw some buffalo and elephants before Ted stopped the car next to an enormous, blue hued spitting cobra. It rose up and spread its hood, which are specially adapted ribs that can be manoeuvred for a more menacing effect. This one must have been around 6-8 feet long and thicker than my arm. It quickly slunk under a boulder, but Ted leapt from the security of the vehicle and, pausing only to grab a big stick, attempted to chase the brute back out into the open. Unfortunately, Hissing Sid wasn't interested in playing and remained in his cool, dark spot.

I was surprised at Ted's pluck. Spitting cobras can shoot venom from the ends of their fangs to a range of about 8 feet, always in the eyes in order to blind the victim, either for a getaway or an attack. Ted rather boldly claimed that he had his glasses on, which was true, but he wore the sort of John Lennon style specs that would have provided next-to no protection at all. Even if I had been wearing safety goggles I wouldn't have fancied trying that stunt.

We passed Maasai giraffe, greater kudu, warthogs and yellow baboons, before seeing our first of many disfigured baobab trees. Elephants enjoy the succulent inner wood, which can hold up to 100,000 litres of liquid, and so they use their tusks to make enormous gouges in the bole, then their trunks to access the juicy pulp within. This leaves gaping wounds in these gargantuan trees. However, the baobabs have evolved the capability of regrowing from fallen branches or mostly destroyed trunks, with new main shoots sometimes adding to the original mass of the plant, and this produces some enormous trees that often look, upon close inspection, like the amalgamation of several tree trunks merged into one that they actually are.

At a muddy warthog wallow, we were told that this would probably eventually become a water hole, as a succession of beasties enlarged what had been a dip in the ground the size of a warthog's pot-like tummy. Once it was big enough to retain a little water during the dry season, its size would be enlarged further and further until it could grow to something that would sustain the multitude of game that wandered this park during the rainless period.

An impala stag was looking importantly over his females and shortly after we found a herd of males, awaiting their turn to do the same. The turnover rate of stag hareem leaders is very high. The cycle begins with a challenge to the existing male alpha from one of the lords-in-waiting, whereupon a duel of strength is initiated by wrestling with interlocked horns. Once the winner is established, he goes off and gets busy with the females, who have just witnessed first hand who the dominant gene belongs to. However, this can leave the newly crowned alpha so exhausted that he is vulnerable to challenges from other males and loses his position fairly quickly. This is a good thing for the species, if not the individual, as it ensures that there is sufficient genetic diversity in the population to prevent diseases causing large scale deaths.

A herd of zebras showed us their rumps, each one's pattern of stripes as unique as a human fingerprint and used by researchers for identification purposes. This got me thinking about why research is being conducted into zebra populations, which are by no means endangered. In fact, zebras are probably one of the animals you can almost guarantee to see on a game drive in East Africa, owing to their comparatively high population and a size and colouration that makes it difficult for them to stay concealed from humans. I suppose it is important to know what the population is in order to have an early warning should levels start to slide. There is also the interest in studying zebras for their own sakes, of course.

The lilac-breasted roller is the most dazzlingly beautiful bird you are likely to see. About the size and shape of a small crow, it has eight different colours in its plumage causing the Dutch bloke to refer to it as 'disco bird.' The roller has a beige head and neck, lilac chest, black and royal blue tail and wings, and an electric blue tummy and shoulders that literally glisten in the African sun whether in flight or twitching on a perch. It looks like a sort of imaginary bird that a young child might paint, making use of all the brightest colours that it doesn't get to use when painting the 'real world.' The roller is thought to mate for life, following a courtship display that includes rocking and rolling dives, loops and twists. Lilac-breasted rollers are carnivorous birds that like to perch at high vantage points to spy out their prey, before dropping onto it, beating it to death and swallowing it whole. It's favourite menu includes lizards, insects, scorpions, snails, amphibians, rodents and sometimes smaller birds.

The doum palms here were much taller than the ones in northern Kenya, and they tended to be less bushy too. Under the shade of a stand of doum palms, a group of lionesses lay, panting in the midday heat. Lions are extremely sensitive to heat stress and adopt a number of thermoregulation strategies to minimize this impact. Lions tend to sleep during the day and are most active during the night, when they hunt and kill most of their prey. They are unable to sweat like humans, so they pant and radiate heat from their skin. This latter reason is why you can often find them lying on their backs in the shade, because the skin on their bellies is thinner than elsewhere which helps heat to release when in this position. Lions also like to sit on rocks, and younger ones sometimes climb trees, to catch potentially cooling breezes.

We found some hooded and Nubian vultures scoffing a carcass

under a bush. As we approached them, there was a terrific tearing sound as one of them ripped a piece of stripey skin from a leg. We had a look at what was left of the zebra, which amounted to just two partly eaten legs, a pelvis and a large piece of hide showing the claw marks that spelled this creature's demise.

A group of elephants was blocking the road on our way back, and we sat there waiting patiently for them to move. These were not the kind of beasties to hurry for a mere rumbling in your tummy. Very considerately, they soon moved off, three adults forming a protective wedge around the youngster. We came across another group who were covered in mud. This has two effects, the first of which is to discourage biting insects that carry disease and the other is thermoregulatory, the mud oozes into the creases and crevices of the elephant's skin and cools the thinner parts of the skin. As the top layer of mud bakes hard, this maintains the moisture in the lower level, keeping the pachyderm refreshed all day. Elephants also have large blood vessels in their ears, which they flap to get air through the thin skin and to the warm blood, which produces a cooling effect.

I was getting eaten alive by tsetse flies, huge horsefly bugs that wreak havoc on cattle stock and can carry sleeping sickness that passes on to humans. I was informed that tsetses in this area didn't carry sleeping sickness, which was reassuring. We stopped by a small stagnant pool, where a couple of serrated-hinged terrapins were frolicking. A flock of helmeted guinea fowl pecked about for lunch and, as we started the engine to head back for our lunch, a group of warthogs fled, tails high in the air.

I was warned that the camp had a resident elephant who went by the name of "Naughty Billy." He had achieved this nickname as a result of the damage he had inflicted on the *bandas*, but I was assured that he didn't *normally* trouble humans. As I walked from my *banda* to my lunch I spotted Naughty Billy and gave him a wide berth. He heard me and turned around to check me out as a potential threat and to show that he both knew I was there and meant business. However, he seemed generally unperturbed and, once I had walked a short distance away from him again, he returned to munching one of the ornamental bushes next to the road.

As I waited in the dining *banda*, sipping an afternoon tea in the most gentile of fashions, I was able to look across the river to where waterbuck, impala, elephant, giraffe and yellow baboon had all come to take their cooling draft. After lunch, I enjoyed that feeling of having nothing to do in the heat of the day. The ground all around me danced, the heat descended on me like a blanket and my eyelids suddenly turned into lead. Yes, I ascertained, there was time to have a siesta before the evening game drive. Perfect.

Almost as soon as we set off on our evening drive, we came across a herd of elephants with a very young calf, of perhaps only two months, still learning to feed himself by copying the adults. A female had enlarged breasts between her front legs and I was just wondering if she was still feeding when, as if in answer to my unspoken question, a juvenile fed from her. It seemed unusual that the calf's trunk wasn't involved in the feeding, but this appendage was used for feeding on solids only.

Just then a young male, who was not yet fully mature enough to leave the herd, lifted his trunk and charged the car. He pulled up short however, as we were stationary and not posing any threat. He just wanted to make sure that things stayed that way. Had he been more serious he would have given us a warning first by shaking his head at us.

We stopped for sodas by a river and at the top of the bank was a sign that read: 'Do not come beyond this point. Crocodiles are dangerous.' Two crocodiles patrolled the water behind the sign, as if ready to prove the truth of the notice. On another chest-high, stone signpost a little lizard sat on the sun warmed summit, like a king atop the battlements of his castle.

Two hippos were doing some sort of synchronised swimming in the river, including dives, somersaults and pirouettes. It looked almost ridiculous but they seemed to be having fun. Hippo dung covered one of the rocks on the bank, a territorial marking, and just to demonstrate how it was done, one of them rose from the river and used its short tail to flick excrement over a wide radius. It's a shame that humans don't have tails. Hippopotamus excrement is actually quite an in depth topic. The method of flicking it, which is mostly done by the male, can spread the muck over 10m, while the female hippo uses its dung as a form of love letter with which to allure males. When a baby hippo is born it lacks the bacteria in its digestive tract to help it break down its food, so the mother feeds its poop to its offspring to help culture the requisite bacteria.

A pair of pied kingfishers flew off noisily when a fish eagle perched itself across the river from them, and we set off back to camp. An eagle owl sat alertly in a tree, looking ready for a night's hunting. These species tend to be solitary for the part of their lives when they are not raising young, which is a shame because the two group names for owls, a parliament and a stare of owls, are brilliant. It made me wonder if the former came from members of parliament being as tight as owls?   A little elephant practised his charge on us before turning tail and rejoining his herd.

I had been giving some thought to the source of some white patches we had seen on trees. I had already discounted droppings from roosting birds, as they were too regularly shaped. I wondered if they were mould growths, but Philip identified them for me as silk moth cocoons.

In light of the afternoon's encounter with Naughty Billy, the walk back from dinner by the scant light of a crescent moon had me extra vigilant and my pulse raced noisily in my ears. Though the walk back was uneventful I was roused from bed during the night and, peering through the blinds, I saw Billy right next to the window helping himself to a midnight feast from a bush that grew next to the *banda* wall.

Next morning we set off for a day-long game drive and we were soon rewarded by the sight of five elephants all lined up, drinking from the river. Upon closer inspection, we saw that three babies were hiding between the adults, sucking up the water into their trunks and squirting it into their mouths in imitation of the grown ups around them.

In the dense forest of low deciduous trees, we came across a herd of roan antelope; black and white striped faces and scimitar horns arched back over their brown bodies. They had a scruff of hair down their necks that looked like brush bristles. The roan antelope is a member of the bovine family and is closely related to the African Cape buffalo and eland. When roan fawns are born, the mothers hide them in long grass and stay close to ensure their safety.

We saw a hillside covered in the perfect grass to feed and hide roans, with just an occasional tree here and there. Ted told us that this had once been a forest but during a heavy period of poaching in the adjoining Ruangwa Park, the elephants had retreated to the safety of Ruaha. However, this added population meant that the environment was now overpopulated and so, being particularly destructive animals, the elephants bulldozed the forests.

On our way down to a gully with a stream in the bottom, we passed a small puddle that was teeming with tiny fish, and I marvelled at the way in which every drop of water had a life clinging to it. From the one side of this gully we watched a large group of banded mongoose running from us on the far bank. Two Senegal coucals were calling to each other in the bush and their song sounded so similar to their names that I wondered if their name was deliberately onomatopoeic.

Another favourite abbreviation I picked up in Africa was LBJ, standing for little brown job. This was the all-encompassing term for birds of a drab colour that are really difficult to identify accurately. Sometimes there may be six or more similar species that might be differentiated by the shade of a bar on their wing, or some such diagnostic which is impracticable in the bush. Even if you get the binoculars onto the bird, either you don't know what to look for or the thing flits away to deeper foliage before you can be sure. A group of LBJs was making quite a racket in the reeds in the stream below. Meanwhile, we spotted some vultures wheeling about on the horizon. This can be a good way to find interesting predators at a kill, but unfortunately we were not able to investigate further as the stream gully proved too formidable an obstacle.

Instead we followed the bed of the stream to where it met a river and admired an enormous, fat croc that was sunning itself on the sandbank. We believed him to be almost 10 feet in length. I did offer to go and lie down next to him to get a better gauge of his size, but fortunately everyone understood this to be the silly joke it was intended to be.

A herd of buffalo halted its advance to the river when they saw us. One of the larger bulls had droopy horns, which hung down like a high court judge's wig. Every one of the buffaloes had oxpecker birds sitting all over them, with their red beaks like vampire's fangs. The relationship between oxpeckers and buffalo (or rhino) had long been thought to be symbiotic, in that each required the other for mutual benefit. However, recent research suggests that the oxpecker might be getting slightly the better deal. The relationship is based on the oxpecker eating the ticks and other insects that bite the buffalo, saving the host the discomfort and potential disease of the parasitic insects with the oxpecker receiving the bugs for its sustenance. The oxpeckers only tend to eat the larger, juicier insects though, leaving the smaller ones to mature into better food, while they continue to feast on the host. Additionally, the oxpecker eats larvae from scars that the buffalo accrue, but reopen the wound to get at them in doing so, thereby opening the way for the next botflies to lay more larvae in the wound. The oxpeckers might even eat the scar tissue from the buffalo.

We came across four giraffes, all with legs splayed as they reached down to drink from the river. Then a huge male lion with an impressive mane walked through the bush in front of us. He crossed the track and made his way into the dense scrub on the other side, followed by a veritable circus of safari vehicles, some of whom left the road (a park no-no) in order to follow the lion more closely. Ted, being a bit of a purist, claimed that he would find us lions without the crowds, and berated those who had left the track in such strong terms that they cannot be repeated.

These words had literally just left his mouth when he plunged the car into the thickest of bush to take us leopard hunting. This hypocrisy amused me no end and I chuckled to myself as we wove in and out of trees and acacia bushes. He had mentioned some get-out clause to his hard line on *bundu*-bashing, to the effect that it was okay where it was justified. I considered this to be a very broad term that left itself open to interpretation. Sadly, there were no leopards to be seen, just plenty of giraffes and impala, and I weighed whether this had been justified or not.

We saw vultures circling and coming down to land again, but when we had crashed through the bush once more to find them, we saw that, instead of leading us to a kill replete with interesting carnivores, they were actually bathing, some in the river, some in the dust, and holding their wings out in the sunshine to dry off. Having seen two black-backed jackals resting in the shade, we stopped by the river to have lunch, watching zebra, giraffes and waterbuck milling about as we munched our sandwiches.

Setting off again we watched a white backed vulture feeding its young high up in a doum palm. There were more vultures wheeling around on thermals nearby and, in that afternoon dreamlike state induced by lunch and dancing African heat, I wondered whether the ability to fly would trump having a tail with which to flick excrement as a "from the natural world" power. The one would offer unparalleled views with minimum effort, as you used the natural heating of the day to push you up and up, but the other would be quite a skill to show your mates.

I was distracted from making a decision on this when we came across a *lugga* that had once had a concrete causeway across it. Successive rainwater floods had mostly washed it away so that all that was left was a ramp that would have looked just the part in an episode of The Dukes of Hazzard. I shared this line of thought with the two American ladies sitting in front of me, and they expressed alarm that this show and the Simpson's, which was the topic a little earlier, were being beamed across the world as examples of American culture. I offered the solace that Daisy Duke's image could offer quite a positive image for many, though this didn't seem to receive a very positive response. I kept to myself that the incumbent president was probably doing greater PR damage to the nation, not wishing to fight over politics.

We were amused by some baboons who were trying to get a seedpod from the very end of a branch. The first reached as far as he could, then fell out of the tree. He seemed to be okay. The next had clearly learned from the first and grasped the branch with both hind feet and his tail to reach precariously for the prize. He was successful and quickly ate his reward before the first could get back up the tree and steal it from him.

Ted told us a story a Tanzanian driver had told him of a group of Japanese tourists he had taken around. When they saw a zebra, they shouted out, "Shimauma!", which is Japanese for the animal. Unfortunately, the driver jumped on the brakes, hearing the Swahili word 'simama', meaning stop. Apparently the urgency with which he stopped catapulted several of the passengers out of the vehicle. They returned with only their pride injured.

The warmth of the afternoon continued to make me feel drowsy and I was finding it hard to concentrate on looking for beasties. I was gradually falling asleep in spite of the unwelcome ministrations of the Maasai flies, who clearly thought it was their turn for lunch, and were biting me relentlessly. Just as my eyelids felt like they were about to glue together, I saw the forms of two lions beneath a bush. "Lion!" I hollered, which woke me up and probably most of the other passengers too, as they gasped, limbs flying everywhere.

The lioness looked asleep, though her chin was turned up in what looked like a most awkward way. The male, who sported a good sized mane, looked more alert, and before long he got up to his feet to give his partner the benefits of his lusty attentions. He climbed on top of the lioness and entered her. He growled quietly throughout, gripping her between his teeth by the scruff of her neck, while she offered the odd snarl of encouragement. It all lasted about ten seconds.

"They'll start again in fifteen minutes," predicted Ted. "And they'll do it repeatedly every fifteen until they're finished. It will take four months until the litter is born and she will breed again in nine months."

Well, we couldn't hang around to check his accuracy for gestation or for the next time she'd be in heat, but we were all sufficiently interested to see how long it would be for round 2 of the current activity to begin. Lo and behold, after a period of fifteen minutes that was so exact it could have been set by a clock, the lion got up again and mounted the lioness. Afterwards, she rolled over exhausted and went to sleep, while he got up, pranced about a bit and peed on a bush. It was almost the exact opposite of the post-coital gender roles for human beings. We left the lovers to it, but fifty yards further along, we saw another big male sat in the shade of a tree. I couldn't tell if he was keeping guard, waiting his turn or delivering pizza.

I didn't know it at the time, but this was to be my last African safari, a day long affair shared with some of Africa's most iconic species, for which I am extremely grateful. I had a few beers with Ted that evening, before retiring for an early night.

I invested the next day in relaxing. I had a lie-in until 8 o'clock, spent the morning reading and writing up some journal entries, whilst I sat overlooking the river. Birdcall filled the air and sunlight flickered through the leaves, dappling the table. The pied kingfishers hovered above the water, their beaks held motionless like spears ready for the attack, and then they dived down in a splash and flew away just above the water. A fish eagle flew past with something in its beak and a family of yellow baboons came down to the river for a drink. This inspired me to go and look into elevenses. Once I had drowned a soda and a bit of cake, I walked back along the sandbank looking for recognisable animal spoor. There were a myriad antelope prints, the spoor of a hippo (about 9 inches wide) and an elephant's (which were about 15 inches wide, like a huge saucer shaped impression in the sand).

Needing the toilet upon my return, I opened the door and was startled by a rustling noise outside the window. A trunk dropped down and picked up some food before disappearing from the top of the window's view, all less than a couple of feet from me (though fortunately with the bathroom wall between us). I didn't make eye contact with Billy, as I didn't want to scare him, and I was looking down the twin barrels of 18 inch long tusks. However, I was able to observe the wrinkles and bristly hairs all along his trunk and mouth before he headed off elsewhere.

That evening we had beers at a hippo pool, where the kids played with boats in the stream, as the hippos crept closer and closer, wanting to get on with their night's grazing. We saw a big croc slip into the river and talked about the strange relationship of mutual respect these two powerful creatures have. They are almost always side by side in rivers and pools, as both prefer comparatively still water, yet neither one ever bothers the other.

Next morning, I negotiated a ride to Iringa with a honeymooning Swiss couple, for which I would pay US$15 towards petrol. We saw more hippos when we stopped at the park gate. They were typically uninterested in the human goings on around them. We drove through the skeletal forest with its copper carpet, and on up the escarpment to take us from the park and towards town. In a great bit of timing, a bus headed to Kyela, on the border crossing into Malawi, swung into the bus station, just as we had stopped and I was able to escape the marauding taxi drivers and board my onward transport.

The only seat left on the bus was one on the back row, where the collisions the back axle made on the potholes flung me into the air, so that it was like riding a bouncy castle. It was one of those African public transport journeys that you half expect to die on, as the speed of the vehicle and state of the road combine to make it mathematically impossible to stay on the surface. But, in one of those strange African anomolies, we did stay on the road. A kiddy in front of me had a toy mobile phone, which played a different beepy tune depending on which button he pressed. I recall hoping after half an hour that the batteries would run out before I had no other choice but to strangle him. Outside was more MMBA.

The bus turned off before reaching Mbeya and started up a good road (as was evidenced by my legible handwriting in my notebook) towards a set of hills called the Poroto Mountains. On the hills was a patchwork of *shambas* growing what looked like tomatoes by the wagonload. A conifer forest stretched up into the clouds at the top of the ridge and it was getting significantly cooler as we climbed up to Tukuyu for another pickup.

The houses in the north of Tanzania had been mainly round, the ones in the centre and east seemed predominantly rectangular, and now in the south they were square houses made of concrete blocks and roofed with tin or thatch. Their fields were full of tea, sugar cane and bananas, reflecting the fact that the southern side of the mountains were a lot moister than the northern slopes, probably due to a prevalent wind from the lake catching vapour and depositing it as the air parcel was pushed upwards. I wondered if I could see Lake Malawi through a gap in the beautiful rolling hills, but it was too hazy to be sure.

We stopped next to what looked like the world's largest collection of bananas, which were loaded onto the roof of the bus in great haste. There was a pleasantly strong aroma of these fruits, but as I inhaled deeply to enjoy it, a big fight broke out between the loaders, which looked like it might get serious, so I shut the window.

The side road to Kyela must be one of Africa's hallmark engineering triumphs, containing as it does the two hallmarks of the continent's communications networks: huge potholes and a few inches depth of choking dust. Still, I arrived without injury or need of an oxygen mask, and booked into the hotel right next to the station, which seemed clean, cheap and friendly. I was amused to find that they used letters instead of numbers for their rooms, but they had arranged the letters in an apparently random fashion, so that it was no use in helping you to find your room. Fortunately, it wasn't a big hotel, as finding your room meant investigating every door.

I had a few things to do upon arrival in Kyela. First up was to find out what time the bus left for Karonga in Malawi, but it turned out there wasn't a bus. The only transport was Dalla Dalla, which would take me to the border. I had more success when I called Isabel to arrange to stay in her house in Dar Es Salaam on my way back through Tanzania. Despite not feeling particularly ravenous, I looked for something to snack on which turned into a bit of an adventure itself. I couldn't find anything that looked like a restaurant, but bumped into a guy with a tiny grill about the size of an ice cream tub on the street outside a doughnut shop. He used the grill to fry me a chip omelette, which was rather good, and I sat on a miniscule stool on the dark pavement, washing down my dinner with a cold Kilimanjaro beer.

I was very excited at the prospect of going to a new country the next day. I always think it's a bit like opening a new box, never knowing what pirate treasures you'll uncover or what Pandora's consequences might be lurking.

Once back at the hotel, I had a beer in my room and the manageress came in to spray for mosquitoes. We had a short conversation in Swahili, which left her in hysterics and I wondered what I had said. There then followed a line of people coming to see me and I wondered if they were coming to listen to my attempts at Swahili, or whether they wanted me to pay for the beer multiple times, which was what they seemed to want. Either way it was a bit confusing.

I went to the toilet, which was an unusual concrete long drop on a step, which I could scarcely see through the cloud of mosquitoes that hovered over it. My cold shower next morning was a death defying stunt with so many insects in the shower. It only takes one bite to give you the lurgy and spraying yourself is of no use because, of course, you're washing it all off.

I took the Dalla Dalla to the border.

MALAWI

Having crossed into Malawi, I was immediately set upon by a lynch mob of currency exchange salesmen, all pressing in close trying to intimidate me into a sale. I found this a bit annoying, but since I did need to change some US dollars into Malawian Kwacha, I asked them what the rate was.

"50 Kwacha," came the reply, which in these circumstances is always an outrageous lie.

The guidebook was of no help in this matter, as it was generally out of date even before going to press, and this was before the time of readily available internet exchange information. I shot in the dark.

"I want 60 Kwacha," he countered. I was surprised at how quickly this was accepted, which told me immediately that I had still given them a fantastic deal. I exchanged only a small amount - enough to get me to a bank in a town. Having enjoyed the interaction with a very friendly border control officer, I got talking to a Yank who was travelling as part of an overland truck package, and I asked if he knew what the official rate of exchange was.

"About 70 Kwacha," was his reply. So I had overpaid by about 15%

I climbed aboard a minibus which was destined for Karonga and the tout took my bag to the boot. However, my enormous bag would not allow the boot to close, so they strapped it to the back of the vehicle by rubber straps which decidedly did not inspire confidence. There was a heavy smell of fish and petrol as the 19-seater loaded up with 26 people and hurtled off. Being somewhat taller than the locals, my head was above the window and I was unable to see anything of the country on this leg of the journey. It rained throughout, which was good for the numerous paddy fields of Kolambera rice we passed, but not so good for tourist prospects.

I got to Karonga, but was told that there would be nowhere open to exchange money until Monday. Karonga didn't really inspire me, being just a small town in the middle of nowhere, so rather than spend two nights waiting here for a bank to open, I pressed ahead to Livingstonia, in the hope that $16 would be sufficient funds.

I was hoping that the bus to Chitimba (the stop off on the junction for the road to Livingstonia) might afford me a better glimpse of the country, but unfortunately they had stacked the bags from the floor to the ceiling in my leg space, not only making it extremely uncomfortable to sit in, but obscuring almost all vision. I was able to see a lake to my left in the east and some highlands to my right. Soon the sun came out, but it wasn't possible to see to the other side of the lake. It was a big one then! And indeed, Lake Malawi, or Nyassa as it was formerly known, is a big one. It is Africa's third largest lake, with an area of 8680 square miles, making it almost as big as Belgium.

The bus was so overloaded that when we stopped at one point, a bloke had to climb out of his window to get out and pee in the verge, as there was no room to clamber over to the door, which was completely blocked with luggage anyway. The back of my seat had somehow wedged itself into my vertebral column and there was so much luggage that I literally couldn't put my feet anywhere. I was keen for this to be but a short trip.

The brief views I had from under the pile of bags were more encouraging. The road was under repair as it made its way down the narrow flat strip between the lake and the highlands, and we passed waterfront villages with lots of dugout canoes pulled up onto the beach as the blue water lapped at them lazily. We started to climb some low hills and scared off a troop of vervet monkeys who ran screaming to their arboreal abode. Herds of zebu cattle with huge horns and humps on their necks were being guided along the highway between eucalyptus plantations. Zebu, which describe a few breeds of Indian cattle, were brought to Africa centuries ago and are popular for their resilience in tropical climates, including a resistance to pests and diseases.

Coming to the bottom of the hills, we stopped at the police checkpoint in Chitimba and I was dispatched from the bus, my luggage launched into my wake. I looked at the road leading up the escarpment and winced. If Livingstonia was at the top of that, this would be quite a hike, I thought. A chap ran up to me and told me that his friend would be driving up at any minute and that I should sit and wait for him. I considered this, but the guidebook claimed the 25km distance could be covered in 5 hours, which would give me just enough time to complete it in daylight if I set off immediately.

"I'm going to start walking and if he comes past, I'll flag him down for a ride," I replied and with that, set off.

The escarpment road was really steep for someone carrying a heavy rucksack and it also dawned on me that I had not eaten anything at all that day. I met a group of fellow tourists coming down, who told me that the walk was well worth it. They had climbed up the day before and were now returning, having thoroughly enjoyed both the walk and the village of Livingstonia. I noticed that not one of them was carrying the sort of burden I was. I later weighed my rucksack and discovered it was 28kg.

The road, which had been built by a Scottish missionary who had somehow acquired a half track with which to carry out the Lord's work, twisted and turned back and forth upon itself like some sort of Alpine goat path gone mad, as it picked its way drunkenly up the sheer ridge face. Well, maybe it wasn't quite sheer but it certainly felt like it.

There were lots of birds twittering and insects rattling and butterflies flapping past to the refuge of the woods as I walked along. Normally, this would have delighted me - the brush with nature to make this a thoroughly enjoyable walk, but I was three hours in, with no sign of the end in sight, and I was absolutely exhausted. Always liking a good challenge, albeit normally in moderation, I struggled gamely on and came across three Germans, who greeted me with good cheer.

"A real die hard, hey?" said one.

"Well, I'm about to die. I don't know if that's the same thing," I offered. Witty, given the circumstances.

They told me that I was about 45 minutes to an hour from Livingstonia, which put me in higher spirits. I stopped at a stream to wash my face and neck in the cooling waters before getting to Manchewe Falls, where two boys sat outside a hut with two soda bottles in front of them. I enquired if they were for sale, to which they replied in the affirmative. I asked how much they would sell me one for and offered them a note. The young capitalists claimed that they had no change, but under the conditions I didn't take much arm-twisting to purchase both. I drowned them in the blink of an eye, only wishing they had been a tad more refrigerated.

The boys pointed me towards a short cut and told me that the rest house was only 30 minutes away. Sadly, the short cut wasn't signposted at all and, unable to find any evidence of settlement still, I made a few wrong turns before finding the correct path. I would be lying if I said I was pleased with this turn of events. I passed some kids who offered to carry my bag. I reckoned it was probably about twice as heavy as they were and suggested they might struggle with the weight. They laughed in a careless manner and boasted of how strong they were. Even so, I didn't take them up on their offer.

An hour after leaving the boys at Manchewe Falls, and a good while longer since the guy in Chitimba had offered me a ride in his friend's car, I collapsed into the rest house only to engage in one of those truly African conversations.

"How much is camping please?" I asked.

"It is 80 Kwacha, and a room is 100."

"That's okay, I'd rather camp, thanks."

"There is no camping."

So that made my decision, and I had to take a mattress, which didn't feel like such a booby prize at the end of my four and a half hour hike up the vertical road. I was ready for food, a shower and sleep.

The rest house was not exactly the Ritz, but the staff were friendly and it felt quite homely, like a deserted farmhouse, which it probably was. Dinner took quite a while to prepare and, while I waited at my table, I met John and Tendai, who were cycling from Nairobi to Zimbabwe, the latter's home country. The boys had cycled up the hill that afternoon and reckoned the distance to be just around 11km. Maybe by bike, but on foot, my friends, it was 25km. (A later investigation into this confirmed the distance at 18km with 900m of altitude gained. Not bad carrying that 28kg rucksack!)

We enjoyed a couple of Carlsberg beers together, brewed in Blantyre in the south of the country. This was the only beer available in Malawi, completely monopolising the market and presumably squirreling the profits off to Denmark. I couldn't see that helping the Malawian economy much. When dinner arrived it was a bit bland on the flavour front but enormously filling. I couldn't finish it off, and I'm normally regarded as something of a trencherman. I got talking to a friendly old Spanish guy called Fernandez, who told me he'd walked up the hill with his bags in only two and a half hours. This was a bit disappointing. If he was younger than 70, then I was a blue bottomed monkey. It was pointed out to me later that this may have been a bit of a fisherman's story. Before retiring to my room, I discovered that Malawi time was one hour behind Tanzanian time. Maybe that explained why it had taken so long to get up the hill? I gave it a moment's reflection as my head touched the pillow and then I was out like a light.

I was woken next morning at 6:15am, by a persistent cockerel who was making more noise than a heavy metal concert. I wondered whether I could have him added to that evening's menu. But grit and determination were still coursing through my veins and, with a bit of effort, I was able to sleep on until 8:30.

I discovered that there was no hot water. In fact, there was only icy water and as it was pretty chipper up in the mountain, I decided to wait until the sun had warmed things up before getting fully submerged in a shower. I stepped out into the garden to find that the morning was blustery and that the lake was covered in a moody grey cloud, which was nevertheless very atmospheric. A group of kids played happily on the lawn as I spent the morning reading and writing.

After a tasty brunch of banana pancakes (which had risen so much they looked like scones) and a 'Ugandan shower' (as the sun never got going) I ventured into Livingstonia, a village claimed to resemble the Scottish hamlets the founding missionaries had set out from. Indeed, the first landmark bore testimony to the creation of the settlement. On a stone cairn, set beneath Scots pines, a plaque read: "Near this spot (a delightfully vague position), Dr. Laws, Dr. Elmslie and Yuraia Chirwa camped the first night and chose the site of Livingstonia. October 1894."

This was actually the third attempt to set up such a mission. The first attempts were made at Cape Clear (in 1875) and Bandawa (1888) which were both abandoned, as their close proximity to the lake, which is at a lower altitude, made them highly malarial. The site at Livingstonia was sufficiently elevated (900m) and far enough from stagnant water that it was less troubled by this potentially fatal disease.

The first house I came across was the imaginatively named House Number One, being the first dwelling of Dr. Laws, before he moved to the Stone House. This was no doubt a very comfortable abode at one point, but now had a ramshackle appearance and a secluded air, perhaps in part because most of the entranceways had been bricked up. As I reached the village green, I sat down and enjoyed the peaceful ambience. The sun came out to throw a little warmth on what was a quite picturesque little village of orange brick houses and overgrown gardens.

The buildings were a halfway meeting point of European and African: they looked quite British in style, but were constructed from sun-dried, mud bricks and tin roofs. The clock on the central tower didn't work, further adding to the impression that time here stood still, and nothing was open. I presumed that this was because it was Sunday, but when I returned the next day, I found a similar lack of commerce taking place.

The village was very well signposted, a distinctly un-African trait, and was permeated by Scots pine plantations, but it didn't look much like any Scottish village I had ever seen. The local building materials, red earth and people, whose colour belied their Bantu rather than Celtic origins, all gave away the village's tropical location. It was, however, an idyllic spot, commanding views of the lake to the east and nestling in the foothills of the Nyika Plateau to the west. No-one could possibly fault Dr. Laws' third choice for establishing his mission.

From there I followed the signposts (what a luxury!) to the church, which was a large brick structure with a high bell tower. As I approached someone shouted down to me, "Hey, white man! Come up here!" I had been pre-warned that this would happen and that it was a moderate scam to try to elicit church donations, so since the views were great from terra firma, I decided not to take the chap up on his offer.

Once inside, the relative monotony of the interior was broken by two noteworthy exceptions. The first was an ornately carved wooden lectern at the southern end, while at the northern extremity was a superb stained glass window depicting Livingstone and his porters encountering some locals, claimed to be chiefs, with Lake Malawi in the background. I found it interesting that this scene should have been chosen over any biblical images, which reflects the sort of cult/hero status this explorer is afforded in the area. To my knowledge, perhaps only Robin Hood achieves this honour without gaining actual sainthood in the UK. Indeed, the good doctor's birthday, March 19, is a public holiday to this day in Malawi.

In the picture, the dress of the African women was little different to how they were dressed while I was there. They wore wrap-around robes, chitenges, with babies tied in, but the men wore just loincloths and carried spears. The men of the village while I was there dressed in a very Western fashion of trousers and shirts. During the reign of the social conservative Dr. Banda, Malawi had some enlightened views on dress code. Women were not allowed to wear trousers or shorts by law, as the former was male attire and the latter showed too much flesh. Instead, they were supposed to wear long skirts or dresses.

Men could also be refused entry into the country for crimes including hair that came below collar length or for keeping 'untidy' beards. I wasn't sure what criteria was given for determining the tidiness or otherwise of facial hair, but the haircut legislation reminded me of the Argentinian police in the sixties, who were given power to administer on the spot haircuts to scruffy-looking, hippy vagrants.

Dr. Hastings Kamuzu Banda was an interesting personality, who wandered the world for decades training, qualifying and working as a medical doctor, before returning to Malawi to be involved in its independence movement on an anti-racism ticket. His political persuasions were not all radical, as he adopted an increasingly dictatorial style over thirty years in power and declared himself 'President for Life' in 1971. Though he indulged in the tyranny of the time, he is to be admired for being an entirely self-made man, the son of poor farmers he worked as a cleaner in a Southern Rhodesian (modern Zimbabwe) hospital to earn enough to get to South Africa, where he worked in the coal mines to pay his way through high school. He suffered racist abuse in Nashville, USA while he went to university, then moved to Scotland to study for his doctorate and established his own practice. He was invited to return to Nyasaland (modern Malawi) to become involved in the political movement against a Federation between Northern Rhodesia (modern Zambia), Southern Rhodesia and Nyasaland, but left, disgusted with the state of affairs, to live in self exile in Ghana. He returned to Malawi and became its first president, already in his sixties, before going on to lead the country for 30 more years.

The stained glass window had Livingstone with his sextant (which some locals believed to have magical properties) and a chest of gold, with which he appears to want to trade. It was odd that the picture had none of the symbols of Christianity, save perhaps the sunlight pouring over the blue mountains in the background. The artwork of the glass was excellent, the highlight and shadows giving a subtle depth to the scene.

From the church I went on to the Stone House, Dr. Law's ultimate Livingstonia abode, which had a good view of the lake. Here I bumped into Cara and Alice, the girls I had met on the ferry back from Zanzibar. Their route through Malawi sounded similar to mine and we agreed to 'look out' for each other along the way.

The museum in the building was very good and crammed a lot of history into two relatively small rooms. It had a collection of farming and hunting tools from the turn of the twentieth century, and a cowhide shield that looked absolutely useless as a means of protection and must have served some purely symbolic function, unless the bearer was regularly attacked by people armed with sharpened sponges. This museum had a very different attitude towards the history of slavery than that held in Zanzibar. The latter, as I have already suggested, seemed to want to forget its past as a slaving entrepot, but Malawi seemed quite happy to tell all. I suppose this was the difference in perspectives between perpetrators and victims of a vicious system.

There were some clippings from books and newspapers displayed on the wall. One account, made by a British person in 1860, claimed that in that year alone 19,000 slaves went through the markets of Zanzibar. Of those, some 4000 were from the nearby Tanzanian coastal region and 15,000 came from the communities living in the area around Lake Nyassa (as Lake Malawi was then known). It was not recorded how many died in transit to the Zanzibari market.

Slavery was a trade twinned with the ivory trade. Slavers could come inland, buy slave bearers and ivory, the one to carry the other back to the coast and on to the lucrative markets throughout Asia and the Middle East. Chained, or tied to bamboo poles, by the ankles, any slave too weak to bear their burden (sometimes in addition to carrying an infant) were discarded. They would be murdered by their 'owners' or simply left where they fell to succumb to thirst, hunger or the depredations of wild animals. The slave trade arrived in Malawi during the nineteenth century and was accelerated by the Yao tribe who arrived as converts to Islam and armed with modern firearms. Natural allies of the Swahili-Arabs, the Yao decimated populations of local Chewa and Maganja tribes, who had recently arrived, fleeing war in the Congo.

It is a truism in this tragic industry, that apportionment of blame cannot be entirely based on racial lines. People of all colours were involved and, if you cast the net of enquiry a little wider, it is possible to find examples of African courts purchasing European slaves who hailed from Greece and other, at the times, impoverished regions of Europe. Indeed, prey could become predator, as in the example of the Yao themselves, who grew so tired of losing their people to the slave trade, that they took up the industry themselves and so decimated populations in their Kilimanjaro locale that they were forced to move into the interior to find new sources of human bondage. Slavery, as in any economy, needs suppliers just as it requires consumers and all races stand guilty of participation in both sides of this horrific equation. This is not in any way an excuse, but rather an acceptance that the history of slavery is more nuanced than popular media would have us all believe.

In 1959, Malawi was gripped by an independence struggle that was at times violent and the colonial administration sent a plane to Livingstonia with a message stuffed into an empty tear gas canister that they should communicate their wishes with the next fly-past by constructing a capital 'I' symbol if they felt safe, or a 'V' symbol if they wished to be evacuated. There was considerable debate amongst the missionaries of Livingstonia that night, but by the morrow they had constructed their reply, "Ephesians 2-14", on the lawns in a brick message visible from the sky.

I imagine the poor pilots flying overhead the next day engaged in a conversation that ran somewhat as follows:

"See anything down there?"

"No. No flags, smoke signals, flares, wait! A message! It reads, "Ephesians 2-14.""

"What does that mean?"

"I don't know."

"Why couldn't they just answer the question as we asked them to? It was multiple choice!"

"I don't know."

"(Insert expletive of choice)."

For those who do not have the Bible memorised, the referenced paragraph reads, "for He is our peace who hath made both one, and hath broke down the middle wall of partition between us." Or in layman's terms, "We're happy to stay, thanks." The original canister was on display in the museum, along with the story, and the crumbling brick letters are said to survive in long grass somewhere nearby, but I was unable to find them, even given these watertight directions.

The room additionally housed a collection of photos depicting the missionary workers from over the years, which I suspect may have held interest uniquely for their descendents, and a collection of Dr. Laws' old stuff, including a film projector, astronomical slides, a sextant and a gramophone. One can only wonder what the impact of these scientific/industrial age items might have been on a people who had contributed the farming and hunting implements on the other side of the room.

There were a couple of good posters on the walls too. One, a promotional poster from 1974, claimed that Malawi was "Livingstone's favourite country" despite the fact that he died twenty years before it ever became a country (or colony). The other stated very clearly, "<u>Beer</u> is not to be taken in the sitting room or veranda," which seemed a somewhat kill-joy attitude.

The second room had long histories of the lives of Livingstone and Henry Morton Stanley. Stanley, it seemed, had to work particularly hard to transform the public's first impression of him as a pompous loud-mouth, into one of grudging respect following his own explorations. There is a part of me that wants to feel a national pride in this Welsh-born journalist and explorer, but Stanley did have a side to him that was somewhere between sycophantic and self-aggrandising, making him a difficult hero to admire.

Leaving the museum, I went in search of a beer shop, or bottle dispensary, in the local patois, but found myself stymied by my lack of local language. Added to this, I had only the vaguest map of a very vague part of the village, which saw me a bit lost in quick order. I discovered a bunch of kids playing football in the street and joined in. If this didn't entirely break down our language barrier, it did seem to help them accept me. They kept asking me "What is my name?", without seeming to understand either the mistake in their question, or my answer, so that I repeated it over and over again. They never grew tired of it though, and I resolved not to either.

On the other hand, my knowledge of Chichewa extended to: "How are you?", "I'm fine," and "Thank you very much," so I wasn't exactly instrumental in any long-winded conversations. This didn't seem to bother the kids overly, as, judging by their remonstrations, they were more perturbed by my failing to control their wayward passes and missing sitting duck opportunities in front of goal. Having built a good sweat against the onset of a chilly evening, I bid the kids a "Zikomo kwambiri," ("thank you very much" - it was all I had) and set out again on my quest.

A kindly old gentleman assisted me, and walked me slowly to the bottle dispensary, two blocks away. His fading clothes no longer clung to the body of youthful strength he must have had to develop the agrarian, silent patience with which he ambled on, leading me unerringly to a fountain of, if not youth, then refreshment. He gave the impression that if the journey had taken several weeks, he would have been quite happy to shuffle along in his capacity of guide, almost certainly the embodiment of the angel upon earth. Or the result of an unhappy marriage, but either way, it produced goods.

On the way back to the resthouse with my swag in tow, a girl called out to me that she wanted to be my best friend. This, in other places around Africa, was a euphemism for, "I want you to pay to sleep with me," but I had misheard her, as a random punter pointed out, and she had said pen friend. There then ensued a rather awkward conversation in which she asked for my address and I had to explain that I didn't have one, as I didn't know where I was going to be living when I returned to the UK. She seemed dissatisfied with my response, but passed it off with a stoically philosophical shrug.

I returned to my accommodation and sat with a good cuppa to warm up, looking out over the deep blue lake to the distant hills of Tanzania on the far side. Behind me, the Nyankoa mountain of the Nyika Plateau watched over us both, man and lake, like a proud father, and I reflected what a beautiful part of the world this was.

However, it did start to get discernibly cold and I got wrapped up warm to eat a filling supper of rice, kidney beans and green goop (which I later discovered was rape leaf, but never established if it was from the same plant that produces the seed oil), this time accompanied by chicken. This chicken was tough but very flavoursome, displaying to excess all the attributes of free-range meat.

That night I had a dream in which I was going to Nkhota Bay (my next destination, on the lakeshore) for a fancy dress party dressed as a chicken. The police stopped me and wanted to know why I was dressed as a chicken. When I explained that I was on my way to Nkhota Bay, they "aaaghed" knowingly, perfectly content with the response. I took this to be a good sign, as I presumed that Nkhota Bay would be a good place to party. I woke up wondering if my premonition would come true.

Getting up at 9 o'clock, Morgan, the man who ran the rest house, asked me why I'd been in bed for so long. I replied that it was because I was on holiday, a reply he seemed happy with and he disappeared to make more of his delicious banana pancake/ scone things. Over breakfast, I decided to take a stroll down to Manchewe Falls.

Lake Malawi is part of the Great African Rift Valley and, as such, is bordered by an escarpment upon which Livingstonia sits. This geological feature is, by definition, pretty sheer, and Manchewe Falls is where the higher rainfall of the Nyika Plateau falls off the sheer escarpment face.

The path to the lookout point is not for sufferers of vertigo, as the one side falls away for about 150m or more. It is made only slightly more tolerable for the faint of heart by the trees that grow out from the cliff face and partially obscure the possible dangers. Once again I was struck by the difference between molly-coddled Britain and the wild African state of health and safety. I assumed that in the UK, a popular cliff-face path might have a safety fence to avoid prosecution, but here people relied on the sort of common sense the west is trying to eradicate by staying to the opposite side of the path to the huge drop. Seating myself on a rock near the viewpoint, I looked out at the vista before me. It was magnificent.

The main waterfall fell in two steps, the first of around 40m, the other of about 80m, and together they comprise the highest cascade in Malawi. In the bowl below and on the cliff face around it was a small ecosystem created by the hot African sun combined with the moisture and spray from the falls. This damp, hot microclimate provided perfect growing conditions for all manner of trees, shrubs and flowers to grow almost horizontally from the escarpment face. Pretty purple flowers sprouted from the cliff face and a bee buzzed busily between blooms. It was hypnotic to watch the sheets of water tumble earthwards to be dashed mercilessly against the hungry rocks below. Wonderful butterflies - yellow and white, orange and black - floated past giving an air of delicacy to this backdrop of power.

Eventually, I moved off to look for a cave behind the waterfall where the locals used to flee to escape the slaving parties. There was a path leading up to one of the smaller falls where I found a crevice that might hold about half a dozen people, but I have to say that I was a bit disappointed if this was it. In my imagination I had built it up to be a vast cavern capable of holding the population of an entire village. I later found that this had been the right place.

On my way back to the resthouse, a motorcyclist named Sylvester stopped to ask me if I wanted a ride down the hill. I said that I would do tomorrow morning and he said that he would call round at seven. Walking on in the sunshine with a pleasant pine breeze tickling the nostrils, I met another chap who had arranged a place for me on a vehicle going from the hospital. We had arranged this the day before and he checked with me that I still needed the lift. I gave him a pen for his troubles and I now had a back-up plan should Sylvester's lift fall through (a wise precaution in Africa).

I passed friendly locals who called out to greet me, but I couldn't tell if they were using the ChiChewa greeting 'Moni' or if they were saying 'morning.' Everyone seemed to be very proficient in English, which was no doubt a missionary legacy, but perhaps they also used it more because the national language of ChiChewa is secondary to the local language in the north.

There was a high-pitched whooping and singing coming from somewhere over the ridge, which sounded like some sort of celebration taking place. The sun disappeared behind a building bank of cloud and it got quite cool again. This made my cold shower somewhat akin to a medieval torture, so I set out for the beer shop to warm up while I stocked up. As I enjoyed the evening calm, Sylvester returned to confirm that all was well for the next morning and everything looked rosy.

Next morning, the sunlight, piercing two gaps in the otherwise all-encompassing grey cloud, shone off the lake like two bright eyes, before dispersing into golden dapples and disappearing. I wondered if these were rays from heaven illuminating the lake for one last time from the missionary town of Livingstonia, or were they serpent's eyes portending something more sinister?

I was beginning to get clues when a message came from Sylvester to say that his bike had broken down and he would be unable to offer me a lift today. I was sorry to hear this news for his sake, but felt that sort of self-gratifying pride that always seems to precede the calamitous fall. I wandered over to the hospital to engage in my back-up plan, only to be told that no vehicles were going to go down the hill today. I pondered my situation as I returned from the hospital, wishing that I had thought of backing up my back-up plan, when I heard a dull thud.

I looked round for the source of the noise and saw a cow sinking slowly to its knees under the weight of the axe that was embedded in its skull. His neck was held fast by two men, whilst a third retrieved his hatchet and, to the interest and amusement of the crowd of a few dozen locals who had gathered around this spectacle, launched it into the cow's head again. The cow then collapsed and I turned away, not wanting to watch, as the crowd, now laughing heartily, obviously did. I suppose beef had to come from somewhere and the promise of a good feed was exciting for these folks.

I took my rucksack and assumed a position in what I thought would be a good spot for hitch-hiking: just where the road from Livingstonia meets the back road from Rumphi to Chitimba at the bottom of the escarpment. Then it started to rain.

It wasn't heavy rain, at least, not at first, but after half an hour I wandered down to a straw roofed shelter to take cover. A Malawian woman passed with a bale of straw balanced impossibly on her head, though it did look like it was pinned into place with a sickle that she had stuck into the top of the dead grass. The bale was about twice the size of the lady. In her left arm she held a baby, who was suckling from her breast, whilst under the right arm she held a large bag of kidney beans. I resolved, there and then, to stop my moaning.

I heard a car approaching, but it was going the wrong way. This happened a couple more times and, in spite of my recent pledge, I cursed my luck: all the traffic going down when I was coming up, and now all the traffic coming up when I wanted to go down. There was some sort of Irish law about this, I was certain.

By this time a group of locals had joined me as the rain had really started in earnest. One of them had a T-shirt with a cheery looking woman on the front, which read, "She gets the blokes because she smokes," which sort of flew in the face of existing western advertising law. Another guy wore a T-shirt with a grinning skull, which read, "Kill 'em all. Let God sort 'em out!" This seemed to be a very twisted Christian belief.

Two others seemed to be fairly normal though, and we had an interesting conversation about the similarities between Swahili and ChiChewa. ChiChewa, means 'language of the Chewa' and was so named at the behest of President Hastings Kamuzu Banda, who was from the Chewa tribe. However, it is a more widely spoken language, recognised as an official language in both Malawi and Zambia, and as a minority language in Mozambique and Zimbabwe. It is more usually known as Nyanja, meaning 'language of the lake," referring to Lake Malawi. Like Swahili, ChiChewa has its roots in the Bantu language group from West/Central Africa, though it doesn't have the influence of Arabic, as Swahili does. Nevertheless, as we sat waiting for the storm to pass, we discovered many words that were similar: *ndovu/njovu*, 'elephant' in Swahili and ChiChewa; *gani/chani,* 'what'; *nyumba/kunyumba*, 'home'; *tatu/ zitatu,* 'three'. You can imagine how the next two hours flew by.

I was looking at the straw roof to our shelter and thinking how incredibly well made it must have been to withstand the storm and keep us dry, when it sprouted a leak, then five more, and began to douse us. I had been waiting for three hours for a lift down the hill and, as the rain paused for a breather, I spotted the opportunity to get away and set off walking back down the escarpment.

I was feeling a bit fed up, the lady with her bale, baby and beans now long forgotten, but I have always been impressed by the power of song to raise even the most downtrodden of spirits. Therefore I sang all the way down the hill, starting with Welsh hymns, sung at the rugby games and at the clubs, and when they ran out and I still hadn't reached the bottom, I began the Queen catalogue. My warbling produced quizzical stares from each of the passersby I encountered, but produced in me a feeling of bonhomie and love for my fellow man.

I decided to take some of the short cuts going down and these, I gathered, were not only the quickest means of descent, but were also the quickest way to a broken ankle, as I stumbled on tree roots, rocks and loose earth, my balance off kilter due to the weight of my rucksack. Even so, the walk down only took me two hours and I celebrated with a soda in Mike's restaurant. Mike was a friendly guy of about my age, who was immensely proud that his name was in my guidebook. He suggested that I have a word with the customs officer at the roadblock to see if he could help me to find a lift with one of the vehicles he stopped.

The corpulent policeman was somewhat stereotypical of Africans in his position. He exaggerated the petty in petty official and talked down to me while not lifting a finger in his work. Though it was frustrating to be treated dismissively by someone who was clearly uninterested in helping me, it was quite comical to watch him strut around like a self-important, pompous TV-star wrestler while no one else took him in the slightest bit seriously. I explained to him that I was hoping to make it to the banks in Mzuzu before carrying on to Nkhota Bay. He sneered and took perverse pleasure in informing me that my plan was doomed. The banks closed at 2pm, it was now 1pm and Mzuzu was two hours away.

The transport system in Malawi is somewhat short of comprehensive (which isn't the exact turn of phrase I used at the time in my notebook), and there was hardly any traffic going through Chitimba that day. Eventually, a minibus stopped and they had room for me. The driver and tout spent ages dismantling my bag only to find that it didn't fit into the minute luggage space. I had to assemble it all over again before they tied it into place with rubber thongs, which they could have done twenty minutes earlier.

An Uzi-wielding policeman stopped us at a roadblock in a lakeside village. Everyone got off to buy food, but I wasn't feeling hungry and stayed on the bus contemplating how strange it was to see waves on a lake. None of the lakes in the UK I had seen were big enough to produce real waves. Setting off again, we climbed a winding road into the dramatic scenery of the inland hills. The rocky outcrops looked like fairytale castles, with tall spires of rock reaching into the sky. A suicidal goat wandered listlessly into the path of our speeding minibus. Perhaps he thought he was a lemming.

I arrived in Mzuzu, welcomed by ominous looking clouds, and set off towards the tourist lodge, where I wanted to pitch my tent. I passed signs for banks and internet access, which was great as these were the services I would require in the morning. The lady at the desk told me where I could find a bookshop in the morning and I got the tent up just in time before the rain started. Though Mzuzu seemed a visually uninspiring town, it seemed that it was going to serve a functional purpose and I felt greatly uplifted by this.

I sauntered into the bar, where the radio DJ was trying to effect a sexy low voice, but was achieving something that sounded more like a prank caller. Here I got chatting to Desmond, who worked in the tourism department. He was well dressed with a dark blue suit and tightly cut hair, and he sat opposite a whisky and water which he was slowly working on. Desmond seemed very keen on Nkhata Bay and enthusiastically endorsed my plan to stay at Njaya Lodge. It was refreshing to be in the company of someone so positive and I offered Desmond a refill on his whiskey and water.

A priest and a businessman, who were obviously friends, joined us at the bar. The priest talked endlessly about how he wanted to change his car for one that was incapable of reaching the far-flung parishes. He had a real chip on his shoulder about having to drive out into the countryside to preach, while his colleagues got to stay in town. I had thought that priests were generally happy to do God's work with whomever, but I suspect he envied the more lucrative parishioners of the bigger towns. I had had many reasons to believe that not all clergymen go into the profession for strictly religious reasons in Africa. It also occurred to me that his colleagues might send him away for a break from his complaining, though that was an uncharitable line of thought.

Inevitably the conversation led to religion and, even though

I offered the opinion that neither politics nor religion were a good mix with alcohol (to which the businessman agreed wholeheartedly, perhaps fed up with the priest's rantings), our dog-collared friend kept prattling on and didn't seem too impressed when I disagreed with his views. I managed to steer the conversation round to Malawian social taboos and was informed that wearing my Kenyan wrap-around *kikoi* cloth, worn by men at the Swahili coast, might not be a good idea here. The priest then set off again on a story about his brother who had answered the door to him wearing his wife's dress when he had last visited. He explained that his brother was an alcoholic, but my thoughts again wandered to ideas of deliberate staging for purposes of avoidance.

Luckily, I was saved by the gong. The dinner gong to be precise, which was an unexpected touch, and I escaped to the dining room. My chicken and chips were excellent, though the radio music was not. Upon retiring to my sleeping bag, a loud howling and yelping from some sort of dog pound in a derelict-looking building behind my tent kept me awake for most of the night and the heavy rain put paid to the rest. Consequently, I woke up unrefreshed in the morning, ready to kill any member of the *canid* family on sight.

I got my money changed, with a precision that got me wondering. At the time, the Kwacha was worth about 1 British pence. In my exchanged money I was given a coin worth 1 Tambala, or a hundredth of a Kwacha. Was it possible that the value of the metal the coin was made from exceeded the value of the currency it represented? And was this common? My shopping turned out to be a bit of a failure though. I couldn't find camera film, mosquito repellent or any books that interested me. I returned to the lodge, showered and shaved off the goatee beard I had fashioned from ten days' stubble growth, giving it up as a bad idea when I saw my reflection in a mirror and mistook myself for a felon.

The tent packed up, I waited for the rain to stop before going to the internet cafe to pay an extortionate amount to check my emails. It was hammering it down when I finished and I had to duck from shop to overhang to shelter to keep my sleeping bag dry, as it was harnessed to the outside of the rucksack. I had covered it in a black bin liner against bad weather, but owing to the width of my rucksack, the plastic bag had been shredded by every door frame I walked through, as it snagged and ripped at the flimsy plastic covering. I was convinced that I was going to be sleeping in a wet sleeping bag that evening and only hoped that the weather might be more clement by the lakeside.

I got on a minibus where I was told to sit next to a girl who had two live chickens in her lap. We waited for a bit for the vehicle to fill up (an indefinite and sometimes seemingly infinite duration) and the girl and her mother got off before the bus departed. Maybe it was a no chicken bus? It is fair to say that on this morning, I was feeling a bit low and negative towards my Malawian experience up to this point and I looked forward to getting to Nkhota Bay in the hopes of things picking up.

Just then a chap got onto the bus selling spoons. I was just wondering what an odd thing it was to have a collection of spoons sequestered in your coat, when another man came on selling what he said was ice cream, despite it being in pots clearly labelled 'yoghurt.' Ah, this was starting to make more sense: a double act!

It has often interested me that on this sort of backpacker trip, you perfect your packing during the course of the journey, so that your belongings fit more efficiently into the space you have. Looking behind me now, I felt what a relief this was. My bag was suspended upside down and was hanging out of the boot, optimistically tied in with the requisite rubber straps. Fortunately, my packing had advanced to a state where I was getting most of my belongings into the main compartments and was able to fully close it. Phew!

My legs didn't fit into the available space and were wedged in at an awkward and uncomfortable angle. I hoped this was going to be the one hour trip described in the guidebook, as I didn't fancy being contorted in this way on a long journey. Just then, the legs on the seat in front of me fell off and the whole weight of the bench, and its four passengers, were now being supported by my knees. I tried to decide what a good analogy for this minibus was, and a sardine tin was the closest I could get, but for three significant differences. The occupants of a sardine tin don't have their luggage on their laps, nor do they bulge out from the tin through windows and doors. But perhaps the most telling difference was that, since sardines in a tin had already lost their lives, they no longer had to fear for them.

We bounced out of a pothole, my head hit the roof and, with a crunch, my sunglasses were broken and my scalp gouged. The sunglasses had lasted an impressive twenty one days though, and I was justifiably proud of my achievement. My minor injury got me thinking on a philosophical bent. African travel seemed to be, to a fairly large degree, centred around dodging potholes, just as in life we try to avoid metaphorical potholes. However, these hiccups can be survived if the right attitude is applied. Stare into the beer mug of self-pity and the potholes seem bottomless and unavoidable, but with a sunnier disposition, anything seems achievable, even if you do find your wheel of life bouncing now and again. This may have been an attitude I was already afflicted with, but travelling made this more poignant and reinforced its value as an outlook on life.

I was just enjoying the prettiness of some nearby hills when the road surface abruptly ended and we were bounced around inside the wagon for half a mile. Except for my legs of course, which were still pinned down by the passengers on the bench. The juxtaposition of pretty hills and tortuous travel goes to show that you can't have everything.

Arriving in Nkhota Bay, I shouldered my pack and set off for Njaya Lodge in Chikale Bay. Nkhata Bay was a small town set in a beautiful little cove on the lakeshore. It had a port for the steamboat Ilala (named after a local tribe) on which I was hoping to eventually travel to Nkhotakota, a town further down the lake. But unfortunately, the ferry was broken down and was under repair.

People were very friendly and pointed me in the right direction without trying particularly hard to sell me anything. I was on the road between Chikale and Nkhota when a bloke called Ahkim sprang from the roadside and told me he was going to show me the way to Njaya. He told me that I didn't need to pay him anything (a refreshing change) as he was employed by the Lodge to escort people there in safety against being mugged. As I looked down at Ahkim, who came up to my chest and was built like an untidy amalgamation of pipecleaners, I wondered if he'd be of any use if it came down to a scrap, but it was a beautiful, sunny day, so I plodded on, chatting amiably with my diminutive guardian angel.

Akhim was good value and surprised me no end when he quoted the entire first scene of Shakespeare's MacBeth. Of course, in spite of reading it a couple of times I don't know it off by heart, so he could have been making up his own version of the Scottish Play, but it sounded convincing and he was happy to have an appreciative ear. We chatted about this and that as we made our way over a small hill, through the neighbouring lodge site, over a beach and to our destination. It looked like a backpacker's heaven. It had a bar, restaurant, pool room and outside a beach where bikini-clad girls cavorted. This, I thought, was a place to relax for a few days.

They had a tab system of payment of which I am not a huge fan. The problem with tabs is that you never really know what you've spent until you go back and get hit in the mouth with it on the next visit. At least paying with cash per drink/plate, you can take out as much as you want to budget, then totter home when you've liquidated your affordable assets. I set the tent up behind the lodge, overlooking the lake and went back to explore the facilities.

Njaya was built by a British couple who decided to sell up their London home and look for a different life on the shores of Lake Malawi. What they had created was something really quite special: wooden *bandas*, a campsite with showers (cold again) and a bar-come-restaurant that was the hub of the site. The staff were really friendly and gave the place a welcoming, family atmosphere.

The menu had a 'Did you know...' section, detailing the kind of random facts about Malawi that fascinate me. The food selection looked pretty good too, consisting almost entirely of burgers and barbecue offerings. The beer was quite expensive by Malawian standards, but the barman, Gilbert, had a habit of replacing finished ones with fresh ones promptly, which endeared him to me greatly and seemed to excuse the hefty price.

It was great to hear western music again after listening to African beepy tunes for quite a while. As I sat greedily scoffing my cheeseburger and chips, I noticed a fascinating batique on the restaurant wall. A bright yellow man had two naked ladies held in a headlock and was somehow contorting himself to grope their breasts. The man had weird spiral eyes, a heart shape over his crotch and fire coming out of his head, which matched the fire emitted by the ladies' backsides. The whole parody was surrounded by stars and moons, and the girls were raising their arms in eerie shock, or was it delight? I was just contemplating what form of mind-enhancing chemicals had been employed to inspire this artwork when, somewhat appropriately, Kool and the Gang began singing one of their disco classics over the stereo system.

Another barman, John, gave me two thorough thrashings at pool before I retired to my tent to attempt another repair job on my jeans. I felt like I was fighting a war of withdrawal here, in the Dunkirk genre. I only had to keep them going until I could return to Britain and replace them. The crotch had ripped open while I was at Ruaha, and I had sewed them up so that they could continue for a while longer. However, the seam was splitting again and I wasn't keen for an uninvited airing of my testicles, so I set to with the needle and thread. This task completed, I settled down for a booze snooze in the afternoon heat.

The lakeside was well known for being a place where cannabis was pretty readily available to those who like to partake. Upon returning to the bar, and receiving my glass of probably the best beer in Malawi, I heard the barman ask, "Do you want grass with that?"

"No, thanks," said I. "I'll just have the beer thanks."

He looked at me quizzically and I realized he had mispronounced the 'l' and was actually offering me a tankard in which to put my beverage. This reminded me of a time I was playing golf in Gilgil with one of the local caddies. I had executed my usual dexterity for the game and, instead of launching the ball in a graceful arc onto the fairway, I had looped it behind some trees.

"Where did that go?" I asked, as I also had a bad habit of not watching where the ball went.

"In the liver," Kibue replied.

"My God! Have I hit someone?" I said, thinking it must be a pretty gruesome injury for the ball to get to this poor person's liver.

"No, no, the liver! You know, with water." A great relief.

That evening I got rather well acquainted with the Malawian brew as I chatted with various travellers and members of staff. Adam and Angela, two students from the UK, were travelling during their summer holiday. They had encountered one of the minor irritations of Africa when people drove up prices because of the colour of your skin. They were finding this challenging as students, and I had found this frustrating during my time in Africa, when I had been earning a wage that certainly wasn't "First World."

I had had a good-humoured argument with David, the waiter, over him charging me double the advertised price for a burger. It came down to some issue over extra goodies that were to accompany the plate, but it made only a very hazy sense, as the conversation occurred some way into my session. In the morning, everything seemed to be okay though, and David took my order for breakfast. The restorative powers of the full English breakfast are without doubt a scientific wonder, and had it been invented this century, I am convinced that a Nobel prize would have been deserving for Mr. E. Breakfast.

Hangover cured, I was again at one with the world. I sat back, put my feet on the table (not only to relax but to keep the table cloth on in the strong wind) and watched as the sun made a determined effort to put his hat on and come out to play after a night of rain. The Rolling Stones were playing laid back tunes and I searched across the lake for a glimpse of Mozambique. Unfortunately, I wasn't able to see it and possibly it would have been Tanzania I had seen if I could have.

Whether it was the effects of the beer from the night before, or whether it was just my usual childish humour, I couldn't be sure, but I chuckled quietly to myself at a woman reading a book called 'Beaver.' Ah, life was good. An Australian girl who I had completely forgotten about from the night before came up and thanked me for the prophylactic tablets I had given her when she had been panicking that her boyfriend was dying of malaria. It turned out that it was more likely a combination of a hangover with food poisoning, as I then recalled I had thought the night before, so she hadn't used them.

After breakfast, I spent the morning lazing in the sun outside my tent and marvelling at how ugly turkeys are. There were three wandering around the campsite with their bald, bobbly skinned heads and flaps of skin hanging down from between their eyes and over their beaks. The locals also kept some guinea fowl which flocked with the turkeys, and somewhat outshone them in the prettiness stakes.

I had a wander through the town of Nkhata Bay that afternoon and discovered a football pitch, craft stalls and a surprising number of supermarkets. Having admired a huge cream and black butterfly the size of a sycamore leaf floating past, I popped into Jonathon's Juice Bar. As I walked in, I was told that the Jonathon after whom the establishment was named had recently died. I offered my condolences, but thought it a somewhat strange greeting.

I struck upon the grand plan of picking up some beers on the way back to the campsite, where I sat outside my tent, pulling on a brew and observing life at Njaya. There was a girl staying there who had a very beautiful body, but also had dirty-looking dreadlocked hair and a big lip spur protruding from below her bottom lip, neither of which I was particularly taken with. The thought of kissing her frightened me, what with having to negotiate that defensive perimeter, and I resolved that six inch nails probably looked better on fence posts.

A group of North Americans, distinguished by the girls all wearing the en vogue continental uniform of bandanas, were wandering about like herd animals. I overheard them discussing which path to take to get back to their *banda* and a lengthy discussion ensued. In true herd fashion, they all trooped off en masse to test the agreed upon route, as splitting up would have been contrary to herd regulations. It occurred to me that I probably looked like some sort of caveman myself, sat outside the open entrance-mouth of my tent, covered in nothing more than a pair of shorts and body hair. Not having a book wasn't proving to be the problem I had feared it might be, as people watching was proving to be equally entertaining.

The staff at the restaurant introduced me to some artists who said they could make a replica of the drug-induced batique for me (though they didn't ask for any hallucinogenic substances). Tosh was great fun to bargain with and a good test for my haggling skills, honed as they were from two years of buying things in Kenya. He was a real stone-face, whose mouth ran at 100mph about all kinds of irrelevancies before he got down to naming prices. After we had both acted our parts to perfection, the price was set and Tosh and his, comparatively mute, assistant left me to enjoy my beer in peace.

A girl walked past with her finger so far up her nostril, she must have been performing brain surgery on herself. She was totally oblivious to my presence and I contemplated shouting a cheery hello to her, just to see what her reaction would be, but in the end I gave in to discretion.

Due to my early start, I was a bit fresh by the time I retired to bed that evening. Next morning, whether due to the hangover or not, I couldn't get my jeans clean when I hand washed them in the sink provided at the facility. I enquired if anyone was available to do a bit of laundry and I was sent to look for "Stand Straight." This gentleman, who had earned his nickname from morning parades, enthusiastically demonstrated just how straight he could stand and it seemed that his posture had really benefited from his drill in the past. However, his attire didn't really meet the parade ground standard, though he probably didn't wear his finery if he was going to get it soaking wet every day doing laundry.

Chores over, I went to the beach for a sunbathe. Almost immediately, a boy of about 10 years old approached me and asked if I remembered him. I did remember being pestered by twenty or thirty kids the previous day, all wanting to sell me hand painted postcards of dubious quality. Judging by what he had in his hands, he must have been one of them. As I further ummed and aahhed, he took off his hat, presumably expecting me to suddenly recognise him, but I was still none the wiser, and he seemed disappointed by this.

On my way back to the tent for a little recuperative siesta, a local guy came past me whistling merrily and waving his fingers in composer fashion. He seemed happy enough and as the sun smiled down on the world, I thought, "why not be?" As I sat there contentedly, it was hard to imagine a more relaxed way of life. So I didn't bother and fell asleep instead.

That afternoon I went for a walk around Nkhota Bay where I bumped into Tosh and his friend, who were supposed to be doing my painting. There was no sign that this was happening, and neither did it appear that it was going to. They were both sat around on the carved wooden stools in their souvenir hut, waiting for people to sell their stuff to. It occurred to me that maybe I had pitched the price too low for the sale to be worthwhile for them, but this might not have been a bad thing, as I was wondering how the purchase of this batique would fit into my budget or packing. Instead, I sat down to play a game called Bao, for which Tosh had many of the wooden boards in his stall. Though I had seen these all over East Africa, I had never played, so what ensued was actually Tosh teaching me to play and either I was a bad student or he was a bad teacher because I just couldn't get the hang of it. It involves moving some form of counters (Tosh had pebbles, but I had seen soda bottle caps and cowrie shells used) which get moved around between carved indents in the wooden board. I never figured out the sequence of this or how you won.

Having given up for the time being, I headed back to the campsite and met Cara and Alice again, who were sunbathing on the beach. We arranged to meet up again that evening for a few drinks. Once back in the restaurant I ordered a sausage and barbecue sandwich, but when it arrived I was disappointed to hear that they had run out of barbecue sauce. Judging by the fact that there was only half a sausage in the sandwich, I reckoned they must have also run out of sausage.

I went back into Nkhata to get something more substantial to eat and met up with the girls. When I met up with them, they explained that they hadn't been out since they started their world trip because they were a bit nervous about going out when they didn't know the lay of the land. They basically asked if I would chaperone them for the evening, which I agreed to. We moved off to the bar where a guy called Winston asked me to play pool with him. I declined the offer but he was very insistent. Even when I explained that I wasn't a very good pool player, this seemed to spur him on and he wouldn't take no for an answer. Soon we were racking them up on a beaten up table in front of an all African audience of a couple of dozen.

Things didn't start well. I went on a break of about 5 balls, totally against the run of my ability, and the balls just kept falling down the holes. The atmosphere started to turn a bit edgy and faces lengthened around us. I thought that this was typical: I had just offered to look after the girls and within half an hour they were going to watch me get beaten up over a pool match. Luckily, my true form shone through and I crumbled dismally at the last, giving Winston the win and the onlookers much to cheer. A few other requests for a game were made, but I turned them down politely and rejoined the girls at the table.

From there the evening got more raucous, as we went to a party at the Butterfly Lodge, where we met up with some other travellers that Cara and Alice had met in Livingstonia, Robert, Felicity and Eddie. After that we came back to town again and danced the remaining night and most of the morning away at Senkhani's Disco, a grubby dive of a place that had disco lights, loud dance music and cold beer in its favour, and not a lot else. I walked the girls home to their hotel and set off on my own to Chikale Bay, where the campsite was. There had been suggestions that this was a dangerous place at night, but as the sun started to rise, I didn't even see anyone. As I had suspected, the people here were too laid back to hassle anyone.

I was unceremoniously jolted awake in the cold shower the next morning, as the mosquitoes buzzed around me in hungry clouds, eager for breakfast and whispering, "Malaria, malaria." It was a slow start to the day. Breakfast seemed to take forever to get to me and I didn't really mind. I stared down at the lake where canoes bobbed on the surface like corks and I still couldn't see to the other side and Mozambique.

I spent a rather listless day, playing pool in the bar area, before heading down to the beach to see what was going on. I sat down in the sunshine and saw a large cloud of what looked like smoke rising from the water of the lake. Upon closer inspection I saw wooden canoes in the water and men swinging baskets over their heads for all they were worth. This cloud was a swarm of chaoborus edulis, small flies that are caught by locals which are pressed into burger-like patties and eaten. David Livingstone was said to have described the flavour as similar to that of caviar, and it got me wondering whether the prospect of eating flies was any worse than the prospect of eating fish eggs. In the end, I wasn't able to find any of these 'delicacies', though a lot of research suggests that eating insects can be a cheap, environmentally friendly way of eating quality proteins. I'd still rather have a good steak myself.

After watching some South Africa Currie Cup rugby in the bar I returned to my tent where I was changing into my mosquito-proof long sleeves and trousers for the evening, when I heard a strange scratching noise coming from under the tent. I pulled up the ground sheet to discover an insect infestation of my own: an army of red ants was on the move under my home. They didn't seem to want to come in, and my mosquito net kept them out anyway, so I just left them to get on with it and returned to the bar.

After watching the blood moon with a beer, I met two Canadians, Andrew and Kathy, who had been building a medical centre near Mzuzu. They tried to teach me the Bao game and I started to grasp something about capturing your opponent's stones and keeping the back row clear, but was still far from an expert by the end of the night. As I settled down to sleep, the ants rustled their noisy lullaby beneath me.

Next morning I had breakfast and went for some Sunday worship on the beach. This, of course, wasn't anything to do with Biblical texts, but more to do with getting a bit of a tan before returning to the sun starved UK. I went to try some sugar cane. People all over Africa eat the stuff straight from the *panga* slash, though it takes a bit of skill to eat without cutting your gums to ribbons. It does give a pleasantly sweet taste (as one might expect) and spitting out the inedible bits is quite fun, but overall it feels like chewing splintered wood, which grows a bit tedious for the small reward that is gained. I should imagine that accidentally swallowing the glass sharp fibres would be unpleasant too.

I lay in the sun's warmth, enjoying some well spent time bikini-watching. It seemed that Sunday was the day that Lilongwe metropolitans came to drink at the beach, judging by the ubiquity of beer bottles carried by the beach goers and the inebriated girl, perched on a rock in the water singing 'My heart will go on' out of tune. There were more beach boys than ever, selling their postcards and paintings; quick with a smile of offer, but clearly disappointed by rebuff. Swimming in the lake was great, with all the advantages of the sea, like sand between your toes and waves, but without the salty taste when you inevitably get some of the water in your mouth. It was just a bit on the cool side for my liking at that time of the year, but I bet it would have been grand during the Malawian summer.

There was a ferry sailing out and I felt a bit miffed as I had hoped to take the ferry to Nkhotakota and had been told the ferry wasn't in service. However, when I asked about it later, I discovered that this was a ferry bound for Likoma and Chizumulu islands, two Malawian territories in Mozambican waters close to their shore. These emerald isles had beautiful beaches to their credit and I had toyed with the idea of visiting, before discovering the ferry wasn't working and that the weather wasn't as fine as I had hoped.

As the last light of the day fought its daily battle with darkness, I watched a fish eagle doing a sort of helter-skelter dive at something piscine in the lake, while dugout canoes bobbed in the water. I listened to some relaxed music as the last rays of sunshine kissed the rippling waters goodnight. A motorboat glided in, absolutely full to bursting with people and I reflected that they obviously filled their boats like they did their buses here.

I watched, amused, as a group of Irish guys came in and all resorted to spelling their own names on the tab list, having failed to get the staff to recognise their Celtic monikers. After a delicious but unfilling Sunday roast (which needed an extra plate of veg and some chocolate to seal up the gaps), I spent the evening drinking with the Irish boys, who were all medical students. They had been doing some voluntary work in a remote village and were here for some well-earned r and r before heading back to their homeland to resume studies.

Having packed up camp the next day, I returned to Nkhata Bay to get transport to Nkhotakota. I had thought that I was big stuff in the African travel experience game, until I clambered aboard the back of the pickup truck that was heading in the southward direction I needed. I sat on the side panel, the small wall that comes up from the sides of the truck bed, and wobbled. A lot. I had to hang on for dear life, as I was only too aware that if I tumbled off, I'd smash my skull on the hard road surface. There was no indication whatsoever that the driver understood the precariousness that his 20-odd passengers faced, squeezed in tight and in prayer. The side panel I was sat on swung out under the weight of its passengers every time we turned left and at every twist of, or bump in, the road the entire population of the truck bed would fall grasping at each other for support in a way that passed imbalance down the line like an unwanted party guest. When a few people had got off, I was able to sit on the wheel arch inside the side panel, and used my former seat as a backrest, but this felt only marginally safer than before. All of my African travels had been mere child's play before this.

The inky blue lake with its cotton crested waves sparkled before us, while pretty rolling hills peeped over our shoulders. We drove through a plantation forest, its trees neatly aligned in rows, and then through a natural one, with vines and epiphytes hanging from arboreal limbs. The coastline was really attractive and Chinteche looked good as I passed through it. Cara and Alice had said that they were going there next, but I wanted to get further south.

A baby cried until its mother thrust a soft, chocolatey-looking breast into its mouth. Another toddler grabbed my fingers and squeezed. He had a very puzzled look on his face, as if he couldn't explain why I had such a funny colour. Two blokes got on board, drinking *chibuku*, a Malawian maize beer, from a cardboard carton that looked like a milk packet. One of them had acquired a milk-like moustache on his top lip, which I assumed he was saving for later enjoyment, and I made a mental note to try this brew, though not from the load suspended on this chap's face.

We were dropped off by a bridge. Well, apparently it had been a bridge at one time. Now some workmen were nearly completing a causeway that would take its place, but the pickup driver did ultimately understand that there were limits to his vehicle's capabilities and we were sent carrying our stuff over the breach.

On the other side we were able to get another ride in an awaiting pickup and I got a seat in the cabin, meaning I didn't have to pray so hard, which was nice.

The second pickup stopped further on so that we could get aboard a minibus. The sun was starting to give everything a pinkish hue as it sank into the hills. Kids in villages waved furiously, and some put their thumbs up, a trait I hadn't seen anywhere else in Africa. One guy left the bus without paying and all the passengers caused a huge uproar. In the end though, there was nothing anyone could do about it, and the freeloader closed the door thoughtfully before disappearing to sleep off his drunkenness.

At a checkpoint a friendly policeman's face broke into an ear-to-ear smile. *"Mule bwangi?* He asked.

I returned his smile. *"Ndele bwino,'* I replied, which I think meant that I was alright. And indeed, now that the immediate threat of death had been removed, everything did seem a bit more alright. I was charged the same fare as everyone else, another unusual occurrence in Africa and I felt a warmth of bonhomie with my fellow travellers. We passed an unfenced airstrip, which I thought to be a potentially dangerous idea, before I was dropped off on the road for the campsite I wanted to go to. A man named Christian and his friend Sam took it upon themselves to show me the site and left me to get the tent up.

Once the canvas was erected, I returned to the office to do the necessary paperwork which included signing in. The guest book included someone who claimed to be a writer from a popular travel guide company, though I had thought they weren't supposed to claim this, in order to maintain the objectivity of their treatment. I wondered if he had tried to get special treatment on account of his career choice. Another patron, a man called John Clark, had listed his occupation as 'waster', which I liked.

Nkhotokota didn't seem to have much to recommend it at first glance. The campsite I had pitched in was nothing more inspiring than a concrete wall lined lawn of around 8 by 6 metres. The town does have some historical significance, as it was a port from which tens of thousands of locals were shipped across the lake to begin a forced march into slavery on the other side. Due to the close connections between the slave trade and the Islamic Omanis from the coast, there is a large Muslim population in Nkhotakota and the call to prayer could be heard at regular intervals throughout the day.

Sam was hanging about when I came out and he took me through the dark village to a bar. It was one of those stereotypical instances where I was the only white man in the place and everyone stopped talking as I approached. I was quite used to it by this time though, and everyone soon picked up their conversations where they had left off.

Sam then launched into a withering and depressing hour and a half monologue about his life as the son of a prostitute and about how he wanted to better himself by becoming a priest, then the story changed and his ambition was to be a policeman, and then another plot twist saw him want to be a businessman. He then told me that he once thought that his calling was to be an athlete and he had run a marathon every day, sometimes two. During his tale, I had run the full gamut of emotions from strong empathy for his plight, to growing tedium with his seemingly endless story, to frustration that he wouldn't leave me alone. I had many similar experiences while I was in Africa, with people seeming to be very helpful and friendly before starting the pitch for what they would really like to be given. It was a sad situation, and it caused me to reflect on whether I was being racist to feel tired of it.

Quite often, when I got talking to a local while travelling in Africa, I would be waiting for the moment when the friendly chat would turn into an appeal for a donation. I had ruminated for some while that the people of poorer countries were in that situation so that richer nations could enjoy their wealth. It came as part of old racist policies of colonial resource exploitation and is perpetuated by a capitalist system that requires low wage earners to churn out the cheap consumer goods that maintain Western countries' high material standard of living. It always made me feel uncomfortable to get caught in a middle ground, where I was earning a lot less than the westerners the tourist prices were pitched at, but more than the locals could realistically, or at least legally, aspire to earn. It didn't seem totally unreasonable that people wanted to individually redress the balance a bit in their own favour, which I could understand. I wanted to help, but wasn't really in a financial position to help many, as my mind was a bit fixated on the student loans that outweighed my annual African salary, even back in the days when student loans in the UK were perfunctory.

I found Sam a bit difficult to shake off, to say the least and returned to the campsite with him still in tow. I bought a carton of *chibuku* on the way back and sat down at a table in the camping compound to try it. It listed its ingredients as: maize, sorghum, yeast, water and enzymes, which should have probably put me off, if I'd had a more sensible head on. I broke open the seal and tipped the fluid down in a big mouthful. *Chibuku*, I discovered, had both the texture and the flavour of bile. I could not understand why anyone would intentionally drink it - this viscous, lumpy material was supposed to move the other direction through the throat. I sat looking in awe at this revolting elixir, unable to fathom its level of depravity. Eventually, I thought to myself, maybe I have this wrong. It can't possibly be this bad and I took a more timid sip. I hadn't been wrong, the stuff was as foul as I had struggled to believe. I offered the rest to Sam, who yummed it up and I bought a bottled lager from the office fridge to wash the God-awful taste from my mouth.

Sam took the proffered drink as an invitation to launch into another tirade which lasted an hour. I wondered to myself just how long he would keep talking if I didn't stop him. I did in the end though, and bought dinner from a man who was cooking *nsima*, which tasted just like Kenyan *ugali*. This seemed sensible enough, as it was probably the same mashed maize flour dish with a different name.

In the morning, I found myself slipping from the campsite earlier than I had let on to Sam the night before, which I felt was a justifiable action. I trotted off to find the famous tree under which Livingstone camped in 1864, when he met Jumbe and other Chewe chiefs, to discuss a treaty to stop the slave trade. Though the treaty was agreed it would be thirty years later when under British rule, the Nyasaland Protectorate Commissioner Sir Harry Johnston asserted the terms of the treaty by force of arms, arrested Jumbe and banished him to Zanzibar.

Having seen what felt like the one sight of Nkhotakota, I decided it was time to leave. The minibus I took from the town had a flat battery and had to be push started at every pickup stop. All the road signs we passed were perforated, a common practice in Africa, which stops people stealing them to make roofing material. We passed maize and cassava fields, which had great termite mounds in them like overgrown molehills.

When we stopped in a village, some kids brought cooked fish to the bus for us to eat, but the overpowering smell of them put me off even more than the idea that they had probably been there for days. Two little boys got off while we ate to have a wee. One had the ingenious idea of trying to urinate really high and looked round with a self-satisfied grin when he had finished. I made a mental note to play that game soon.

I saw firewood neatly stacked by the roadside, cut to equal size and built into beautifully presented bundles. It seemed odd to me that they would take such exquisite care to stack their firewood when they had no inhibitions whatsoever about throwing litter all over the place. Women by the road carried water on their heads. I have tried carrying stuff on my head and it does seem the best place to carry your luggage as your entire body can support it in a more balanced way than is offered by carrying in the hands or perhaps on the back. Still, it takes some practice, from what I could tell, and probably a bit of building up of the neck muscles too.

Houses in this area were tiny two room blocks that seemed a bit inadequate considering the average family was seven people strong. Then again, most of their activities could be done outside, which significantly increases your home area, so the inside was only a sleeping space. Men were making carved wooden furniture and displaying their wares at the roadside, like huge open air department stores. A bloke got on the bus and had to lean over me (it was overcrowded again). His breath absolutely reeked of fish and I wondered to myself if that was what crocodile's breath smelled like.

It started to get more hilly as we approached Lilongwe. The capital of Malawi was bigger than I had expected it to be. I got a minibus to the City Centre, where I had to find the US Embassy. I wandered into the embassy district and kept searching until I stumbled across the Stars and Stripes flapping away over a manicured, emerald lawn. Here I was to meet Jennie's sister Megan, who worked as a nurse there. I had never met her before and had been invited by Jennie, another of the parents from the school I worked at. It is often with trepidation that we meet these new hosts upon whom we have been thrust, but Megan was absolutely adorable, with a luminous smile and generous nature par excellence. She immediately offered to take me to buy my return ticket to Dar Es Salaam (which I think was for the reason of careful planning, rather than because of any poor first impression I had made… I think).

We had to go through the central market area which heaved with people, smells and colours. Huge metal plates were erected on stands like barbecues, with a bowl shaped hollow in the middle in which to fry chips, chicken and fish. They looked ingenious in their simplicity. Bright vegetables and fruits were arranged in pyramids on wooden trestles with noisy hawkers shouting their properties to gaily dressed shoppers, bustling in the African midday heat.

Megan dropped me at her house and it felt so good to have a warm shower and a shave. The hot water cleansed me of the smells of African travel: a heady concoction of sweat, dust, goat, chicken, manure, other people's sweat and in Malawi, seemingly unavoidably, pungent cooked fish. I now smelled of soap, after-sun lotion, shampoo and minty teeth, while my face was a baby's bottom. All in all, this felt like a status promotion.

I ate regally that evening before retiring to bed. Having left the fan on I spent the night dreaming that I was hitch-hiking in helicopters, which was a bit strange. It was good to sleep in a comfortable bed again after several days camping, and I treated myself to a lie in. When I finally roused myself, I discovered mold growing on the handle of my toothbrush, which I didn't suppose was too healthy. I enjoyed an excellent breakfast and was given the liberty to lounge at will. I spent my time talking with their son, Bryce, and playing video games.

I also started reading a new book, "Round Ireland with a Fridge," by Tony Hawks. This was a laugh-out-loud comedy, but included an interesting excerpt from Nigel Walker. In this he explained that he had quit Olympic sprint hurdling to give playing rugby for Wales a go. His rationale was that he never wanted to get too old for it and spend the rest of his days saying "if only." This struck a real chord with me as this was pretty much the reason I was in Malawi, exploring the world and was generally an outlook on life I embraced warmly.

In the afternoon, Bruce convinced me to go out and play golf, a sport at which I do not excel but do enjoy, and we headed down to the Lilongwe club for a nine hole round. I had warned Bruce to expect ineptitude, and on the second hole, the opportunity arose for me to offer buffoonery of the highest calibre. Having dribbled the ball 80 yards-or-so up the fairway (but kept it on the fairway, which was good for me), I noticed a tractor and trailer up ahead, where two gentlemen were shovelling off tobacco twigs to fertilise the grass. I joked with Bryce that we should award extra points for hitting the obstacle. I settled down, kept my head steady, waggled the head of my club and buttocks, swung back and let it fly.

We squinted for the ball in the bright sunlight but were rewarded instead with a metallic twang as the ball smashed, full-steam ahead into the tractor. The two groundsmen dived for cover, quite reasonably fearing for their lives, as the ball inexplicably came to rest between them in the tobacco straw of the trailer bed. Before I could hop onto the trailer to play the ball from where it lay, in the true spirit of the R and A, the caddy threw the ball onto the fairway, offering an apology to the groundsmen in a language I couldn't understand and could therefore only assume was expletive laced.

On the sixth fairway, I teed up, swung like billy-o and was deafened by an explosion that sounded like glass shattering. I dived onto the floor, covering my head and assumed the foetal position. The club's head had snapped off on contact and had cleared a distance greater than that achieved by the ball, which Bruce found thoroughly amusing. This event had the unfortunate effect of scaring the pants off me, to which I attribute the 3 ½ holes to 5 ½ defeat I suffered. Bruce would perhaps more reasonably point out that he was a better player than I was, but that was splitting hairs. I was able to even up the overall score at the pool table however, and we began discussing a plan to go out into Lilongwe to discover some of the brighter nightlife spots.

Ben and Megan lent me their pickup to take Bryce out and have a few drinks with him. I met Eddie, Robert and Felicity in one of the bars, but they disappointed by accepting a round of drinks and then disappearing without any of them offering to return the favour. As any self-respecting Brit knows, this was poor pub decorum and I never saw them again to offer them the benefit of explaining the error of their ways. We went on to another bar where lots of Bruce's teenaged friends were getting absolutely tanked up. They offered me their favourite cocktail shooters and I tried a 'pancake', which was Aftershock with a layer of Sambuca on top, then a flaming Sambuca. At this point I decided that carrying on this way was probably going to get the borrowed car beaten up on the way home, which was a poor way to repay Megan's hospitality, so I drank sodas for the rest of the night, while the teenagers cracked on.

After a bit of a lie in, I got up to watch 'Muppets in Space' with Bruce while his head recovered. Once he started to feel a bit more human, we visited the Lilongwe Nature Sanctuary, which was an area of preserved forest right in the centre of the capital. Here there was an interesting information board on the benefits of termites. I hadn't really thought this much before, but they are an integral part of the ecosystem, as they are able to break down tough plant fibers, turning dead and decaying wood into fertile soil. They also have an aeration effect on the soil, and accelerate the recovery of soils after fires.

There were colonies of weaver birds, bright yellow with onyx faces. Their nests look like male genitalia and the females choose their mates by inspecting the males' nests for the best made offerings. I had always known that tidying my flat was worthwhile. I found a sign that explained that bamboo was a grass and could grow 4 feet in a single day, but there was no sign of any bamboo. It wasn't the only thing that was scarce. Other than a monitor lizard and a hyena's whoop, there were precious few beasties to be seen. I had held out hope of seeing a bush pig there, but I reckon they were too tasty to hang around in plain view.

That evening I chatted with Ben who had lived in Malawi for many years and shared with me some interesting stories about the country. The European town planners had planted a forest ring around the city to provide firewood for the African families who lived nearby. However, they hadn't conducted their research properly, so when they planted the *malina* trees, they did so without realising that they were planting just about the only tree in the region that didn't burn. Therefore the trees were never cut down and provided a welcome sanctuary in which criminals could hide to evade the law.

The AIDS crisis was having a nationwide adverse effect on the Malawian economy at the time, in a similar way to many other African countries. Companies were finding that it was impossible to keep up with the rate at which skilled workers, who were dying from the virus, needed to be replaced. It seemed that newly appointed skilled workers, with their accompanying higher earnings, could afford to pay prostitutes an extra stipend to not use condoms, with the inevitable tragic effect.

That night I stayed up to watch the film "Sixth Sense", which has a clever twist in the plot. That night I dreamt that I was unwittingly dead. I'm a bit soft like that.

The next day was to be my last in Malawi, as I was booked onto the bus for Dar Es Salaam that night. Megan took me into town where I wrote some postcards and bought some stamps that were so big that they left no room for the address. No doubt this would pique the interest of collectors, but it was rather impractical. I passed a man who was collecting old plastic bags. He looked homeless and I speculated that he intended to sell the plastic bags. It was amazing to see the industry of this guy, all to make a few coins for something to eat. I glanced at the vendors in the market, selling all kinds of strange stuff. One had a selection of Christmas cards that, when opened, sang carols in ChiChewa. This was particularly unnerving as it was only August.

I went to Ali Babas, an establishment to avoid if you are hungry. It took ages to get a menu, though it was very busy and I suppose I was lucky to get a table. However, as I was killing time this was okay. Dozens of blokes marauded me with the same question, "Yes, boss?" showing me the same newspaper, which could have been the only print in town. I ordered a medium pizza and, at length, was brought a monster! As I tucked into my mountain of dough, tomato sauce and cheesy topping, a small boy walked up to the table and started fumbling in his trousers. I was surprised, to say the least, but fortunately his father appeared just in time to stop him peeing in the plant pot next to me.

There were lots of beggars around the restaurant. Malawi is one of the poorest countries in the world, according to GDP data, and the restaurant was attracting a significant white clientele, seen by most poorer Africans as potential gold mines. A cripple and then a salesman approached me to ask for money, which always made me feel uncomfortable. I knew how rich I was perceived to be, but I didn't feel rich, scraping together savings to travel and with a student debt to look forward to upon my return to the UK. I made my usual firm negative response with an apologetic smile, which seemed to be taken the way I wanted it to be taken.

On my way to the toilet, I saw a poster advertising a group called Queen Almost who were going to play a tribute act in Lilongwe about a week later. It seemed a shame that I would miss them, as, having seen the house of Freddie's birth in Zanzibar, I could've made this a tribute tour of my own. Returning to my seat, a hawker approached me and we haggled over some gifts for my parents.

I picked up my bag and hiked into the old town. I had memorised some landmarks to help me find the road where the buses left from. I found the Kandodo Supermarket okay, but someone had removed my next identifying feature, a rack of loud, distasteful cardigans! It reminded me of a conversation I had had with the head teacher on directions to the school in Kenya. He had drawn the main highway and marked a right turn with zebras. "They're always there," he had claimed. I reckoned he was right... about 90% of the time. Anyway, in Lilongwe I got the wrong turn but found my way to the bus station through some back streets.

I had great difficulty communicating with the guy in the ticket booth. I asked to get on the next bus and he kept telling me to leave my luggage in his kiosk. Eventually, we seemed to draw the threads of our seemingly disparate conversation together.

"Now, now?" he queried, confirming my preferred departure time in a somewhat surprised manner.

"Yes, now, now," I replied, relieved at the minor breakthrough.

"There isn't a bus until half past six." So he had been offering to look after my luggage for an hour and a half until my return for the bus.

I decided to wait on the street-side and people watch. A VW camper van spewed dust, rumbling through town at a snail's pace. I should get a lift on that, I thought to myself, before realising it was heading in the opposite direction to the one I wanted. Turning further to take in my surroundings, a man brought a teddy bear up to his face and made cutesy faces at me while waving the bear's arm. I found this a little unsettling.

Just then, someone leapt out of nowhere and clutched me by the knees. He wanted to be a gospel teacher, he claimed, could he have my address? I told him the priceless truth (which I will have to remember when it is no longer the truth) that I didn't have a permanent address, as I was in the process of moving house and I didn't know where I would end up. This seemed to satisfy Aaron, and he gave me his address instead.

Someone else approached me and said, "Hi, Mr. Man," which I thought was a strange greeting. He stood in front of me grinning with the pride of a man who has performed his words well, before turning on his heel and disappearing. I had just enough time to wonder if sitting on the bus would have saved me these odd interactions, when Aaron returned, steaming drunk and with a large-breasted prostitute on his arm, whom he boldly introduced as his wife. I wasn't sure that this was behaviour becoming of a gospel teacher, but on second thoughts maybe it was?

Eventually, following a debilitating debate over seating, we were off and I tried to get some of the restorative. It was difficult to sleep on the bus as it wasn't very comfortable at all. Fortunately, the trip was only going to be 28 hours and I succumbed soon enough. We arrived at Malawian emigration first thing in the morning, where I discovered that it was a lot more hassle to get out of the country than in. The officials needed precise locations and dates for every part of my stay.

As I left the emigration office, a random bloke, claiming to be a police officer, asked to see my passport. I asked him for his ID and he told me that this was his office, with a nod of his head to indicate the building behind me. I pointed out that anyone could say that and that without ID he wasn't seeing anything. He shrugged and told me to go through. The chap in front of me turned and said he wished he'd thought of that. When asked to present his document, he had cooperated and then been asked to leave his Malawian money with the 'officer'.

The Tanzanian immigration office wasn't open and we had to wait. I began to worry that, since the bus driver hadn't counted us off the vehicle, he probably wasn't counting us back onto it either, so I might get left behind. But in the quirky, normal African way, having no system seemed to work, with the added perk that we weren't allowed back onto the bus until we had carried our bags 50 metres from where they had been thrown off the bus to be put back on exactly where they had come from. No bag checks had taken place and it all seemed a bit pointless. The guy from the line told me he'd never visit Africa again and, though I could see why, it seemed a shame. Tedious and nonsensical as it was at times, Africa was also magical and full of human warmth.

Our driver for the next leg seemed to be the slowest in Africa. He crawled up the mountain range and I waited for the downhill side where he would surely race in lunatic fashion, but was disappointed to discover he seemed almost slower still. I supposed that he was at least driving safely, though I felt impatient, as if we would never get anywhere. I glanced out of the window and watched a tortoise speeding past us. I couldn't see us arriving before midnight... of some day next week.

We stopped in Morogoro, where the bloke sat next to me was eating something that smelled of apple with a loud smacking of his lips and tongue. I couldn't decide if this was making me feel ill or hungry. Back on the bus, MMBA rolled slowly past as the landscape danced in the heat haze.

We got into Dar at 11:15 and I rang Isabel, who didn't sound like she had received my email. I felt guilty about turning up so late and dragging her out to pick me up. There was the usual crew of taxi drivers attempting to get me into their wagons. The planet Mars stood out from the glare of the city lights, suspended between electricity cables.

Isabel took me back to her place, where I got a good night's sleep. I woke up with an aching neck, from where I had fallen asleep with my head on my chest or against the window in the bus. It had not been the most comfortable 28 hours of my life. I spent the rest of the morning finding out what a hammock was all about. I think it was the first time I had used one, but I soon found the right balance. It may have been a kid's hammock, or perhaps I had enjoyed my hosts' hospitality a little too much, because whatever position I got into my arse touched the grass.

I was now reading a book of Anglo-Welsh poetry. When I read Michael Burns' 'A Welsh Love Letter' I howled out loud with laughter, as the humour was so Welsh. It also made me think of home. Does absence make the heart grow fonder? It had certainly underlined for me how much things meant to me. I remember those days at Isabel's home with mixed emotions. It was a lovely few days, spent relaxing and chatting. However, at the same time I knew that a dream was about to end. I had been living out a long held ambition to the fullest I possibly could. I wanted so much for it to carry on and to go to South Africa via all the countries in between. I felt like I could have stayed on the road forever.

But I was also looking forward to seeing my mum and dad, finding out how far my dad had got with building the extension. I was looking forward to seeing my brother, who had come out to visit me for three months and would be more able to sympathise with some of the feelings and experiences I might have. I was looking forward to seeing my friends, some of whom I hadn't seen for a while but to whom I had been sending these journals. I was looking forward to being with Ceri, with whom I had established a relationship while living in a different country. It was as if I had put off real life for the period I had spent in Africa.

On the other hand, there were also things to be a bit nervous about. I had no job in the UK and I would have to find one quickly. It was unlikely to be in an idyllic school full of delightful children, but I would have to wade through the mountains of bureaucracy that the UK feels is essential in teaching. I would be living in the same house as the girl I had mainly had only an email relationship with until this point. I would have to find out why the banks had mishandled my student debts while I was away. I would have to wake up from this dream.

I was certainly more aware of why I loved my home. My family, friends, the familiarity of people, places, my taste in music and decent beer. But at the same time I had raised my aspirations for travel. I had seen new places, met new people, observed different everyday lives and learned new languages and views on life. I had made new friends. All in all, it had been a success.

That night we had a dinner of chicken liver on the roof. I am not fond of any type of offal, and I had to work hard to enjoy this. But the setting beneath Sagitarius, the company and the cooling winds made the meal excellent. I listened to Isabel talking to her partner, Mike, who was a doctor. Though most of what they talked about was unintelligible to me, I did overhear, "I'll be operating all day." Everyone should have the opportunity to hear a doctor say that in earnest at some point in their lives.

I spent the next day getting money exchanged and paying for my bus ticket to Nairobi. When I arrived back for lunch, Cornelius, the house boy, had prepared another liver dish. I found it very tasty though, so perhaps I was getting the taste for it. After an afternoon completing my travel preparations, I enjoyed another rooftop meal with Isabel and Mike, testing the wine goblets I had bought for mum and dad (checking for leaks!).

The next day I went through the 'luggage ticket' attempted scam again, and suffered through some African music videos which were playing without the volume on. Two fat guys dressed like clowns, some scantily clad girls and two topless male dancers attempted to silently gyrate themselves free of an acute bout of constipation. Not a Tanzanian highlight.

At the border, I got a surprisingly good deal for my exchange and then settled in to watch the super-heavyweight contest of the century, as a Maasai crone haggled the price of a necklace with a Jewish chap. It was riveting.

The journey from the border was uneventful and when I arrived in Nairobi I shared a taxi ride with the Jewish guy, and told him I admired his haggling skills. I rang Mark and Jean from a bar and stayed up drinking beer with them. They showed me the video they had taken of the Under 11 rugby team I had helped coach as they won the seven-a-side tournament and we cheered like we were watching live. It was a great way to end the trip.

Soon after I climbed aboard a plane headed for Heathrow. I had been in Africa for two years and now it was time to return home.

GLOSSARY OF SWAHILI TERMS

Askari   A security guard or night watchman

Banda   A small hut or chalet

Baridi   Cold

Bibi   Literally girl, but can be used as a polite form of address to a younger woman

Buibui   The full length, concealing dress of the Muslim women. Normally black coloured.

Dhow   A wooden boat with a triangular canvas sail.

Duka   A market stall or collection of market stalls.

Jambo   Hello

Kahawa   Coffee

Lugga   Dried up river bed.

Makuti   Banana thatch roof or building with one.

Matatu   The minibus taxis that hurtle along the roads of Kenya. The name originates from the three shillings it once cost to get from Kisumu to Nairobi (*tatu* is three in Swahili)

Morani   (Massai) Warrior or the warrior lodge that the young Maasai men attend to become warriors.

Mzungu   White person or European. *Mzungu* roughly means 'bell-ringer'.

Ndovu   Elephant

Nyama   Meat. *Nyama choma*, meaning 'roast meat', is very popular in Kenya.

Nyani   Baboon

Panga   A large knife used for all sorts of purposes from cutting firewood, to gardening to a weapon. It is the African *machete.*

Pole (sana)   Sorry (very)

Rafiki   Friend

Safi   Literally means 'clean', but is also used to mean 'excellent'.

Shamba   A plot of land on which crops are grown and goats are tethered.

Shifta   An armed bandit.

Shuka   (Possibly Maasai) Maasai wrap around cloth. Looks like a Scottish tartan and can be worn around the waist, over the shoulders or in a variety of creative ways. Always has red in the pattern somewhere.

Tumbo   Stomach

Printed in Great Britain
by Amazon